Vocational Impact of Psychiatric Disorders

A Guide for Rehabilitation Professionals

Gary L. Fischler, PhD
Director
Institute for Forensic Psychology
Minneapolis, Minnesota

Nan Booth, MSW, MPH
Licensed Independent Clinical
Social Worker
Institute for Forensic Psychology
Minneapolis, Minnesota

AN ASPEN PUBLICATION®
Aspen Publishers, Inc.
Gaithersburg, Maryland
1999

The author has made every effort to ensure the accuracy of the information herein. However, appropriate information sources should be consulted, especially for new or unfamiliar procedures. It is the responsibility of every practitioner to evaluate the appropriateness of a particular opinion in the context of actual clinical situations and with due considerations to new developments. The author, editors, and the publisher cannot be held responsible for any typographical or other errors found in this book.

Aspen Publishers, Inc., is not affiliated with the American Society of Parenteral and Enteral Nutrition.

Library of Congress Cataloging-in-Publication Data
Fischler, Gary, 1955–
Vocational impact of psychiatric disorders : a guide for
rehabilitation professionals / Gary Fischler, Nan Booth.
p. cm.
Includes bibliographical references and index.
ISBN 0-8342-1251-X
1. Vocational education—Psychological aspects Case studies.
2. Vocational rehabilitation Case studies. I. Booth, Nan, 1949– II. Title.
[DNLM: 1. Mental Disorders—rehabilitation Case Report.
2. Occupational Health Case Report. 3. Rehabilitation, Vocational Case Report.
WM 40 F5293v 1999]
RC454.4.F576 1999
616.89′03—dc21
DNLM/DLC
for Library of Congress
99-30253
CIP

Aspen Publishers, Inc., grants permission for photocopying for limited personal or internal use. This consent does not extend to other kinds of copying, such as copyingfor general distribution, for advertising or promotional purposes, for creating new collective works, or for resale. For information, address Aspen Publishers, Inc., Permissions Department, 200 Orchard Ridge Drive, Suite 200, Gaithersburg, Maryland 20878.

Orders: (800) 638-8437
Customer Service: (800) 234-1660

About Aspen Publishers • For more than 35 years, Aspen has been a leading professional publisher in a variety of disciplines. Aspen's vast information resources are available in both print and electronic formats. We are committed to providing the highest quality information available in the most appropriate format for our customers. Visit Aspen's Internet site for more information resources, directories, articles, and a searchable version of Aspen's full catalog, including the most recent publications: **http://www.aspenpublishers.com**
Aspen Publishers, Inc. • The hallmark of quality in publishing
Member of the worldwide Wolters Kluwer group.

Editorial Services: Kathleen Ruby
Library of Congress Catalog Card Number: 99-30253
ISBN: 0-8342-1251-X

Printed in the United States of America
1 2 3 4 5

Dedicated to the cooperative spirit that makes teams effective.

Table of Contents

Preface . . . . **xiii**

   About This Book xiii

   Disorders Left Out xiv

   Case Examples and Treatment Issues xv

   A Final Word xvi

**Introduction: Psychiatric Disorders and Vocational
Functioning** **1**

   The Role of DSM-IV 1

Part I—Feeling Bad **7**

Chapter 1—Mood Disorders **9**

   Major Depression and Dysthymia 9

   Jack 10

      What Depression Is Like 10

      Depression's Effect at Work 12

      Working with Depression 13

      Summary: Depression's Effect on Vocational Abilities 17

      Summary: Vocational Strategies and Accommodations 19

   Bipolar Disorder, Manic Phase 20

Paula. 20

What a Manic Episode Is Like 20

A Manic Phase's Effect at Work 23

Working with Bipolar Disorder 24

Summary: Bipolar Disorder's Effect on Vocational Abilities . . . 28

Summary: Vocational Strategies and Accommodations 30

Chapter 2—Anxiety Disorders **33**

Agoraphobia and Social Phobia. 34

Ron. 34

What Agoraphobia and Social Phobia Are Like. 34

Agoraphobia and Social Phobia's Effect at Work. 36

Working with Agoraphobia and Social Phobia 38

Summary: Agoraphobia and Social Phobia's Effect on
Vocational Abilities 42

Summary: Vocational Strategies and Accommodations 44

Posttraumatic Stress Disorder 44

Susan 45

What Posttraumatic Stress Disorder Is Like 45

Posttraumatic Stress Disorder's Effect at Work 47

Working with Posttraumatic Stress Disorder. 48

Summary: Posttraumatic Stress Disorder's Effect on
Vocational Abilities 52

Summary: Vocational Strategies and Accommodations 54

Obsessive-Compulsive Disorder 55

Larry. 55

What Obsessive-Compulsive Disorder Is Like 56

Obsessive-Compulsive Disorder's Effect at Work. 59

Working with Obsessive-Compulsive Disorder 60

Summary: Obsessive-Compulsive Disorder's Effect on
Vocational Abilities 63

Summary: Vocational Strategies and Accommodations 65

Chapter 3—Somatoform Disorders **67**

Somatization Disorder 68

Marianne 68

What Somatization Disorder Is Like 68

Somatization Disorder's Effect at Work 70

Working with Somatization Disorder 71

Summary: Somatization Disorder's Effect on Vocational
Abilities. 75

Summary: Vocational Strategies and Accommodations 77

Part II—Problems Getting Along **79**

**Chapter 4—The "Odd" Cluster: Paranoid, Schizotypal,
and Schizoid Personality Disorders** **81**

Paranoid Personality Disorder 82

Martin 82

What Paranoid Personality Disorder Is Like 83

Paranoid Personality Disorder's Effect at Work 85

Working with Paranoid Personality Disorder 86

Summary: Paranoid Personality Disorder's Effect on
Vocational Abilities 92

Summary: Vocational Strategies and Accommodations 94

Schizotypal Personality Disorder 94

Shelly 95

What Schizotypal Personality Disorder Is Like 95

Schizotypal Personality Disorder's Effect at Work 97

Working with Schizotypal Personality Disorder 99

Summary: Schizotypal Personality Disorder's Effect on
Vocational Abilities 105

Summary: Vocational Strategies and Accommodations 107

Schizoid Personality Disorder 107

Ed 108

What Schizoid Personality Disorder Is Like 108

Schizoid Personality Disorder's Effect at Work 110

Working with Schizoid Personality Disorder 111

Summary: Schizoid Personality Disorder's Effect on
Vocational Abilities 115

Summary: Vocational Strategies and Accommodations 117

**Chapter 5—The "Dramatic" Cluster: Borderline,
Antisocial, Histrionic, and Narcissistic Personality
Disorders 119**

Borderline Personality Disorder 120

Carol 120

What Borderline Personality Disorder Is Like 121

Borderline Personality Disorder's Effect at Work 123

Working with Borderline Personality Disorder 125

Summary: Borderline Personality Disorder's Effect on
Vocational Abilities 130

Summary: Vocational Strategies and Accommodations 132

Antisocial Personality Disorder 133

Rocky 133

What Antisocial Personality Disorder Is Like 134

Antisocial Personality Disorder's Effect at Work 136

Working with Antisocial Personality Disorder 138

Summary: Antisocial Personality Disorder's Effect on
Vocational Abilities 141

Summary: Vocational Strategies and Accommodations 143

Histrionic Personality Disorder 144

Peggy 144

What Histrionic Personality Disorder Is Like 145

Histrionic Personality Disorder's Effect at Work 147

Working with Histrionic Personality Disorder 149

Summary: Histrionic Personality Disorder's Effect on
Vocational Abilities 153

Summary: Vocational Strategies and Accommodations 155

Narcissistic Personality Disorder 156

Gerald. 156

What Narcissistic Personality Disorder Is Like. 156

Narcissistic Personality Disorder's Effect at Work 159

Working with Narcissistic Personality Disorder. 161

Summary: Narcissistic Personality Disorder's Effect on
Vocational Abilities 166

Summary: Vocational Strategies and Accommodations 168

**Chapter 6—The "Anxious" Cluster: Avoidant,
Dependent, Obsessive-Compulsive, and
Passive-Aggressive Personality Disorders. 169**

Avoidant Personality Disorder. 170

Connie 171

What Avoidant Personality Disorder Is Like 172

Avoidant Personality Disorder's Effect at Work. 174

Working with Avoidant Personality Disorder 176

Summary: Avoidant Personality Disorder's Effect on
Vocational Abilities 181

Summary: Vocational Strategies and Accommodations 183

Dependent Personality Disorder 183

Bill 184

What Dependent Personality Disorder Is Like. 184

Dependent Personality Disorder's Effect at Work 187

Working with Dependent Personality Disorder. 189

Summary: Dependent Personality Disorder's Effect on
Vocational Abilities 193

Summary: Vocational Strategies and Accommodations 196

Obsessive-Compulsive Personality Disorder 196

Judy 196

What Obsessive-Compulsive Personality Disorder Is Like ... 197

Obsessive-Compulsive Personality Disorder's Effect
at Work.. 200

Working with Obsessive-Compulsive Personality
Disorder 201

Summary: Obsessive-Compulsive Personality Disorder's
Effect on Vocational Abilities. 205

Summary: Vocational Strategies and Accommodations 207

Passive-Aggressive Personality Disorder 208

Ray 208

What Passive-Aggressive Personality Disorder Is Like 209

Passive-Aggressive Personality Disorder's Effect at Work. 211

Working with Passive-Aggressive Personality Disorder 212

Summary: Passive-Aggressive Personality Disorder's Effect
on Vocational Abilities.............................. 216

Summary: Vocational Strategies and Accommodations 218

Part III—Problems with Reality. 221

**Chapter 7—Schizophrenia and Other
Psychotic Disorders 223**

Schizophrenia 223

Kelly 223

What Schizophrenia Is Like 224

Schizophrenia's Effect at Work. 227

Working with Schizophrenia 228

Summary: Schizophrenia's Effect on Vocational Abilities. . . . 234

Summary: Vocational Strategies and Accommodations 236

**Conclusions and Implications: The Role of
Psychological Assessment 237**

Beyond Diagnosis. 238

Personality Factors 239

The Case for Supported Employment 240

Disclosure of Disability 241

Appendix 243

References 247

Index 249

Preface

ABOUT THIS BOOK

This book offers a guide to many of the DSM-IV diagnoses that vocational rehabilitation professionals are likely to encounter in their work. Its organization is congruent with DSM-IV's classification, but it includes only those disorders that best and most clearly illustrate the difficulties encountered by these clients and the professionals who serve them.

Variables, such as severity, comorbid psychiatric conditions, personality factors, and general intelligence, can combine to create an almost infinite number of nuances and permutations, which is why diagnosis is art as well as science. No exact formula exists, or can exist, for helping or working with a particular person. In addition, each individual will react differently to his or her diagnosis. However, the framework offered here can serve as an example and guide to decisions about how to provide effective rehabilitation services (Figure 1).

Part I describes disorders characterized by subjective distress; the client feels bad. DSM-IV classifies these disorders on Axis I. They have been popularly known as neuroses and are very common. Chapter 1 addresses mood disorders: major depression, dysthymia, and bipolar disorder. Chapter 2 is devoted to the anxiety disorders, including agoraphobia and social phobia, posttraumatic stress disorder, and obsessive-compulsive disorder. Chapter 3 discusses the somatoform disorders, which involve unexplained physical symptoms.

Part II describes disorders characterized by a chronic pattern of problems in relating to others, acting impulsively, or engaging in illegal behavior. The client may or may not feel bad but experiences significant problems in situations that require dealing with other peo-

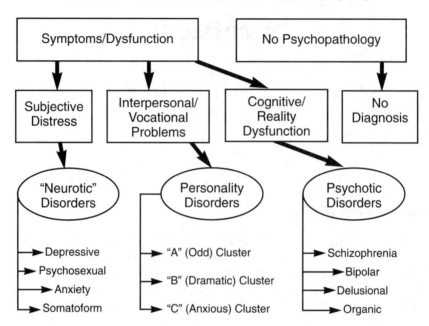

Figure 1. While diagnosis is as much art as science, it provides an important framework for rehabilitation decisions.

ple. These disorders often go unrecognized. Their effect is insidious and pervasive, and their ability to disrupt the workplace and the work experience is extensive. They are the personality disorders, classified on Axis II. Part II covers each personality disorder identified in DSM-IV, grouped in clusters based on similar traits. These are the "odd" cluster, found in Chapter 4; the "dramatic" cluster, in Chapter 5; and the "anxious" cluster, in Chapter 6.

Part III addresses psychotic disorders. Schizophrenia and related disorders are discussed in Chapter 7. These are Axis I disorders, characterized by difficulties in accurately perceiving reality. They have a profound effect on a person's ability to function at work and in every other aspect of life.

DISORDERS LEFT OUT

Several very common conditions, including learning disorders, organic disorders, and substance abuse disorders, are not discussed here.

People who have such disorders do not compose a homogeneous group and cannot be described or understood as such. Diverse factors cause these disorders and affect their expression. Recognizing them and responding to them in the workplace, however, can be a fairly straightforward process.

Learning disorders, of which dyslexia or reading disorder is the most common, show themselves as deficits in one or more specific cognitive or academic abilities. They are not necessarily related to general intelligence or to mental or emotional health. A person of average or above average intelligence might have difficulty learning to read or write, learning a foreign language, or learning arithmetic. Once identified, such deficits can be readily dealt with either through appropriate vocational planning or through relatively simple workplace accommodations.

Organic disorders, called cognitive and amnesiac disorders in DSM-IV, are caused by neurological damage or insult, such as head injury, stroke, or toxic reactions to substances like drugs and alcohol. Different organic causes lead to different intellectual, cognitive, or memory deficits. The term "organic disorder" refers to a diverse set of intellectual and personality problems, including lasting or permanent changes, which are not consistent from person to person. Identifying the particular deficit in a particular individual is an essential step in vocational planning for that person.

A great deal has been written about substance use disorders and their effect at work (cf. Falvo, 1991). Those who struggle with such disorders are an extremely diverse group, some of whom function quite well and others not at all. Many mental health and personality disorders are exacerbated by substance abuse, and in those cases the underlying disorder must be addressed. When substance abuse is the primary factor affecting vocational planning, issues such as absenteeism and lack of reliability are usually at the forefront. A straightforward approach, relying on clear expectations and consequences, is often the most useful. In general, however, people who are actively abusing chemicals cannot benefit from vocational rehabilitation until they experience a sustained period of sobriety and make a commitment to a sober lifestyle.

CASE EXAMPLES AND TREATMENT ISSUES

Illustrative case material in each chapter describes specific psychological and psychiatric symptoms and their vocational impact. Drawn from actual cases, the examples represent composite pictures, with

personal details changed to protect privacy and clinical details selected to provide clarity. Each case study consists of a description of
the disorder, details of its effect on vocational functioning, and an example of how a rehabilitation professional might respond to the difficulty in order to bring about a successful resolution.

In reading through the cases, one notices that each of the people
presented is in great need of mental health care and would seemingly
benefit from psychotherapy, medication, or a combination of the
two. If such a referral were accepted, and if the treatment were highly
successful—if, for instance, Jack (Chapter 1) never had another major
depressive episode or Carol (Chapter 5) stopped her self-destructive
behavior—the workplace difficulties that these or any of the other
disorders create would be considerably less problematic.

Unfortunately, some people with the disorders described here either refuse to accept a referral for psychotherapy or psychiatric medication, or are unable to benefit significantly from treatment. Those
who cannot change, and the professionals who work with them,
must instead learn to cope with and accommodate their symptoms
and their interpersonal problems as best they can. The right work setting and the right kind of support on the job can help them do so,
and this book is meant as a guide in that regard. An interdisciplinary
team approach, including a vocational rehabilitation professional, a
psychologist, a workplace supervisor or human resources representative, and perhaps a social worker, psychiatric nurse, psychiatrist, or
other helping professional familiar with the situation, is invaluable.

A FINAL WORD

Psychological and psychiatric disorders often occur in combination
with each other, and they always occur in the context of the client's
life. Axis I and Axis II diagnoses can mask each other, so that a major
depressive episode might hide an underlying passive-aggressive personality disorder, or a substance abuse disorder might develop as an
attempt to cope with anxiety. Making effective use of diagnostic information requires looking closely at all factors affecting a client's life
and mental health. To this end, the World Health Organization
(1997) offers a model of factors affecting "disablement," a concept
formerly referred to as "disability" (see Figure 2). The model suggests
that disablement is a complex interaction between the disorder and
environmental and personal "contextual" factors. The interaction is
not always predictable, and it is reciprocal, with the contextual factors affecting the disorder and vice versa.

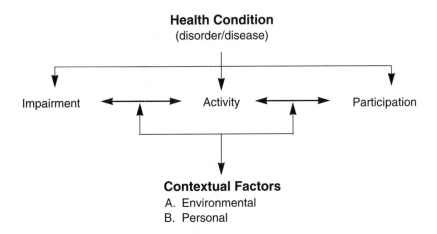

Figure 2. Disablement is a complex interaction between a disorder and contextual factors.

Source: Reprinted with permission from International Classification of Impairments, Activities, and Participation. A Manual of Dimensions of Disablement and Functioning. Beta-1 draft for field trials. World Health Organization, Geneva, ©1997.

For example, if a person with generalized anxiety disorder avoids others because of embarrassment, and has trouble concentrating when experiencing stress, certain contextual factors could be altered to reduce the impact on participation (formerly referred to as "handicap") in the workplace. Changes could include relaxation techniques or medication to reduce anxiety (a personal factor), allowing the person to take a time-out when feeling especially anxious, and encouraging coworkers to be tolerant and supportive (environmental factors).

Incorporating this model along with the DSM-IV multiaxial system provides a biopsychosocial perspective that is broader and more useful than a strictly medical model. It places the emphasis not on the psychiatric diagnosis, but on the interaction between diagnostic symptoms, work environment, and personal factors. Such an inclusive view, while recognizing limitations in a realistic and pragmatic way, focuses instead on strengths, coping ability, and creativity in structuring the work environment.

Just as effective vocational rehabilitation of people with physical disorders requires an understanding of the nature, extent, and effects of the disorder, effective rehabilitation of people with psychiatric disorders is best accomplished in conjunction with a thorough psychiatric or psychological evaluation.

Introduction: Psychiatric Disorders and Vocational Functioning

Psychological and psychiatric disabilities—disorders involving emotion, behavior, cognitive ability, and interpersonal skills—present a unique set of challenges for employees and employers, and for professionals who work in the field of vocational rehabilitation. Unlike physical disabilities, mental health, behavioral, and emotional problems are rarely visible. The criteria for defining them are complex, and their impact in the workplace can be difficult to understand. Nevertheless, such disorders are extremely common, and their effect on job performance can be profound.

THE ROLE OF DSM-IV

The *Diagnostic and Statistical Manual of the American Psychiatric Association,* fourth edition, known as DSM-IV *(American Psychiatric Association, 1994),* is the latest classification of mental disorders, continuing an evolving system of defining diagnostic categories that began with the appearance of the first manual in 1952. It offers specific diagnostic criteria based on a consensus of current thought and understanding. It serves as a guide to making diagnoses of mental disorders and as an aid to research, communication, and treatment.

DSM-IV defines mental disorders by means of a multiaxial system, which attempts to map the complexity of factors relevant to mental health. A diagnosis may be made on one or all of the five axes:

Axis I refers to clinical syndromes, such as depression or anxiety, and to learning disorders.

Axis II refers to personality factors—long-standing patterns of thinking about and relating to other people, the environment, and oneself—and to mental retardation.

1

Axis III refers to physical conditions.

Axis IV describes current psychosocial stressors, such as unemployment, the death of a family member, or being a crime victim, which can affect mental health and level of functioning.

Axis V contains a rating scale for Global Assessment of Functioning, on which a rating of 1 indicates overwhelming and debilitating symptoms, such as the imminent threat of hurting self or others, and 90 indicates almost no symptoms.

Psychiatric disorders are assigned number codes on Axis I and Axis II, and one individual may have several diagnoses on each. When clinical syndromes and personality disorders occur together, the conditions are known as comorbid, which is often the case; research indicates that up to 90% of mental health patients who have an Axis I disorder also have a personality disorder coded on Axis II.

A summary of DSM-IV appears in the Appendix. Looking at it, one notes that Axis I disorders are organized from the broad to the specific. Within a broad category, such as mood disorders, appears a specific disorder, such as major depression. Each disorder is then further specified with descriptions of its severity and associated features, for example, major depression, moderate, without psychotic features.

The relevance of such diagnostic information for vocational rehabilitation professionals becomes obvious when we look at some of the dimensions on which a psychological or psychiatric disorder can adversely affect job performance, as in Table 1.

Cognition refers to intelligence, memory, academic skills, and the ability to use these skills. It is the ability to acquire knowledge, to plan, to make use of one's perceptions, and to reason out problems or difficulties. Some jobs require high levels of cognitive ability, while others require relatively little, but its absence or impairment is problematic in any work setting. The effect on cognitive ability is obvious in mental retardation and brain injury. A depressed or anxious person may not be mentally retarded, but the symptoms of major depression, anxiety, and other psychological disorders often include problems with memory and concentration, which in turn adversely affect cognitive ability.

Pace is the ability to perform job tasks at a reasonable or competitive speed, or at a steady and predictable rate. It is the ability to get the job done on time and to work at a rate that is in accordance with the needs of coworkers and the workplace. An employee who cannot keep up the pace, who slows other workers down, and who is sometimes fast and sometimes slow affects performance and morale for everyone. A depressed person may lack the energy to keep up the

Table 1   Psychological Factors in Job Performance

Psychological Factor	Effect on Job Performance	Diagnostic Examples
Cognition	Intelligence, memory, academic skills and the ability to use these skills.	Mental retardation; brain injuries; schizophrenia; depression; anxiety.
Pace	The ability to perform tasks at a reasonable speed.	Depression; obsessive-compulsive disorder; passive-aggressive personality disorder.
Persistence	The ability to stay with a task until it is complete.	Bipolar disorder manic phase; attention deficit hyperactivity disorder; histrionic personality disorder; somatization disorder; schizophrenia.
Reliability	Coming to work every day in spite of personal or emotional problems.	Agoraphobia; somatization disorder; avoidant, antisocial, and borderline personality disorders; major depression; bipolar disorder manic phase.
Conscientiousness and motivation	Wanting and trying to do a good job; persisting until it is accomplished.	Antisocial, schizoid, and passive-aggressive personality disorders; major depression.
Interpersonal functioning	The ability to accept supervision, to get along with coworkers or the public.	Bipolar disorder manic phase; posttraumatic stress disorder; antisocial, passive-aggressive, schizoid, borderline, and narcissistic personality disorders.
Honesty, trustworthiness	The ability to be truthful, direct, and straightforward, to refrain from such things as lying and theft at work.	Antisocial personality disorder; borderline personality disorder; chemical dependency.
Stress tolerance	The ability to withstand job pressures such as deadlines or working with difficult people.	Schizophrenia; posttraumatic stress disorder; somatization disorder; agoraphobia; major depression.
Job-specific requirements	E.g., typing speed, conflict resolution skills, "people skills."	Depends on requirement.

pace, an obsessive-compulsive person may be paralyzed by the need to perform the task perfectly, and a passive-aggressive person might respond to a requirement by delaying and procrastinating.

Persistence means staying with a job or task until it is complete, even if one is distracted, frustrated, or bored. Throwing up one's hands in an impulsive rejection of the work, procrastinating, avoiding, cutting corners, leaving parts undone, all show lack of persistence, and all adversely affect the workplace. Someone in the manic phase of a bipolar disorder is simply too disorganized and distracted to be persistent. A person experiencing the symptoms of somatization disorder may feel physically unable to go on. Attention deficit hyperactivity disorder impairs a person's ability to stay focused on a task. People with histrionic personality disorder tend to become easily bored and frustrated.

Reliability means coming to work every day and staying all day, in spite of personal or emotional problems, stress, or psychological or physical symptoms. It means being honest and straightforward. A reliable person is one others can count on and trust to show up, do the work, and take responsibility. An unreliable person causes extra work for others and delays in getting work done. People with agoraphobia struggle every day to get out of the house and get to work, and some days they don't make it. Those with avoidant personality disorder also sometimes feel overwhelmed by ordinary life and don't make it to work. Those with borderline personality disorder may become so involved in their own internal conflicts that the needs of the workplace are secondary, while those with antisocial personality disorder have little regard for rules and schedules.

Conscientiousness and motivation translate into wanting and trying to do a good job and persisting until the desired result is accomplished. A motivated, conscientious person not only does the work, but does it as well as he or she is able and takes pride in a job well done. Many people become less conscientious when troubled by psychological disorders or personal problems. Those with antisocial or schizoid personality disorder, however, seem indifferent to the needs of others and to what others think of them and may show little interest at any time in doing a good job. Motivation is the will to succeed, the belief that one can succeed despite difficulties, the belief that doing one's best is important. An unmotivated worker sees little reason to make the effort to do well. Depression has a major effect on motivation; someone who feels hopeless and wants to die is unlikely to believe that trying hard will make a difference. Similarly, people with dependent personality disorder think very little of themselves, do not believe they can succeed, and are unmotivated to try.

Interpersonal functioning has to do with the ability to accept supervision, criticism, and directives, to get along with coworkers, to work effectively with the public. Poor interpersonal skills cause major problems in the workplace, even if the worker is exemplary in every other way. Personality disorders by definition often involve interpersonal difficulties, some more than others; someone with a dependent or avoidant personality disorder is likely to be easier to get along with than someone with a passive-aggressive, antisocial, or schizoid personality disorder, though he or she may still present difficulties in the workplace. The manic phase of bipolar disorder also creates interpersonal problems because the person can become unreasonable and extremely irritable. People with posttraumatic stress disorder may have learned not to trust, either other people or their own perceptions, and may have difficulty getting along with others as a result.

Honesty and trustworthiness reflect the ability to be truthful. Honest employees can be trusted not to pilfer from the till and not to embezzle from the business. They can be trusted to keep accurate account of their time and to do the work they are paid to do. They are direct and straightforward in their workplace relationships and can be trusted not to engage in manipulation or harassment of others. Antisocial personality disorder, borderline personality disorder, and chemical dependency all involve traits that compromise trustworthiness. A chemically dependent person may lie, manipulate others, or steal to support a drug or alcohol habit. People with borderline personality disorder experience highly unstable emotions, leading them to manipulate others in order to meet their own emotional needs. Those with antisocial personality disorder have little regard for laws, rules, or any other structure meant to keep order in society; they are likely to lie, cheat, steal, and use other people as they please.

Stress tolerance is the ability to withstand the everyday pressure of job demands, such as meeting deadlines, or of the interpersonal environment, such as working with difficult people, without significant decline in job performance or an exacerbation of psychological or physical symptoms. Some workplaces are more stressful than others, but an inability to handle moderate or fluctuating levels of stress causes problems for the worker in any workplace. Most psychological disorders involve a reduction in stress tolerance and are made worse by stressful situations. A person with schizophrenia in its residual phase may become actively psychotic again under stress, even ordinary workday stress. Anxiety disorders and somatoform disorders are also vulnerable to the effects of stress.

Job-specific requirements include such traits as above average judgment required of human service professionals, above average conflict-resolution skills required of law enforcement professionals, high "people skills" required of public relations personnel, high typing speed requirements for word-processing personnel, high intelligence required of rocket scientists, and so on. Many jobs have such requirements, and many psychological disorders preclude meeting them. Helping the client find the right fit is a crucial part of a rehabilitation counselor's role.

Whether an employee's disorder affects these psychological dimensions severely or only mildly, it can have major implications for all involved in the workplace, including supervisors, coworkers, and troubled employees themselves. Understanding a disorder's expression allows for effective planning and a better outcome in the vocational rehabilitation process.

PART I

Feeling Bad

We all feel sad or nervous sometimes; such feelings are part of the human experience. Mysterious physical complaints—a strange weariness, an unexplained ache—plague many of us from time to time. As bad as we may feel, most of us, most of the time, take these things in stride and go on with our daily lives until we feel better. But our feelings and symptoms leave the realm of the normal and become disorders to the extent that they cause us problems at work or in relationships, limit our choices about what we do and say, and diminish our ability to live full lives.

People suffering from mood, anxiety, or somatoform disorders are in a great deal of distress. They would not choose their lot. They cannot simply "snap out of it," much as they would like to and no matter how many times people tell them to. But they can limit the painfully debilitating effects of their symptoms by making life decisions that increase their ability to function. A vocational rehabilitation professional who understands the specific problems these disorders present in a work setting is in a position to offer concrete and effective counseling that will improve functioning and quality of life for the client.

CHAPTER 1

Mood Disorders

Mood is the general, prolonged emotion through which all life experiences are filtered. A mood disturbance can go either down, toward excessive sadness, or up, toward excessive elation.

An episode of major depression is agonizing and overwhelming. Its symptoms can be so severe that hospitalization is the only way to prevent suicide. A person may experience one or many major depressive episodes in a lifetime. Dysthymia is milder and more chronic than major depression. It produces long periods of diminished ability to function or work normally, in which the person can't imagine feeling better or doing more.

The manic phase of a bipolar disorder, at the other end of the mood continuum, sends a person reeling into wild and uncharted territory, unable to make sensible decisions or to behave in a reasonable, organized way. It sometimes requires hospitalization to prevent dangerous or injurious actions to self or others.

The vocational problems created by major depression or bipolar disorder are acute, severe, and extremely disruptive. Those created by dysthymia may be constant and oppressive. All of these disorders cause serious distress in the workplace.

MAJOR DEPRESSION AND DYSTHYMIA

Major depression occurs in up to 25% of the adult female population, and up to 12% of the adult male population; it affects twice as many women as men. It can strike at any age but typically shows up for the first time during the mid twenties. Dysthymia is more common among close relatives of people with major depression than among the general population. It is likely to start early in life and likely to be chronic. Each year, about 10% of people diagnosed with dysthymia experience their first major depressive episode. About half of those go on to have a second episode, 70% of those have a third episode, and 90% of those a fourth. As many as 15% of the people diagnosed with severe major depression die by suicide (American Psychiatric Association, 1994).

Jack

Jack's room was dark and silent when he woke up. He closed his eyes, fighting off consciousness. He felt exhausted, he hadn't slept enough, he couldn't possibly be awake; but sleep would not return. He groaned and turned over. His first thoughts were of death, how easy it would be to die, how little he would be missed, how worthless his life was. If only he had the energy to do something about it. Thirty-nine, twice divorced, estranged from his children, unemployed for the fifth time in as many years—he felt no interest in his life, no desire to ease his loneliness, no hope that anything he did would make any difference. He lay still, waiting to gather enough energy to get up and make himself a cup of coffee, wishing he would just die instead.

What Depression Is Like

- Depressed mood, tearfulness
- Lack of interest in life, low motivation
- Sleeping problems
- Poor appetite
- Irritability
- Pessimism, defeatist attitude, low self-confidence, feelings of worthlessness, guilt
- Poor concentration, memory, and decision-making abilities
- Preoccupation with death

Depressed mood, tearfulness. Jack feels sad, down, blue, bummed out, or empty most of the time. He cries a lot, sometimes for no reason he can see, and he feels ashamed if it happens when anyone else is around. His mood has been generally low for a long time, but lately it's become more than he can stand. He's felt this bad before, several times before, in fact, and he's even gone to see a psychiatrist about it, at his second wife's insistence.

The psychiatrist never did much good though. Jack didn't like the pills the doctor gave him; they took weeks to work, then they didn't seem to work all that well anyway, and they had weird side effects.

The doctor wanted him to try something else, but Jack quit going. He also didn't like the psychotherapist the doctor sent him to. He could never think of anything to say to her, and he was irritated that she was always so damn cheerful. He quit going to her, too. This time, he feels too hopeless and alone even to think of getting help.

Lack of interest in life, low motivation. Most days, Jack has almost no energy. He feels worn out, weighted down, as though he were moving through water. Sometimes just getting himself washed and dressed exhausts him. Sometimes he stops halfway through something he's doing, like mowing the lawn. He feels too tired to go on, and he doesn't care about the result. The idea of trying to find a job is enough to send him straight back to bed. Even things he used to enjoy—fishing, hiking, playing his guitar, going to movies, hanging out with his buddies—seem like way too much effort. Most of his friends have stopped calling him, because he never wants to do anything.

Sleeping problems. Some depressed people sleep all the time, but Jack's problem is the opposite; he can't sleep. He wakes up in the middle of the night, or too early in the morning, and can't get back to sleep. Sometimes, tired as he is, he can't even fall asleep when he gets into bed, so he usually stays up as late as he can watching TV, hoping that'll help.

Poor appetite. One thing Jack used to love was food, any kind of food. He was even a pretty fair cook and did most of the cooking for the family during his second marriage. But now, he doesn't care if he eats or not. Even if he makes it to the grocery store, thinks of something to eat, and prepares a meal for himself, he usually doesn't finish it all. He thinks he's lost weight but hasn't bothered to weigh himself.

Irritability. Most people who know Jack don't know he's depressed. He snaps at his mother when she calls to ask how he's doing. He gets mean and sarcastic with friends who want him to go out. He loses his temper with anyone who asks how his job search is going. In fact, his habit of being withdrawn and generally irritable was one of the reasons he lost his last job. Most people think he's just bad-tempered.

Pessimism, defeatist attitude, low self-confidence, feelings of worthlessness, guilt. Jack feels like he's failed at everything he's tried. "Give me something to do," he says, "and watch me screw it up." His first marriage, to his high-school sweetheart at age 18, ended less than a year later, his fault, he's sure. His second marriage lasted five years and produced two children. That was a good time in his life. He had a computer programming job, he liked it, and he did well for a while. But he doesn't blame his wife for leaving him when that job fell apart; she deserved better.

He would like to be more involved with his children and feels guilty that he isn't, even though it's hard because his ex-wife moved them out of state and would never talk to him about letting them visit. He gave up trying. He's hopeless about trying anything, whether it's work or relationships, but feels guilty about not trying. When he does talk to people, he feels guilty about "bringing them down, too." He feels like he deserved to lose his jobs—"I was never that great at any of them"—and does not deserve another chance.

Poor concentration, memory, and decision-making abilities. One of the most frustrating things for Jack is that he can't seem to keep his mind on anything. He'll turn on the TV to watch the news, and five minutes later find himself staring off into space. He can't remember what he did the day before, whether or not he did his laundry, how long it's been since he saw his mother, or what the clerk just said to him in the check-out line. He can't decide what shirt to put on in the morning, derides himself for being indecisive about such a stupid and inconsequential thing, still can't decide, and doesn't get dressed. In his last job, as a clerk at an auto-parts store, he couldn't make a decision about which part a customer needed. He lost the sale, and the next day he lost the job.

Preoccupation with death. Jack has never tried to kill himself, but he's sure thought about it. Right now, he thinks about it all the time. Sometimes he thinks his life isn't worth living. Other times, he wishes he were dead. And sometimes he starts to think about how he would do it, what method would be the most certain. Nearly every day he drives past a construction site near his house. He watches the crew repairing a bridge and he thinks about how easy it would be to "fall" from one of the high girders into the river below. Death seems like the easiest way out.

Depression's Effect at Work

- Low motivation, poor initiative, low energy
- Poor ability to stay on task, many mistakes
- Irritability, hypersensitivity to criticism, poor stress tolerance

Low motivation, poor initiative, low energy. When he's depressed, Jack does as little as he can to get by at work. He stays out of the boss's way, so he won't get any extra tasks. If he has to learn something new, like the new computers at the auto-parts store, it takes him a long time. Weeks after everyone else was comfortable with them, Jack was still asking for help. Once, in a burst of energy, he agreed to reorganize a couple of shelves in the stock room, but he left the job unfinished because it seemed too hard. He has no endurance; he can't stick with things. He comes in late, leaves early, and some days he doesn't come in at all.

Poor ability to stay on task, many mistakes. To his boss, Jack didn't seem to care how well he did his job. To Jack, just showing up seemed like a huge effort, about the best he could do most days. If something didn't get done fast enough, or well enough, or at all, he was likely to leave it for someone else to fix. Many times at the auto-parts store, his orders would not get forwarded in time to the supplier, or they would contain major mistakes, or he would leave out important details, because he couldn't concentrate, he couldn't remember things, and he couldn't decide what to do. His boss couldn't count on him.

Irritability, hypersensitivity to criticism, poor stress tolerance. Jack felt guilty and extremely frustrated with himself; he knew his work performance was bad, but he couldn't seem to make it better. He backed off as much as he could from his coworkers and usually responded with irritation or anger to anything they said to him. Everything sounded like criticism, especially if it came from his boss, and he just didn't want to hear it. He figured they all talked behind his back, complaining about him. When his boss asked him to redo something or to correct a problem with a customer or supplier, he felt overwhelmed and stressed out and couldn't handle the task.

Working with Depression

Jack was looking back at a long string of failures, and he couldn't see any way to turn things around. He didn't believe he could make the changes in attitude and behavior that he needed to make. He couldn't even think of what they were. He felt stupid, even though he got average grades in high school and completed two years of college. His self-esteem was zero. His motivation was zero. His hope for the future was zero. But the truth is, he could work.

When he realized that he was nearly out of money and facing the danger of losing his house, fear overcame the inertia of Jack's depression. He knew that he had to do more than read the want-ads, respond half-heartedly to a few, and hope someone would offer him a job. He began to think more seriously about suicide—it would solve all his problems. He actually went to a gun shop, but did not make a purchase, and found himself shaken and frightened by the direction his thoughts were taking.

He tried going to an employment agency, but felt put off and intimidated by the crisply efficient receptionist, and left without filling out the form or seeing a counselor. He remembered that his ex-wife's brother had gone to some state agency for help getting a job after recovering from a motorcycle accident. Jack didn't know what the agency was, and he didn't know if they would help him. Feeling desperate, not hopeful, he looked at the state office listings in his phone book until he found one for vocational services. He called the number and made an appointment.

Making this much effort on his own behalf had taken a great deal of energy for Jack, and it actually helped lift his depression a little bit. He remembered something he had heard from his psychotherapist during one of the few visits he made—that being active was the best cure for depression. He didn't believe it, but he did feel some slight relief, enough to allow him to keep the appointment he had made to see Sandy, a vocational counselor who works for the Department of Rehabilitation Services.

After getting as thorough a picture as she could of Jack's vocational history, Sandy wasn't sure exactly what had caused his repeated failures. She knew he was depressed, but she didn't know if there were underlying factors. She didn't know how high his intelligence was. She didn't know if he had a problem with alcohol or drugs. She didn't know if he had neurological or medical problems that could contribute to his difficulty concentrating and his low energy. She wanted more information, so she referred him to a psychologist for an evaluation.

The results were pretty straightforward. Though Jack had some features of avoidant and passive-aggressive personality disorders, his overriding difficulty was depression. His chronic dysthymia had caused him problems, but it was the dips into major depression, with its severe and acutely painful version of the symptoms, that had cost Jack his jobs. The psychological report strongly recommended a referral for medication and psychotherapy, citing the demonstrated effectiveness of this combination for many people with Jack's type of depression.

With this information, Sandy could begin to think about a job situation that would allow Jack the possibility of succeeding. She knew it wouldn't be easy. He would need encouragement and a great deal of emotional support to begin the process, to stay motivated, and to stick with it. Once in a job, he would need some workplace accommodations to help him cope with his symptoms. She knew he had little hope of succeeding without treatment for his depression, and she knew he had failed at treatment in the past. She took a strong stand on the issue. She insisted that he accept the referral. She told him that receiving her services was contingent on his giving treatment a shot at helping him.

Jack didn't really like Sandy. He appreciated her nonjudgmental approach to his situation, but he resented her air of confidence and capability. Still, he thought she might be his last chance, and he felt a tiny glimmer of hope that she could actually help him. He found the information in the psychological report, some of which she had shared with him, to be an accurate assessment of his condition and to be useful in helping him understand what he was going through. He found her efforts to discover his vocational interests and needs gratifying; he had never thought before about trying to find a job that actually suited him. So he agreed to her terms.

On visiting the psychiatrist, Jack learned that a lot had changed since he first tried antidepressant medication about 15 years earlier. After three weeks on a new medication, he had to admit that he felt better, had more energy, slept better, enjoyed his food again, and was not bothered by side effects. His psychotherapy experience was not quite so successful, but he had agreed to 10 weekly sessions, and he attended all of them. By the end of the 10 weeks, he did feel that he understood the cyclical nature of his depression and how to cope with it a little better. He was no longer suicidal.

Jack and Sandy began to look closely at exactly what had gone wrong with his previous jobs and to consider what kinds of situations might work better. He told her about wishing he could work with the construction crew on the high bridge, but they both agreed that he didn't need any job that came with a suicide risk. He lost his computer programmer job because of concentration and memory problems; he couldn't come up with the right solutions when he had to. He once had a job in an assembly plant; he thought he ought to be able to handle that, but he couldn't keep up the pace consistently, and he threw off the timing for everyone on the assembly line. The job at the auto-parts store was low stress in some ways, but it required him to take the initiative in solving customers' problems. He had to make decisions, deal with complaints, and confront suppliers, and he often felt overwhelmed.

Jack's interests and aptitude tend toward things rather than people, concrete rather than abstract. Because of his depression, he is more likely to succeed in a low-key job where the tasks and expectations are relatively simple and straightforward and are pretty much the same from day to day without a lot of surprises or changes. Clear guidelines or protocols would help him, so he wouldn't have to make decisions.

Flexibility with respect to how much and how fast he worked, and with respect to the exact hours he worked, would help him. He could work alone but would probably do better as part of a supportive team, in order to prevent isolation.

Sandy felt that Jack was ready to start applying for jobs. She worked with him on some sample application forms, helping him phrase his job experience and his frequent job changes in positive language. She helped him identify his strengths as an employee, something he had never thought of before. He filled out applications for several possible employers. Sandy role-played job interviews with him, and eventually he was offered one, and then another. Neither job worked out, and Jack's natural pessimism and defeatist attitude began to threaten his new-found confidence. He skipped a scheduled appointment with Sandy, then felt guilty and was afraid to call her. She called him several days later and told him he had to continue the process even though he felt discouraged. She told him she had another possibility for him to check out.

Through her placement resources, Sandy knew of a large manufacturing company that was looking for an inventory manager. Jack thought that any job with the word "manager" in the title was beyond his capabilities, but Sandy encouraged him at least to find out what it entailed. She coached him on what to say when he called for information, and he made the call from her office. The job consisted of working with two other people in a supply room, keeping track of parts, supplies, and equipment. It involved some computer work, some ordering, and some contact with people from other departments within the company. Sandy thought it sounded perfect for him, and Jack decided to apply.

When he was hired, his first comment to Sandy was, "I wonder how long it will take me to mess this up." She told him that she would be available to him for the first few months of his new job, and she encouraged him to do something he had never done before: be straight with his supervisor about his depression. To Jack, his struggle with depression was a shameful secret, something he did his best to hide. He couldn't imagine voluntarily telling anyone, especially his boss.

But Sandy convinced him that the disclosure would help him in several ways. First, his boss couldn't provide the necessary accommodations, such as scheduling flexibility and clearly spelled-out daily tasks, unless he knew what Jack needed. Second, his coworkers would be more likely to offer encouragement and emotional support if they knew he was depressed than if they thought he was just standoffish, irritable, and slow to learn. Third, the next time he began to slide into a major depressive episode, his coworkers or supervisor could recognize what was happening, and Jack wouldn't have to lose his job over it.

On his good days, Jack feels like a valued and contributing member of the work force. On his bad days, he shows up, if maybe a little late, and does a reasonably good job because his boss has helped him establish a predictable routine for each day and he doesn't have to think or make decisions. Staying on his medication will help him, as will the routine of his job and some renewed interest in things he used to enjoy. Still, Jack is likely to struggle with periodic episodes of major depression all his life. If he knows that, and his supervisor knows it, he can cope with it better. The episodes are likely to be shorter and less disruptive, and Jack can keep his job.

Summary: Depression's Effect on Vocational Abilities

Level of Impairment

1. no impairment
2. mild—minimal impairment with little or no effect on ability to function
3. moderate—some impairment, which limits ability to function fully
4. serious—major impairment, which may at times preclude ability to function
5. severe—extreme impairment

Understanding and Memory

Remembers locations and basic work procedures

1_____ 2___X___ 3_____ 4_____ 5_____

Understands and remembers short, simple instructions

1___X___ 2_____ 3_____ 4_____ 5_____

Understands and remembers detailed instructions

1_____ 2_____ 3___X___ 4_____ 5_____

Concentration and Persistence

Carries out short, simple instructions

1___X___ 2_____ 3_____ 4_____ 5_____

Carries out detailed instructions

1_____ 2___X___ 3_____ 4_____ 5_____

Maintains attention and concentration for extended periods of time

1_____ 2_____ 3_____ 4___X___ 5_____

Can work within a schedule, maintain attendance, be punctual

1_____ 2___X___ 3_____ 4_____ 5_____

Sustains ordinary routine without special supervision

1___X___ 2_____ 3_____ 4_____ 5_____

Can work with or close to others without being distracted by them

1___X___ 2_____ 3_____ 4_____ 5_____

Makes simple work-related decisions

1_____ 2_____ 3___X___ 4_____ 5_____

Works quickly and efficiently, meets deadlines, even under stressful conditions

1_____ 2_____ 3_____ 4_____ 5___X___

Completes normal workday and workweek without interruptions due to symptoms

1_____ 2_____ 3_____ 4___X___ 5_____

Works at a consistent pace without an unreasonable number or length of breaks

1_____ 2_____ 3_____ 4___X___ 5_____

Social Interaction

Interacts appropriately with general public

1_____ 2_____ 3___X___ 4_____ 5_____

Asks simple questions or requests assistance when necessary

1_____ 2___X___ 3_____ 4_____ 5_____

Accepts instruction and responds appropriately to criticism from supervisors

1_____ 2_____ 3___X___ 4_____ 5_____

Gets along with coworkers without distracting them

1_____ 2___X___ 3_____ 4_____ 5_____

Maintains socially appropriate behavior

1____X____ 2_____ 3_____ 4_____ 5_____

Maintains basic standards of cleanliness and grooming

1____X____ 2_____ 3_____ 4_____ 5_____

Adaptation

Responds appropriately to changes at work

1_____ 2_____ 3____X____ 4_____ 5_____

Is aware of normal work hazards and takes necessary precautions

1_____ 2____X____ 3_____ 4_____ 5_____

Can get around in unfamiliar places, can use public transportation

1____X____ 2_____ 3_____ 4_____ 5_____

Sets realistic goals, makes plans independently of others

1_____ 2____X____ 3_____ 4_____ 5_____

Summary: Vocational Strategies and Accommodations

To optimize the chances for vocational success, a person with major depression needs:

- A referral for medication and psychotherapy to help reduce symptoms.
- Simple, straightforward tasks and expectations to aid memory and concentration and help develop a sense of mastery.
- Predictability, little change in tasks and expectations from day to day.
- Clear guidelines and protocols, possibly written out and posted.
- Flexibility with regard to pace of work, timing of breaks, exact hours worked, and possibly days worked, to accommodate medication effects and fluctuations in energy level.
- To work as part of a team or work unit, in order to minimize loneliness.
- To disclose history of depression to supervisor, if supervisor is likely to be supportive, in order to be provided with necessary accommodations and social support.

BIPOLAR DISORDER, MANIC PHASE

About 0.4%–1.6% of the people in the general population will experience a manic episode in their lifetime, and, of those, 90% will go on to have a second episode, a third, fourth, and more. In between episodes, 70%–80% will return to being fully functional, but 20%–30% will continue to experience mood fluctuations, as well as interpersonal difficulties. Gender and ethnic differences have no effect on the prevalence of bipolar disorder, but close relatives of those who have had a manic episode are more likely than the general population to be diagnosed with either bipolar disorder or major depression. Manic episodes can bring violent behavior, abuse, serious occupational and relationship problems, and, in 10%–15% of the cases, suicide (American Psychiatric Association, 1994).

Paula

At 3:00 in the morning, Paula was still up. Not only up, but feeling great. Not just great, terrific. On top of the world, out of this world, in outer space, in the stratosphere. She was buzzing around her apartment, planning a surprise gourmet dinner for her boyfriend—she'd been meaning to call him to come over for hours, but kept getting distracted; she remembered the incredible drawing she'd started, and that reminded her of all her ideas about how to change her job; she went to call her boss, but on her way to the phone she passed her open closet door and decided to gather up all the clothes she didn't like to pack in a box and give away. Who needed dull clothes? She had so much to do, it was a good thing she didn't need sleep anymore. Why didn't she realize before how brilliant she was, how creative, what magnificent ideas, what incredibly important projects to offer the world? She started off again to call her boss, even though she was still mad at him for putting her off this afternoon. It was 4:30 a.m., and this time she made it to the phone.

What a Manic Episode Is Like

- Abnormally elevated, expansive, or irritable mood
- Grandiosity
- Reduced need for sleep
- Increased sociability, hyperactivity
- Pressured speech, distractibility, racing thoughts, flight of ideas
- Flamboyance

- Poor reality testing, hallucinations, delusions
- Poor judgment

Abnormally elevated, expansive, or irritable mood. In her manic phase, Paula felt euphoric, elated, high, on top of the world, and she laughed loudly and frequently. But she could quickly slip into a nasty, irritable state, as she had that afternoon with her boss. She had gone to him at the end of the day with a whole list of great suggestions, fantastic ideas for work she wanted to do, clients she wanted to get, advertising campaigns she knew would just dazzle everyone. He was unimpressed. In fact, he asked her to leave his office. So she told him off, at length and in no uncertain terms.

Grandiosity. Her performance on her job as a graphic designer in an advertising agency has been solid, though not stellar. But in her manic state, Paula is certain that her ideas are unmatched for creativity and brilliance, and that she is by far the best person to carry them out. Her self-esteem has taken off, sky-rocketed, gone through the roof. She feels like the most attractive, desirable, intelligent, fascinating, charming, and knowledgeable person on earth, whose words are pearls of wisdom or hilariously funny, and whose plans are perfect and should never be questioned.

Reduced need for sleep. Paula has slept only about three hours in the last five days. She's 30, and this is her third manic episode, the first in three years. She had been stable for so long that she thought she could go off her medication, even though her doctor told her otherwise. She knew the first night she didn't sleep what was coming, but was already too caught up in the high energy and euphoria to do anything to stop it.

Increased sociability, hyperactivity. Paula has always been active and sociable, with lots of friends and interests. But now, while manic, she is a whirlwind. She joined a committee to reelect her favorite political candidate and makes dozens of phone calls daily on his behalf. She hands out leaflets on street corners for a local religious organization. She decided to go to graduate school, and has gone to the admissions office several times, trying to get the entrance requirements waived. She started to paint a mural on an outside wall of her apartment building and went into one of her angry tirades when the owner came to stop her. She has been calling people, including her boyfriend, her boss, and old friends from college, in the middle of the night, oblivious to the fact that they are not glad to hear from her. One night she stood on the corner near her apartment handing out all the cash she had on hand, including her collection of rare coins.

Pressured speech, distractibility, racing thoughts, flight of ideas. Paula is always talkative, but in her manic phase she's almost impossible to interrupt. She talks loud, she talks fast, and she doesn't make much sense. She goes off on tangents, and then off on tangents of tangents, and never gets back to what she started with.

In her latest conversation with her boss, for example, she knew she was a little disorganized in presenting her ideas; she had so much to say that the words just seemed to tumble out, and she jumped from thought to thought much too fast for a "plodding ignoramus," which is what she called him, among other things, to follow. She was talking about a design, heard someone cough in the hallway and went off about germs in the air, flashed on some movie she had seen and started to act out a scene from it, remembered the boyfriend she had seen the movie with, burst into loud and dramatic laughter, and then dropped her voice to a conspiratorial stage whisper to describe their sex life. She was amazed when her boss asked her to leave the room and started ranting against him and "the stultifying, mind-numbing, creativity-draining, idiotic organization" he worked for.

Flamboyance. Normally a fan of sophisticated outfits and subtle accessories, Paula has ransacked the back of her closet looking for the red sequined sweater, the ankle-length circle skirt with the tropical bird print, the fringed velvet cape, the skin-tight day-glo running suit. She wears everything with scarves, belts, hats, and all the jewelry she can find. She has forgotten about personal hygiene or hasn't taken the time to attend to it. She wears much more make-up than usual, adding more whenever she thinks of it; her eye-shadow and mascara and lipstick are deepening and expanding and taking over more and more of her face.

Poor reality testing, hallucinations, delusions. At times, Paula slips out of reality altogether and begins to believe she is the reincarnation of the artist Georgia O'Keefe, or maybe some other great artist. At these times, she can't imagine why she bothers working at all, much less at an advertising agency, and can't understand why people don't show her more deference. Sometimes she believes they do show her the respect she deserves; she thinks she hears people on the street referring to her as the artist when they point and smile.

Poor judgment. After calling her boss at 4:30 in the morning and being dissatisfied with his response—he told her to get help or she was fired, then hung up on her—Paula decided to quit her job and leave town. She began packing her suitcase and went on to pack several boxes. She packed her dishes and glassware. She packed her grandmother's silver coffee spoons. She packed all the clocks in her apartment. She did not pack any extra clothes or toiletry articles. She loaded the boxes and suitcase into her car and drove to the mall. It wasn't open yet, so she got back in her car, got on the interstate, and drove until she ran out of gas. Luckily, she was near a town, and she was able to coast to the bottom of an exit ramp. She left the car there and started walking. Three young men drove past in a pick-up truck. They offered her a ride, and she was happy to accept.

A Manic Phase's Effect at Work

- Inflated self-concept, reduced level of interpersonal functioning
- Excessive, inappropriate motivation
- Distractibility
- Distracting to others
- Poor judgment, poor stress tolerance
- Workplace danger

Inflated self-concept, reduced level of interpersonal functioning. In the several days leading up to her manic phase, Paula had been increasingly unable to accept any kind of feedback or direction from her boss or her coworkers. She would either go off on a long litany of complaints and accusations against them, or ignore what was said to her and continue her incessant and apparently disorganized activity. She believed that her work was exemplary, though she could not have said exactly what her work was at that moment. She saw her boss and coworkers as irritating distractions.

Excessive, inappropriate motivation. At the same time, she demanded new responsibilities; she wanted to see her designs all the way through production, she wanted to contact clients personally, she wanted to travel to other cities to get new business. She thought she could do the impossible and would not tolerate being thwarted. But, as was obvious to anyone watching her, she could not seem to get anything done. She used her time unwisely, spending hours talking about her plans, perfecting one part of one design, or making lists and sub-lists of her ideas. Her desk was a mess, and she became more disorganized with each passing day.

Distractibility. Paula was trying to work on so many things at once she couldn't stay focused on any of them. She produced great quantities of work during this time, but finished nothing. While pieces of what she did were quite good, most of her work was unusable. She made phone calls seemingly at random; she would talk on and on with no apparent purpose and then hang up suddenly.

Distracting to others. In the days leading up to her manic phase, Paula would frequently interrupt others' work to share a funny story, to talk about her own ideas and projects, or just because she couldn't sit still. As the manic phase intensified, her mere presence disrupted the teamwork in the office. Her loud voice, constant talk and laughter, incessant activity, and unrealistic appraisal of her ability—not to mention her increasingly bizarre appearance—made it difficult for anyone to get any work done.

Poor judgment, poor stress tolerance. Over a matter of a few days, Paula's presence quickly became not only a business liability but an actual danger in the workplace. She was unreasonable. She was irrational. She was unpredictable and unreliable. Her behavior was either belligerent and provocative, or dramatic and bizarre. She made split-second decisions and acted on them with no thought of possible consequences. She came and went as she pleased. She seriously jeopardized business relationships and ruined some interpersonal relationships on her work team. Stress intensified her erratic behavior; if someone disagreed with her, asked anything of her, questioned her, or thwarted her, there was no telling what she might do.

Workplace danger. Paula never actually presented a physical danger in her workplace, but she might have. People in a manic phase can become verbally aggressive and unpredictably violent. In their state of high energy and poor judgment, they can make inappropriate sexual remarks and aggressive sexual advances. In tenuous contact with reality, they can misinterpret others' innocent behavior as sexually seductive, provocative, or threatening, and act accordingly.

Working with Bipolar Disorder

For three years, very mindful of the painful after-effects of her two previous manic episodes, Paula was extremely conscientious about her medication. Going off it almost certainly precipitated the most recent episode, which eventually spun itself down, but not without its own painful consequences. She ended up in the hospital, back on medication, and back home only after several precarious days in an unfamiliar town while her mental state continued to deteriorate.

The young men in the pick-up truck who offered her a ride by the side of the road may or may not at that moment have had the best intentions toward her, but they quickly understood that something was seriously wrong, that her speech and behavior were far from normal. They had the compassion and good sense to bring her into town to the local sheriff's office, and they told the deputy where her car was.

Paula had left home with no identification of any kind. She told the deputy her name, but was hazy about other details. Her energy level was still high, but her euphoria and expansiveness had faded to a kind of confusion. Her manner was irritable and belligerent.

The nearest hospital didn't have a psychiatric unit, but it kept Paula and medicated her until her identity could be established and arrangements could be made for her brother to come and get her. He had spoken to her psychiatrist, who admitted her to the hospital she had been in twice before. She was there for three weeks before her proper medications could be reestablished and her mood stabilized.

When not manic, Paula is charming, creative, and energetic, with a wide variety of interests. People like her. She functioned well in her various pursuits and at work as long as she structured her life carefully, with regular mealtimes and a regular sleep schedule, and stayed on her medication. Her job at the advertising agency, which she had for over a year, was a good choice for her, because it allowed her a creative outlet, it involved lots of people contact, and at the same time it was a fairly structured environment, with guidelines, deadlines, and time frames. But it wasn't enough to keep her on track.

Before her first manic episode, which happened when she was in college, Paula had a job working rotating shifts in a hospital. Her sleep schedule became so unpredictable that she didn't even know when she stopped sleeping. She was manic for weeks before her behavior became so bizarre that she was forced into a hospital and put on medication. The nurses and the psychiatric social worker told her that maintaining a regular sleep schedule was almost as important as staying on medication in preventing a recurrence. Still, a few years later, she volunteered to help out on a rape crisis hot line. She began waking up in the middle of the night to take calls, and, sure enough, she became manic again within a few weeks.

Paula's vocational success rests on her ability to maintain mental health stability, which she can do only to the extent that she lives a structured and predictable life, something that doesn't come easily to her. She likes action and activity, she likes spontaneity. She fully understands the importance of staying on her medication, but it takes the edge off her energy level, and she sometimes thinks it holds her back. Like many people with bipolar disorder, she is in some denial about the devastating effects of each manic phase and, especially after not having experienced one for a while, remembers the elation and euphoria and high energy as very enjoyable.

For several years after she graduated from college, Paula was self-employed as a freelance artist and designer. She loved the freedom and the fact that she could work as much or as little as she liked, whatever hours she liked, at whatever pace she liked. She did quite well for a while, though it was a whirlwind existence, and she was several times very close to the edge of a manic phase. Her life, her business, and her finances became increasingly chaotic, and it all fell apart very quickly after she began volunteering for the rape crisis line and her sleep schedule was disrupted.

Paula is achievement-oriented and energetic, but she cannot succeed in running her own business because she can't meet high demands for focus and concentration, and she needs ongoing help with her organizational skills. She needs someone to help keep her on track, to check in with her routinely, and to monitor her judgment and decisions. Though she continues to find it very appealing, working on her own in an unstructured setting is not an option for Paula.

While she was hospitalized that second time, about three years prior to her most recent manic phase, Paula established a relationship with Sonia, the social worker on the psychiatric unit. They were close in age, and Sonia also had an interest in art and design. Before Paula could be discharged, Sonia knew that she had to be stable with regard to her mood and her medications, and that she had to have a structured situation to return to.

As part of her discharge planning, Sonia arranged for Paula to stay in a small halfway house near the hospital in order to allow her to establish a routine and maintain a source of support as she continued to stabilize. During the three months that Paula stayed in the halfway house, Sonia left the psychiatric unit, but continued to work in the hospital's outpatient mental health clinic. She saw Paula weekly.

Paula began to feel better and to regain her confidence. She wanted to get a job, and she asked for Sonia's help. Other than her freelance experience, Paula had not had a job that allowed her to be creative and use her artistic ability. Sonia saw the opportunity to do so as central to Paula's ability to stay on track; she had a feeling that even if her mood remained stable, Paula would not stay long in a job situation that didn't allow her a creative outlet.

Sonia helped Paula to prepare a résumé and put together a small portfolio of her work. They worked together on interviewing skills, though, when not manic, Paula had little difficulty convincing people to hire her. Using employment resources that Sonia had, and some contacts of Paula's from her freelance days, they explored the job possibilities. Paula eventually took a job for a small sign-painting company. She painted signs in bright colors with broad brush strokes that said things like "Today's special—peas—29 cents a can."

Paula moved back to her apartment, but she stayed in touch with Sonia. She was extremely careful to keep a regular schedule and to stay on her medication. She continued to look for a more challenging job and was thrilled when the opportunity at the advertising agency came up. She called Sonia to celebrate, and after that their contact was less regular than it had been.

Paula's most recent manic episode was less sudden than it seemed. She had been thinking for several months about going off her medication. She believed she could remain stable but somehow feel better. She was becoming bored with her strict routine and began to allow herself some variations. She requested and was allowed to work on a high-pressure, high-intensity, short-timeframe project at the advertising agency; her boss was very pleased with her contribution, and she was elated by the experience. At the time she made the decision to quit her medication, her mood was already elevated and her need for sleep reduced. She recognized the danger signals and could have averted a manic episode, but succumbed to denial instead.

As she started to regain her mental stability in the hospital, Paula was devastated to realize the extent of the damage she had done to her life, especially to her job. She was certain that she had so severely damaged her relationships at work that she could never return there or even hope for a letter of recommendation from her boss. Frightened, ashamed, and depressed, she began to talk to Sonia, who still worked in the outpatient clinic.

Sonia was not so sure that all was lost. She remembered what a good fit the advertising agency had been for Paula and that Paula's boss had liked her work. She urged Paula to call him, explain what had happened and why, and ask him to give her another chance. Paula felt unable to make the call; the soaring self-confidence of her manic phase was reduced to deep shame about the episode. So, with Paula's permission, Sonia made the call.

She offered a thorough explanation of bipolar disorder and of Paula's particular situation. Paula's boss was willing to listen; he had been concerned for her and had learned from her brother about her hospitalization. Paula then called him herself and asked for her job back. He was willing to let her come back, on the condition that she stay on her medication and that she talk to Sonia, her doctor, her brother, or to him, when she felt her mood begin to change. He also said that one more episode like the last one would mean the end of her employment there; he didn't think his agency or his other employees could survive another period of turmoil like that.

Coaching Paula's boss and coworkers to recognize the early signs of a manic episode might help them help her to head it off. Their noticing and pointing out changes in her behavior might make the difference for her before it's too late. In addition, a structured setting, with clear guidelines, expectations, and timeframes, and with a built-in system for regular feedback would help keep her on track. Sonia offered to meet with Paula, her boss, and any coworkers who wished to attend, to provide such information.

The primary responsibility for Paula's mental health, however, rests with her. She will probably always be drawn to situations that involve creativity, high energy, and lots of contact with people—to situations that excite her and represent a potential danger to her mental health. Despite her best efforts, she may be unable to avoid some manic episodes. But to the extent that she understands her disorder and how to cope with and manage it, and to the extent that she surrounds herself with informed, supportive people, she can keep the disruption in her life to a minimum.

Summary: Bipolar Disorder's Effect on Vocational Abilities

Level of Impairment

1. no impairment
2. mild—minimal impairment with little or no effect on ability to function
3. moderate—some impairment, which limits ability to function fully
4. serious—major impairment, which may at times preclude ability to function
5. severe—extreme impairment

M = while manic; R = in remission

Understanding and Memory

Remembers locations and basic work procedures

1____R____2_____3____M____4_____5_____

Understands and remembers short, simple instructions

1____R____2____M____3_____4_____5_____

Understands and remembers detailed instructions

1____R____2_____3_____4____M____5_____

Concentration and Persistence

Carries out short, simple instructions

1_____R_____2_____3_____M_____4_____5_____

Carries out detailed instructions

1_____R_____2_____3_____4_____5_____M_____

Maintains attention and concentration for extended periods of time

1_____R_____2_____3_____4_____5_____M_____

Can work within a schedule, maintain attendance, be punctual

1_____2_____R_____3_____4_____5_____M_____

Sustains ordinary routine without special supervision

1_____2_____R_____3_____4_____5_____M_____

Can work with or close to others without being distracted by them

1_____2_____R_____3_____4_____5_____M_____

Makes simple work-related decisions

1_____R_____2_____3_____4_____5_____M_____

Works quickly and efficiently, meets deadlines, even under stressful conditions

1_____2_____3_____R_____4_____5_____M_____

Completes normal workday and workweek without interruptions due to symptoms

1_____2_____R_____3_____4_____5_____M_____

Works at a consistent pace without an unreasonable number or length of breaks

1_____2_____R_____3_____4_____5_____M_____

Social Interaction

Interacts appropriately with general public

1_____R_____2_____3_____4_____5_____M_____

Asks simple questions or requests assistance when necessary

1_____R_____2_____3_____M_____4_____5_____

Accepts instruction and responds appropriately to criticism from supervisors

1_____R_____2_____3_____4_____5_____M_____

Gets along with coworkers without distracting them

1_____R_____2_____3_____4_____5_____M_____

Maintains socially appropriate behavior

1_____R_____2_____3_____4_____5_____M_____

Maintains basic standards of cleanliness and grooming

1_____R_____2_____3_____4_____5_____M_____

Adaptation

Responds appropriately to changes at work

1_____2_____R_____3_____4_____5_____M_____

Is aware of normal work hazards and takes necessary precautions

1_____R_____2_____3_____4_____5_____M_____

Can get around in unfamiliar places, can use public transportation

1_____R_____2_____3_____4_____M_____5_____

Sets realistic goals, makes plans independently of others

1_____R_____2_____3_____4_____5_____M_____

Summary: Vocational Strategies and Accommodations

To optimize the chances for vocational success, a person with bipolar disorder needs:

- To take prescribed medication consistently in order to reduce severity of mood swings.
- A structured lifestyle with daily routines and a structured work setting with clear guidelines and expectations, to help modulate mood.
- Clear and predictable timeframes and deadlines.
- An outlet for creative or social energy to minimize boredom.
- Clear limits with regard to behavior and dress, as needed.
- Flexible scheduling to accommodate effects of medication and fluctuations in energy level.

- Regular feedback about job performance and social interaction, if appropriate.
- Help from a rehabilitation professional in disclosing the nature of bipolar disorder to appropriate others at work, in order to engender necessary social support and structure.

CHAPTER 2

Anxiety Disorders

Persistent and irrational fear is the hallmark of anxiety disorders. If the fear is simple—heights, snakes, closed spaces—then dealing with it vocationally is fairly simple, too; one does not become a tour guide at the Sears Tower, a snake handler at the zoo, or a member of the U.S. Navy submarine crew.

Agoraphobia and social phobia, however, present a more complex set of vocational problems for the people who suffer from them, because they involve fears in almost every conceivable life circumstance. People with agoraphobia fear their own feelings. They fear situations and places. They fear going out and they fear being unable to get out, being embarrassed if they try, and needing help when none is available. People with social phobia fear other people. They fear being watched and judged, and they fear acting in a way that will embarrass them in front of others.

Posttraumatic stress disorder stems from a terrifying real-life experience, which the person relives over and over again, unable to move on from it, to forget it, or to put it into perspective. Frightening scenes and sounds intrude into daily life in unpredictable ways, keeping the person constantly on the alert and ever watchful.

Obsessive-compulsive disorder requires a person to perform a repetitive series of meaningless actions, in a vain attempt to ease anxious feelings. The actions become not only an end in themselves but an additional reason to fear; in the obsessive-compulsive mind, leaving out a part of a ritual or doing it wrong could have dire consequences.

These disorders are difficult to cope with in the workplace, not only for the people who suffer from them, but for their coworkers as well. The fears are overwhelming to experience and debilitating if not confronted. They interfere dramatically with work performance.

AGORAPHOBIA AND SOCIAL PHOBIA

Social phobia typically develops in mid-adolescence, often after a childhood characterized by shyness more extreme than normal. It might last a lifetime but vary in intensity depending on life stressors. Its lifetime prevalence can range from 3%-13%, depending on the level of impairment considered. It is associated with other anxiety disorders, including agoraphobia and panic disorder, and is likely to precede them. Ninety-five percent of people diagnosed with agoraphobia also have, or have had, panic attacks. Three times as many women as men are diagnosed as having them. Panic attacks are most likely to begin between late adolescence and the early thirties. Agoraphobia varies in its relationship to panic attacks; it may be chronic regardless of the presence or absence of panic attacks, or its symptoms may decrease as panic attacks decrease (American Psychiatric Association, 1994).

Ron

The morning was cool, but Ron felt sweat rolling down his back under his shirt. He paced back and forth, clenching and unclenching his fists. His hands were clammy. His breath came fast and shallow; he tried to take a deep breath but could not. A wave of nausea washed over him, and he sat down on the bench, holding his head in his hands, trying to fight off dizziness. He was terrified of the ordeal facing him. Each time it seemed harder, not easier.

He looked up and saw the bus. He began to tremble, his whole body shaking. The driver flung the door open, and waited, impatient, watching him, Ron thought. His heart pounded. Somehow—he could not say how he did it—he forced his legs to support his weight, to carry him up the steps into the bus. Somehow, he handed the driver his card to punch, took it back, put it in his pocket, and turned to find a seat. The bus was crowded, the aisle impossibly long and narrow. It wavered in front of him. His knees buckled. He clutched the railing. This was it. He was sure he was dying. No one here could help him. He had to get out. He heard the door close, felt the bus lurch into motion. He had to get out.

What Agoraphobia and Social Phobia Are Like

- Intense anxiety, panic, in a broad range of situations
- Avoidance of anxiety-provoking situations
- Physical symptoms of anxiety

Intense anxiety, panic, in a broad range of situations. Ron is terrified of being in any situation he might not easily be able to get out of. He is terrified of needing help when none is available. As painful as riding the bus is for him, he finds it preferable to driving alone through the long tunnel on his route to work. It was in that tunnel that he had his first panic attack, although at the time he was sure he was having a heart attack and was about to die; he's still not completely convinced that wasn't the case. He was willing to trade his fear of being alone and helpless in the tunnel for his fear of the crowd on the bus. Being dead seemed slightly worse than being embarrassed, although to Ron, in his state of anxiety, it's a meaningless distinction.

He is terrified not only of crowds, but of individual people. The idea of being watched and judged by anyone at any time, of doing or saying anything that might draw him notice, is among his worst fears. He is 35 and single, and he lives in the house he grew up in. His father died about 10 years ago, just before Ron's first panic attack in the tunnel. His mother went into a nursing home about a year ago. He has worked for 12 years as a data-entry clerk at the same company his father worked for. His boss knew his father and for that reason has been pretty patient with Ron and his symptoms. Her patience is wearing thin, however, especially after Ron started missing work because he couldn't cope with the bus ride.

Avoidance of anxiety-provoking situations. Ron gave up driving to work because he couldn't deal with the tunnel. He would often get off the freeway at the exit just before it, which put him in a maze of city streets in a bad neighborhood, an equally frightening situation. He would arrive at work late, soaked in sweat, and shaking. The bus ride is nearly as difficult for him, and there are days when he can't make himself do it. On those days, he calls in sick. He brings his lunch to work and eats alone at his desk because he can't go into the cafeteria at noon. He never goes to movies or restaurants or ball games or the mall. He can't stand in lines. He doesn't leave his house at all unless he has to. He used to get his sister to go out with him sometimes, but she moved to her own apartment and now he is alone.

He stopped going to the grocery store nearest his house, because once a check-out clerk commented on his choice of ice cream, and he felt humiliated. He inadvertently let his mother's rose bushes die during an early frost, and now he can't face his next-door neighbor for fear she will say something to him about it. Once, a young woman was waiting at his bus stop. He walked to the next stop rather than wait with her. When he was young, his mother let him stay home from school on days he felt too nervous to go. He finished high school with the help of a private tutor.

Physical symptoms of anxiety. Ron has full-blown panic attacks, with pounding heart, sweating and trembling, feelings of choking, shortness of breath, and pain in the chest. He feels nauseous and dizzy. He is afraid he will completely lose control or die. He has come to understand that these symptoms are connected to his fears and not to actual physical problems. He also understands that at times his fears are excessive and his behavior unreasonable, but that only increases his embarrassment and reticence. Having a panic attack is a big part of what he tries to avoid.

He has been to his family doctor several times about the physical symptoms, and he followed up on the doctor's referral to a psychologist when there were no medical findings. Despite what he has learned about his fears and his panic attacks, he is not fully convinced that he doesn't have a medical problem, a heart condition, maybe. He found the visits to see the psychologist extremely difficult and unrewarding. The office was in an unfamiliar part of town, he had to ride in a crowded elevator, and he was sure the receptionist disliked him. Also, he couldn't make much sense of the psychologist's treatment program, which involved "confronting" his fears. Ron figured he was already confronting his fears as much as anyone could, and he would much rather avoid them. He quit going after three visits.

Agoraphobia and Social Phobia's Effect at Work

- Restricted behavioral choices
- Hypersensitivity to criticism or rejection
- Decreased energy level, slow pace, inefficiency
- Poor interpersonal functioning, reduced stress tolerance

Restricted behavioral choices. In his 12 years on the job, Ron has been able to create a manageable situation for himself, but one that his coworkers resent and that his boss is under pressure to change. Ron simply doesn't do certain kinds of work. He does not respond to anyone who comes into the office, even if he is the only one in the room. He does not make or accept telephone calls. He does not help train new employees, though he is one of the more experienced workers. He does not work late, even if his project requires it, because then he might be left alone in the building. His work station is nearest the front, because he felt trapped in the back of the room.

His work group rotates the responsibility of reporting on their activities at the departmental staff meetings; Ron does not take his turn, because being the center of attention makes him too anxious. Sometimes he gets out of going to staff meetings altogether. He also does not take his turn at picking up department mail from the mail room, because doing so involves walking through the crowded lobby.

Hypersensitivity to criticism or rejection. To Ron, any criticism is evidence that his anxiety is warranted, and the possibility of being criticized terrifies him. He avoids his boss, because she might tell him about something he did wrong. He avoids his coworkers, because he senses their disapproval of him. He doesn't ask questions, even if he runs into a problem, because he doesn't want to risk embarrassment or be criticized for not knowing. He avoids new responsibilities or changes in expectations. He puts so much energy into avoiding criticism that at times his productivity suffers. He has no desire to make his work more interesting or challenging or to seek advancement; to do so might get him noticed, it might be embarrassing, and it might be criticized.

Decreased energy level, slow pace, inefficiency. Fearful as he is of making mistakes, Ron works slowly and methodically, even, or maybe especially, on "rush" projects. His efforts are successful: he doesn't make many mistakes. But he doesn't get much work done, either. At the end of a mistake-free day, his output is about half that of less conscientious coworkers. He spends a long time making sure he understands exactly what needs to be done, even if he has done it many times before. He checks and rechecks his work at regular intervals. He stops to worry about whether or not he understands it correctly.

Sometimes other worries intrude—will someone ask him a question, will they want him to go pick up the mail, how can he endure the bus ride home, is his heartbeat irregular, are they watching him? Sometimes he stops working for a while until his worries subside. Sometimes his worries overwhelm him, and he doesn't have the energy to go on.

Poor interpersonal functioning, reduced stress tolerance. At those times when he is forced to respond to other people, Ron becomes nearly tongue-tied. He can't communicate or express what's on his mind. Often, he can't answer simple questions, especially if he senses some criticism. He would rather not respond than stand up for himself. Situations that wouldn't bother most people—the location of his work station, for instance—can be sources of extreme stress for Ron. The feeling of being trapped in the back of the room became so consuming that for a while he got very little work done. Still, it was his boss who proposed a solution; Ron had been unable to speak up and ask for what he needed.

Working with Agoraphobia and Social Phobia

Ron is highly motivated to do well at work, if only to avoid the humiliation and embarrassment of doing poorly. His job allows him to relate primarily to his computer screen and very little to other people. His boss has a soft spot for him and has shown unusual patience with his problems. She has made some reasonable accommodations for him and some that go beyond the reasonable, resulting in resentment among his coworkers. Still, Ron's work performance is marginal at best and his continued employment tenuous.

High on Ron's list of worries is the possibility that he might find himself looking for work, and it sends him into a panic. He imagines himself forced to take a job as an usher at a stadium, or in sales, or telemarketing, or some other frightening scenario, and feels he would truly rather die. He never had to interview for his current job, because of his father's help, and the idea of doing so, even for a similar job that he knows he can do, is terrifying. These worries absorb him and do nothing to enhance his performance.

When his boss asked Ron to meet with her and an EAP (Employee Assistance Program) counselor from the human resources department one afternoon, Ron felt ill and nearly left at lunch time. He knew that the purpose of the meeting was to discuss his series of mediocre performance reviews and the increasing tension among his coworkers over what they saw as preferential treatment for him. His boss had assured him that she had asked for help from human resources because she wanted to resolve the problems, but Ron was sure he would be fired and that he would embarrass himself in the meeting.

Over the years of his struggles with agoraphobia and panic attacks, Ron had read many self-help books on the subject and had seen it addressed on various television programs. He did not believe that the generally advocated self-talk and relaxation techniques were at all helpful, but sometimes, in desperation, he tried anyway. Before meeting with his boss, he closed his eyes and focused on his breathing, attempting to clear his mind of negative thoughts. He was able to enter her office in a highly anxious, but not panicked, state.

He felt immediately intimidated by Dan, the EAP counselor. Dan was younger than Ron, he appeared fit and confident, and he greeted Ron with a friendly heartiness that frightened him. Embarrassed by his sweaty palms, Ron kept the handshake as brief as possible and sat down quickly.

Dan talked about Ron's 12 years of service to the company. He noted that such loyalty was rare. He mentioned Ron's father, who had also been a loyal, long-term employee. Ron listened nervously, fidgeting with his hands, not looking up. Dan went on to say that during the past 12 years, things had changed, the department had grown, the workload was heavier, new procedures and new technology had changed the expectations and requirements. Ron glanced at his boss; she smiled reassuringly. Dan said that he had a proposal for Ron to consider. Ron shuddered; he might not be fired, but he might have to attend classes or support groups in order to keep his job, like a chemically dependent coworker had to do.

But Dan's proposal was worse than that. He said that he wanted Ron to take his place as a fully functioning member of the work team, sharing responsibilities equally with his coworkers. Starting the next day, he would meet with Ron several times over the next few weeks to figure out how they could accomplish that. Dan said that he had confidence in Ron. He said that with a few accommodations to help with his problems, Ron would feel more confidence in himself and be more accepted by his coworkers. Ron said nothing, but he felt that he might as well quit right then.

Nevertheless, he did keep his appointment with Dan the next day. Dan had reviewed Ron's performance reviews from the last 12 years. He started by talking about Ron's strengths: Ron likes the detail-oriented nature of the data-entry work he does, and he's good at it when he doesn't feel too stressed and can concentrate. He is conscientious and thorough, and his work, though slow, is accurate and complete. He doesn't mind the limited opportunity for interaction with others; he feels better working undisturbed on his own.

Unfortunately, his boss's well-intentioned efforts to help Ron deal with his anxiety by allowing him to reduce his level of responsibility have created tension between him and his coworkers. In his overconcern about social acceptance and his hypersensitivity to criticism, he is painfully aware of their attitude toward him, he fears their ridicule, and much of his time and energy is spent in avoiding them. When Dan told him that much of his coworkers' dislike stemmed from his avoidance of certain aspects of the job, Ron could understand their point of view, but he couldn't see what he could do about it. He explained to Dan that certain situations made him nervous, and that he might have a heart condition.

Dan asked Ron about his medical history and about his brief experience with the psychologist several years ago. Ron was not happy with his family doctor; he thought that his physical symptoms were severe enough to indicate a medical and not just a psychological problem, he was sure the doctor had missed something, and he was hurt and annoyed that he kept telling him to see a psychologist. He had not found his visits to the psychologist helpful, either, and he said so, but he gave his permission for Dan to talk to both his family doctor and the psychologist, and to review records of his visits there.

At their next meeting, after he had reviewed his history, Dan asked Ron about stress in his life outside of work. Looking back, they saw that Ron's symptoms were worse at times of difficulty at home. He had always been a nervous person, but his panic attacks didn't start until shortly after his father's death about 10 years ago. At that time, his mother, who also suffered from anxiety, became ill and depressed, and she was worried about the family's financial situation, about which she knew nothing. The task of going through their father's papers and figuring things out fell to Ron's sister, then 20, who didn't hesitate to let him and their mother know how much she resented their dependence on her.

The financial situation was not dire—the house was paid off, there was a life insurance policy, and Ron's mother was eligible for a pension—but the relationships in the household became increasingly strained. Ron's mother became fanatical about keeping the house and yard in perfect order. Yet she herself became less and less able to carry out the necessary tasks, and she relied on Ron and his sister. She never left the house, and she was critical of their efforts. She was sympathetic of Ron's difficulties with anxiety, however, and she urged him not to stress himself by doing things that made him nervous.

Ron's symptoms worsened again about a year ago, when his mother's arthritis and other medical problems forced a decision about her care. Again the burden of dealing with things, and of making the arrangements for nursing home care, fell on Ron's sister. Resentful of Ron's inability to cope, she became more and more involved with her own friends and her own life, and eventually moved out. Ron had never lived alone before. He missed his mother's understanding and support and his sister's ability to manage things. He did his best to maintain the household schedule he had known, but with no support or companionship, his anxiety became increasingly overwhelming.

By the time of his third meeting with Dan, Ron was beginning to feel less threatened by the process. He believed that Dan took him seriously, understood his problems at least a little bit, and wanted to help him keep his job. He found some relief just in talking about his situation and his feelings. But he still didn't know exactly what changes Dan would require of him, and he didn't think he would be able to make them.

He certainly didn't like Dan's first recommendation—that he accept a referral for psychotherapy, and possibly join a support group. But

Dan insisted. He said that the county mental health center offered a program specifically for agoraphobia, social phobia, and panic attacks. The program included psychology aides, students trained to provide support and hands-on help to people who were trying to do things that they had been avoiding because of anxiety. If Ron had someone with him, someone who understood what he went through, as he boarded the bus, drove through the tunnel, or entered the lunchroom at noon, he could gradually learn to be less frightened in those situations. He would be less lonely, and his life would be less limited.

Dan went on. He thought that if Ron had some measure of control over his work environment, he might be able to improve his performance. If he could work unobserved by others, work at his own pace without worrying about being judged for it, and work on a flexible schedule, he might be less fearful and preoccupied. This meant moving his work station again, away from the front of the room. Dan suggested a spot about halfway back, near the exit to the back stairway. Ron could then come and go that way if he wanted to, without passing through the busy room.

If he had the option of working with a companion on such tasks as the staff meeting presentation, the mail pick-up, and projects requiring staying late, he might be able to take his turn as needed. Ongoing feedback about what Ron does well—his low error rate, his efforts to be conscientious—would make him feel part of the team, even if he preferred to work alone. Dan said that he would meet again with Ron and his boss to help implement these changes.

Equally important to Ron, however, was the atmosphere in the office. He believed that Dan's suggestions would help, but he wasn't sure they would reduce the level of resentment his coworkers felt toward him, or his own anxiety about them. He wanted to blend in, not be singled out. Dan urged him to try it out—any effort he showed toward become a functioning member of the team would likely improve his coworkers' tolerance of his needs. Dan also thought there might be one or two coworkers who would be sympathetic to Ron if he disclosed his problems to them. When Ron thought about it, he remembered a quiet young woman who had recently started working there; she seemed almost as shy as he was, and he thought maybe he could talk to her.

Ron's anxiety disorder will be a life-long struggle for him. He can ease the burden by staying in regular contact with people who understand it and can support him. He can learn to use relaxation and other coping techniques. He can increase his confidence by following a regular routine, even when he feels especially bad. He can reduce the limitations on his activities by gradually expanding them, with support from others. And he can perform adequate work in a setting where people are willing to make reasonable accommodations for his needs when he can identify and express them.

Summary: Agoraphobia and Social Phobia's Effect on Vocational Abilities

Level of Impairment

1. no impairment
2. mild—minimal impairment with little or no effect on ability to function
3. moderate—some impairment, which limits ability to function fully
4. serious—major impairment, which may at times preclude ability to function
5. severe—extreme impairment

Understanding and Memory

Remembers locations and basic work procedures

1____X____2_____3_____4_____5_____

Understands and remembers short, simple instructions

1____X____2_____3_____4_____5_____

Understands and remembers detailed instructions

1____X____2_____3_____4_____5_____

Concentration and Persistence

Carries out short, simple instructions

1____X____2_____3_____4_____5_____

Carries out detailed instructions

1____X____2_____3_____4_____5_____

Maintains attention and concentration for extended periods of time

1_____2_____3____X____4_____5_____

Can work within a schedule, maintain attendance, be punctual

1_____2_____3____X____4_____5_____

Sustains ordinary routine without special supervision

1____X____2_____3_____4_____5_____

Can work with or close to others without being distracted by them

1_____ 2_____ 3_____ 4_____ 5___X____

Makes simple work-related decisions

1_____ 2_____ 3___X___ 4_____ 5_____

Works quickly and efficiently, meets deadlines, even under stressful conditions

1_____ 2_____ 3_____ 4___X___ 5_____

Completes normal workday and workweek without interruptions due to symptoms

1_____ 2_____ 3_____ 4_____ 5___X____

Works at a consistent pace without an unreasonable number or length of breaks

1_____ 2_____ 3_____ 4_____ 5___X____

Social Interaction

Interacts appropriately with general public

1_____ 2_____ 3_____ 4_____ 5___X____

Asks simple questions or requests assistance when necessary

1_____ 2_____ 3_____ 4___X___ 5_____

Accepts instruction and responds appropriately to criticism from supervisors

1_____ 2_____ 3_____ 4_____ 5___X____

Gets along with coworkers without distracting them

1_____ 2_____ 3___X___ 4_____ 5_____

Maintains socially appropriate behavior

1___X___ 2_____ 3_____ 4_____ 5_____

Maintains basic standards of cleanliness and grooming

1___X___ 2_____ 3_____ 4_____ 5_____

Adaptation

Responds appropriately to changes at work

1_____ 2___X___ 3_____ 4_____ 5_____

Is aware of normal work hazards and takes necessary precautions

1____X____ 2_____ 3_____ 4_____ 5_____

Can get around in unfamiliar places, can use public transportation

1_____ 2_____ 3_____ 4____X____ 5_____

Sets realistic goals, makes plans independently of others

1_____ 2____X____ 3_____ 4_____ 5_____

Summary: Vocational Strategies and Accommodations

To optimize the chances for vocational success, a person with agoraphobia or social phobia needs:

- As much control as possible over work environment to reduce anxiety about the unknown.
- To work unobserved by others to the extent possible, to minimize self-consciousness.
- To work at his or her own pace, without judgment by others, to minimize self-consciousness.
- Flexible scheduling to accommodate medication effects and fluctuations in symptom severity.
- To have the option of working with a partner on some tasks, to reduce loneliness and increase social support.
- Ongoing positive feedback about things done well.
- A referral for cognitive-behavioral psychotherapy, and perhaps medication, to help cope with social discomfort.
- To disclose problems to coworkers who are likely and able to be supportive, in order to reduce self-consciousness and embarrassment when symptoms increase.

POSTTRAUMATIC STRESS DISORDER

Prevalence rates for posttraumatic stress disorder vary widely, depending on the population studied and the methods of gathering information. It may occur in 1%–14% of the population. In groups at risk for developing the disorder, such as combat veterans, victims of natural disasters, or victims of violent crime, the rate is from 3%–58%. Posttraumatic stress disorder can occur at any age and in people with no predisposing conditions. Factors such as social support and personality variables play a part in determining the severity and duration of the disorder, as do the characteristics of the traumatic event that triggered it (American Psychiatric Association, 1994).

Susan

Each night before going to bed, Susan stands at her window in the dark, looking up and down the street and all around the parking lot below, looking for danger, looking for signs of trouble in her quiet neighborhood. One night as she stepped back from the window a white pick-up truck caught her eye and set all her senses on edge. She watched it pass under the street light on the corner, then slow and turn into the parking lot of her building. It had one dim headlight.

She slammed down the window blind and ran to her apartment door. It was securely locked, as always, but she checked it to be sure, reset the chain, and pulled a chair in front of it, the back of the chair under the door knob. She ran into her bedroom, barricaded that door, too, and huddled under the blankets on her bed. The truck she had seen was her brother Dell's.

She hadn't seen Dell since he went to prison, but she could see him plain as day now, just as he had always been, his face contorted in anger, his voice slurred with liquor, his rough hand on the back of her head, demanding, threatening, menacing. She felt the force of his blow across her face just as she had that day, the day she turned 17, the day she shouted back and fought him and refused to do what he had forced her to do so many times before.

She lay still and tense, expecting to hear his boots in the hallway, his fist pounding on her door. Trembling, she listened. Clutching the blankets around her, she crept from her bedroom and toward the front window. She inched the blind open and looked out. The truck was parked under a street light near the building. It wasn't white, but yellow. She didn't recognize the guy behind the wheel. He was smiling, leaning out the window, talking to a man and a woman, who were laughing at something he'd said. It wasn't Dell.

What Posttraumatic Stress Disorder Is Like

- Exposure to trauma
- Reexperiencing the trauma
- Avoidance of stimuli associated with the event
- Persistent symptoms and problems

Exposure to trauma. Posttraumatic stress disorder is something combat soldiers, plane crash survivors, and crime victims have in common; it is a reaction to a horrible event. For Susan, the event occurred in her childhood. Her brother Dell abused her physically and sexually from the time she was 7 and he was 12. He threatened her, mocked her, and humiliated her in front of his friends. Once, he held a pillow over her face until she thought her lungs would explode.

Susan's parents drank and fought with each other. Their fights were often physical, but their verbal battles were just as vicious. Susan once watched her father hold a gun to her mother's head and dare her to move. Her mother laughed when Susan told her about Dell's sexual demands. Her only suggestion was that Susan not let her father find out.

Susan is 43. She has seen no one in her family, including Dell, for 15 years. She is currently separated from her third husband. She has a son from her first marriage; he joined the army when he turned 18, and she does not know where he is.

She has sought help for her problems several times; once, she attended a 10-session women's support group, and after that she tried an incest survivor's group at a rape crisis center. She tried individual psychotherapy on four separate occasions, with four different therapists. None of it helped her very much. She couldn't really connect with the other group members or the therapists; she didn't trust any of them. She didn't see why she should talk about what happened to her, or listen to other people talk about what happened to them, when all it did was make her cry and feel worse.

Reexperiencing the trauma. For Susan, seeing a pick-up truck similar to the one her brother drove 15 years ago was enough to make her feel like a child again, alone and scared and helpless. Time has done nothing to dim her memories; they are vivid and intrusive and often triggered by things she sees or hears. When her son turned 12, she began to see a resemblance to Dell, and she withdrew from him; he spent his adolescence with his father, who Susan had left years earlier because of his foul temper. She wakes up at night sometimes in a cold sweat from her dreams. Her second and third marriages failed in part because she could not make an emotional connection; being close felt dangerous. In many of her interactions with men, she finds herself feeling, and sometimes acting, as though she were helpless and in danger.

Avoidance of stimuli associated with the event. Susan feels bombarded on a daily basis by memories of her childhood, and she does her best to screen them all out. She left her home town and moved to a different state. She has no contact with her family or with anyone she knew as a child. She avoids children. She has no family photographs or mementos. She doesn't watch certain TV shows or movies or read about child abuse in the newspapers. She doesn't drink or spend time with people who do. She cuts off relationships with anyone who reminds her even slightly of family members or of herself as a child. She recently quit her job because of a female coworker named Del.

Persistent symptoms and problems. Susan often feels depressed. Her nights are restless; she doesn't sleep well. She tends to be irritable and sometimes lashes out at people. She can't keep her mind on things. She is on edge all the time, tapping her feet, drumming her fingers on the table, looking around, checking things out, scanning her surroundings. She feels like she can't let up for a second. Still, for all her vigilance, she is likely to scream and jump if she hears a sudden noise or if someone comes up behind her unexpectedly.

Posttraumatic Stress Disorder's Effect at Work

- Inconsistent pattern
- Reduced stress tolerance for events associated with the traumatic event
- Low energy, poor endurance, high error rate

Inconsistent pattern. Susan has been working since she was 17 and has had dozens of jobs. The longest time she ever held a job was a year, in a gas station when she was 19. She's done OK at work—she's never been fired—but she tends to quit after a short time for reasons mysterious even to her. She gets nervous, she gets edgy, she takes a dislike to someone, she's afraid she'll goof up, the place doesn't feel right anymore.

While she's there, she gets along OK with others, but usually keeps her distance. Sometimes she can go along for a few weeks and everything's fine, work is no big deal. Then, for no reason she can figure out, she'll "lose it," start to feel scared, maybe have a flashback at work, maybe start to think about things and forget where she is for a few minutes, maybe start to shake. Once she broke down crying when she overheard a loud argument between two coworkers. All of this is confusing to Susan and even more so to people she works with. None of her supervisors have had any idea how to handle it.

Reduced stress tolerance for events associated with the traumatic event. Susan doesn't like pressure. She doesn't like being criticized. She doesn't like loud voices or sarcasm. She doesn't like any kind of confrontation, whether it involves her or not. She doesn't like being ordered around. She doesn't like being asked, no matter how nicely, to do unpleasant tasks. She doesn't like surprises or sudden changes. She finds ordinary workplace tensions and demands extremely stressful. Solving the kinds of workplace problems that come up every day feels beyond her. Bigger stresses—conflicts, aggression, crises, time pressure, mistakes—feel overwhelming.

Low energy, poor endurance, high error rate. Susan feels tense and edgy but rarely energetic. She doesn't usually get enough sleep to feel like working very hard. She is preoccupied much of the time and sometimes actually out of touch with her surroundings; she has flashbacks, she has sudden intense memories, and sometimes she feels like she's back in her room at home, with Dell about to open the door. She doesn't always pay attention to what she's doing, and often she doesn't care too much about the result.

Working with Posttraumatic Stress Disorder

Susan feels helpless and out of control much of the time. She feels unsafe, on the edge of danger, unable to protect herself or to find protection. She lives in the present, day to day. She doesn't have a sense of the future; she can't imagine or visualize the rest of her life. She especially can't imagine being able to exercise any control over it. She doesn't set goals, and she doesn't have a clear idea of what kind of work she might like. She knows plenty about her deficiencies but little about her abilities.

Many of her work situations have made her symptoms worse. She once took a job in a daycare center; she worked less than a day and knew she couldn't continue. She once worked on an office cleaning crew, which required her to be alone in the building for most of the shift with a male coworker; he was nothing like Dell, but she quit after two days. She's worked in a lot of convenience stores, all-night restaurants, and factories. Some of them were all right, but some were in bad neighborhoods, the customers were impatient and demanding, her coworkers were loud and abusive, or her boss was critical and aggressive. For all the jobs she's had, not one stands out as desirable or suitable. She does not regret leaving any of them.

Susan graduated from high school with average grades, and she took some secretarial training, but didn't complete the program. She has never had a problem finding a job when she needed one, being willing to take anything, not caring what it was, knowing she would probably quit soon anyway. She stayed on her last job, as a night-shift cashier in a large truck stop on the interstate, for 10 months. When she quit, she began looking for work again right away. She doesn't enjoy time off; idleness and unstructured time both bore her and increase her sense of apprehension.

Unfortunately, this time Susan had some trouble finding a job. It was late June; high school and college kids had already been hired for many of the kinds of jobs she usually took. Her spotty work history was beginning to catch up with her; she had a wide variety of experience, but no longevity. Many employers wanted consistency and reliability and were reluctant to consider her application when younger, more promising applicants were available. She had never interviewed well, and after being rejected several times she became less and less able to present herself in a positive light. Her rent was paid for the month, she had gas in her car and food in her kitchen, and even a little money in the bank, but she felt more and more nervous as the days went on. A neighbor in her building suggested that she apply for unemployment benefits, and Susan thought she might as well.

The man at the unemployment office was brusque and unfriendly. Susan was not surprised to learn that she was ineligible for any benefits. On her way out, she noticed a brochure describing the vocational rehabilitation program, whose office was on the next floor. Without thinking much about it, she went in and set up an appointment to see a counselor. The appointment was a week away; she figured that if she found a job before then, she wouldn't bother to keep it.

The week went by with no job offers. Susan went to her appointment at the Department of Rehabilitation Services because she didn't know what else to do, not because she thought it would help. Diane, the vocational rehabilitation counselor, began the interview with small talk—the weather, a new movie, the food at a restaurant across the street—trying to put Susan at ease. Susan hated small talk. Her responses were brief and noncommittal. Her guard was up; she was almost challenging Diane to do something helpful.

Diane took the hint and began the process of taking a thorough vocational history. Susan couldn't remember all the jobs she'd had, but she did her best to provide accurate information. She was relieved that Diane seemed neither surprised nor judgmental. Diane also asked about her medical and social history and her current situation. Susan was reluctant to reveal much about her family background, but she did sign a release of information form so that Diane could get records from the psychotherapist she had seen most recently.

Diane then began asking questions about Susan's vocational preferences, her ideal job, her goals for the future, what she saw herself doing in five years time. Susan had never considered these questions before, and she didn't know how to respond. She remembered phrases she had heard from psychotherapists or from support group members, phrases like "take charge of your life" and "your future is up to you." Such ideas had never had much meaning for her, but applying them to her work life seemed to make sense. Maybe she did have choices.

After Susan had completed some interest and aptitude testing, she and Diane met again. Diane wanted Susan to consider training in a specific field, rather than simply finding another short-term, low-skill job. Susan was ambivalent; she felt some safety in the easy out afforded by the kinds of jobs she had had, and was reluctant to commit herself into the future. On the other hand, her current difficulty finding a job, the fact that she was not getting any younger, and the notion that she could take some action on her own behalf, combined to convince her to work with Diane and see what happened.

Unfortunately, the testing results were inconclusive; Susan didn't show strong interests or clear abilities. She was disappointed. She felt that she was getting nowhere and might as well quit the process. Diane assured her that such test results were not unusual, and that there was still much they could do to find the right work situation for her.

They began discussing in detail each of her last jobs, trying to find a pattern to what had worked better and what had not worked at all. Susan recognized that she preferred job situations that involved specific tasks with a beginning and an end to those with less structure. She also preferred working alone, or at least independently, to working with others or as part of a work team. But Diane pointed out that too much isolation made her feel vulnerable and distracted.

Diane also noticed that Susan did better in those situations in which she had some control over her work environment. She thought that if Susan had a choice in such things as whether and when to work alone or with others, how fast or slow to work, when to come in and go home, how much work to take on at one time, and how her work space should be arranged, she would probably feel safer, be a better worker, and be able to stay on the job. That such choices were possible in a work setting had never occurred to Susan.

Diane asked Susan about her unfinished secretarial training, now nearly 25 years old and badly out of date. Susan thought it was useless to her at this point, but she remembered that she had been able to develop some skill as a typist and that she had liked the typing part of the work. Diane told her about a six-week word-processing training course at a nearby community college. Susan would learn basic computer skills and several word processing programs. But by this time Susan was very concerned about her financial situation; she didn't think she could make it for six more weeks without a job. She recognized the benefits of Diane's idea, but again she nearly quit working with her; she wanted a job, any job, now.

Diane had a hard time understanding Susan's lack of a future orientation. To her, six more weeks to help guarantee a better future made perfect sense. But Susan couldn't see past her next rent due date. Diane helped her apply for short-term financial assistance and food stamps, and Susan agreed to complete the training program.

During and after the training program, they met several more times to work on job search and interviewing skills. Susan took an extra three-day course in medical terminology and, following up on Diane's contacts, eventually got a job transcribing medical reports in a large hospital. The workload was fairly heavy, but the job was based on reports produced, not hours worked. Susan could work at her own pace and pretty much choose her hours. She had her own workspace, which she arranged the way she wanted it. She was rarely alone in the office, even when she worked late at night, but all the transcribers worked independently, so she could also choose how much she wanted to interact with others.

Diane had also been concerned about Susan's social isolation and lack of leisure-time activities or interests. She believed that a more rewarding life outside of work could help Susan succeed in a job. She urged her to return to therapy or a support group, but Susan adamantly refused. She went into a bit of a tirade over it. She said that she was through with therapy, it had never helped her, and she would never talk about her childhood with anyone ever again.

On a whim, and almost as a joke, Diane suggested that Susan get a dog. They both laughed, but Susan thought about the idea. She liked animals but had never considered herself a suitable pet owner; it involved commitment and continuity. One day, though, she made a visit to her local humane society. A few days later, she went back and adopted a puppy, a German Shepherd mix. She took the dog training course offered at the humane society and found that relating to dogs was much easier for her than relating to people.

Over time, Susan developed an interest in dogs and dog training. She began volunteering at the humane society, helping to socialize puppies, and working with the training classes. She was able to form a strong bond with her own dog, and she found that having him around helped her to feel generally safer. She met other dog owners and, though she never formed any close friendships, she found the company of casual acquaintances in the parks and on her walks pleasant.

Susan did not always have an easy time with the word-processing work. She often found it tedious. She struggled continually with her error rate and at times had difficulty meeting the weekly quota of work. Still, the quiet and predictability of the office setting and the level of control and independence that she had there helped her to stay with it. Diane had suggested that she let her supervisor or one or two coworkers know something about the problems she struggled with, or at least give them some general information about posttraumatic stress disorder, so they could help provide emotional support for her. Predictably, Susan refused. She did, however, gradually develop a friendship with another woman about her age who also kept odd hours, and, without ever learning much about each other, they helped keep each other going.

Two years after she had last met with Diane, Susan sent her a note thanking her for the suggestion that she get a dog. She mentioned in passing that she still had the medical transcription job.

Summary: Posttraumatic Stress Disorder's Effect on Vocational Abilities

Level of Impairment

1. no impairment
2. mild—minimal impairment with little or no effect on ability to function
3. moderate—some impairment, which limits ability to function fully
4. serious—major impairment, which may at times preclude ability to function
5. severe—extreme impairment

Understanding and Memory

Remembers locations and basic work procedures

1___X___ 2_____ 3_____ 4_____ 5_____

Understands and remembers short, simple instructions

1___X___ 2_____ 3_____ 4_____ 5_____

Understands and remembers detailed instructions

1_____ 2___X___ 3_____ 4_____ 5_____

Concentration and Persistence

Carries out short, simple instructions

1___X___ 2_____ 3_____ 4_____ 5_____

Carries out detailed instructions

1_____ 2____X____3_____ 4_____ 5_____

Maintains attention and concentration for extended periods of time

1_____ 2____X____3_____ 4_____ 5_____

Can work within a schedule, maintain attendance, be punctual

1_____ 2____X____3_____ 4_____ 5_____

Sustains ordinary routine without special supervision

1_____ 2____X____3_____ 4_____ 5_____

Can work with or close to others without being distracted by them

1_____ 2_____ 3_____ 4_____ 5____X____

Makes simple work-related decisions

1_____ 2____X____3_____ 4_____ 5_____

Works quickly and efficiently, meets deadlines, even under stressful conditions

1_____ 2_____ 3_____ 4____X____5_____

Completes normal workday and workweek without interruptions due to symptoms

1_____ 2_____ 3____X____4_____ 5_____

Works at a consistent pace without an unreasonable number or length of breaks

1_____ 2____X____3_____ 4_____ 5_____

Social Interaction

Interacts appropriately with general public

1_____ 2_____ 3____X____4_____ 5_____

Asks simple questions or requests assistance when necessary

1_____ 2_____ 3____X____4_____ 5_____

Accepts instruction and responds appropriately to criticism from supervisors

1_____ 2_____ 3_____ 4_____ 5____X____

Gets along with coworkers without distracting them

1_____ 2____X____3_____ 4_____ 5_____

Maintains socially appropriate behavior

1_____ 2___X___ 3_____ 4_____ 5_____

Maintains basic standards of cleanliness and grooming

1___X___ 2_____ 3_____ 4_____ 5_____

Adaptation

Responds appropriately to changes at work

1_____ 2___X___ 3_____ 4_____ 5_____

Is aware of normal work hazards and takes necessary precautions

1___X___ 2_____ 3_____ 4_____ 5_____

Can get around in unfamiliar places, can use public transportation

1___X___ 2_____ 3_____ 4_____ 5_____

Sets realistic goals, makes plans independently of others

1_____ 2___X___ 3_____ 4_____ 5_____

Summary: Vocational Strategies and Accommodations

To optimize the chances for vocational success, a person with post-traumatic stress disorder needs:

- Help in identifying skills, abilities, and workplace needs, due to vague sense of future needs and poor planning ability.
- Predictability and structure in the work setting to help reduce fear of the unknown.
- To have the option of working independently, but not in isolation, in order to feel in control of personal space.
- The opportunity to arrange work space as needed.
- Flexible scheduling to accommodate medication effects and fluctuations in symptoms.
- Flexibility with regard to pace of work to accommodate fluctuations in memory and concentration.
- Social support at work and outside of work to increase sense of psychological and physical safety.
- An understanding of the nature of posttraumatic stress disorder and help from a rehabilitation professional in disclosing it to appropriate supervisors or coworkers, to help engender support and to provide necessary accommodations if symptoms increase.

OBSESSIVE-COMPULSIVE DISORDER

Obsessive-compulsive disorder occurs equally among men and women, and, though until recently thought to be a rare disorder, it appears in 2.5% of the population. Though it occasionally comes on suddenly, most people experience a gradual onset, usually starting in adolescence or early adulthood. It tends to begin earlier in life for men than for women. For most people, it is a chronic disorder, though the symptoms may vary in severity depending on such factors as life stressors. Some people show a consistent and progressive deterioration in functioning, while others experience symptoms only once in a while, with no difficulties in between. The disorder occurs more often in close relatives of those who have it than in the general population (American Psychiatric Association, 1994).

Larry

Larry collected his light jacket, his umbrella, and today's paper—it was today's, wasn't it? He checked the date on the paper, then the date on his watch, then folded the paper into the precise size and shape he preferred for carrying it under his arm, and checked the date again. Yes, it was today's. He glanced at his watch again, then at his kitchen clock. Plenty of time to get to the bus.

He looked out the window. Should he wear his jacket or carry it? Wear it or carry it? He put the jacket on, felt too warm, took it off, and folded it carefully. He looked out the window again, thought the sky looked cloudy, unfolded the jacket, and put it on, zipping it all the way up. He looked around his kitchen: coffee maker, off; water in the sink, off; toaster, unplugged. He checked his watch and the kitchen clock—still plenty of time.

Holding his umbrella and the paper, he took his keys out of his pocket, went through them once or twice, then selected his apartment key, and stepped out the door. He tested the key in the lock to make sure it was the right one, then closed the door and locked it. He unlocked it again, opened it, and looked around at the coffee maker, the kitchen sink, and the toaster. He checked his watch and the clock. He'd have to hurry now.

He closed the door and locked it. He jiggled the handle several times to make sure it was locked. He unlocked it to see if it would open. It did. He locked it again, and jiggled the handle maybe 10 or 12 times, just to be sure. He walked down the hall, almost to the stairway. He wasn't quite sure he'd locked the door; he couldn't remember doing it.

He walked back and repeated the jiggling, unlocking, opening, locking, and rejiggling routine. He walked down the hall, down the stairs, and outside. He checked his pocket for his keys. He checked his watch. He checked his pocket again. Keys were still there. He was hurrying down the sidewalk checking his watch when his bus roared past.

What Obsessive-Compulsive Disorder Is Like

- Presence of obsessions
- Presence of compulsions
- Recognition of excessiveness, emotional distress

Presence of obsessions. Larry is obsessed by the ordinary worries of daily living. He is consumed by such possibilities as leaving his toaster plugged in and burning down his building, leaving his door unlocked and being murdered on his return home, being exposed to germs, having body odor, failing to floss properly, not being prepared for the weather, and on and on. These concerns both limit and dictate his behavior. They occur predictably in certain situations, and they also intrude on his mind at inconvenient times, distracting and upsetting him.

Larry is troubled by other obsessions as well. Frightening, disgusting, or embarrassing thoughts and impulses often intrude on him at the most inopportune times. When talking to his former boss, a kindly, proper woman of 60, he might think about dirty jokes he heard on late-night TV. Several of his former coworkers are of a different race than Larry; though he dislikes all forms of racism, he might find himself on the verge of repeating racial slurs when he sees them. Sitting in a restaurant, he might experience vivid images of the other diners smeared with food. On the bus, he might have to suppress an impulse to squeeze the thigh of the person sitting next to him. In church, he could become absorbed by thoughts about whether or not the minister showered that morning and, if so, what he looked like. He has never acted on these thoughts in any way, but he is terrified that he will; he feels at their mercy.

Presence of compulsions. Larry has several strategies for dealing with his obsessive thoughts. He tries to ignore them, or push them aside, or focus on something else, but with little success. He tries to neutralize them by acting in such a way as to prevent their cause; if he checks his apartment door enough times, he won't have to worry about whether it's actually locked or not. This also doesn't work, and it forces Larry into a pattern of compulsive behaviors.

He gets up at 4:00 in the morning so he can spend the required amount of time on his personal hygiene. He washes his hands at length and in a prescribed manner after he touches something that might be unclean, after he shakes hands with anyone, or after he sneezes. He counts the people on the bus over and over again. Every time the bus stops and someone gets on or off, he starts his count over again. He counts silently and without turning his head in any direction, so no one will know what he is doing.

Walking from the bus stop into work, he repeats the word "savior" over and over in his head, for fear that failure to do so will result in too much work for him to handle when he gets there. If he has to shake hands with anyone, he places his right hand behind his back immediately afterward, rubs it with his left hand, and repeats "stay clean" over and over in his mind until he can get away to wash his hands. He does a similar thing if someone sneezes near him.

He begins counting to himself when talking to people, to keep from repeating the intrusive comments that fill his mind. He always stands in what he believes to be a down-wind position from the person he is talking to, in case he has body odor. After lunch, he tries not to be near anyone at all for fear he will pass gas. He checks and rechecks almost everything he does, in case he made a mistake or left something out. If he missed a step in one of his rituals, or thinks he might have, he starts over from the beginning.

Recognition of excessiveness, emotional distress. Larry knows that his behavior is not normal. He understands, at least some of the time, that his thoughts and his rituals are unreasonable, excessive, and bizarre. He knows that the things he feels compelled to do are for the most part unrelated to the things he fears—that repeating "stay clean," for instance, will not prevent disease. His wife left him because of his difficulty. He lost three jobs because of it, most recently because of missing his bus and coming in late once too often, violating a probation imposed by his boss in an attempt to change his behavior.

Recognizing the severity of his problem, however, does not suggest a solution. In fact, it adds to his pain and embarrassment. He feels humiliated by the nature of his rituals and the amount of time they take. He is deeply ashamed of what goes on in his mind and the efforts he must continually make to cope with it. He struggles constantly for some sense of control over his thoughts and behavior. He has little time for leisure activities or friends. His obsessions and compulsions fill his life.

Larry's parents recognized early in his childhood that he seemed to have some problems. They sought advice from their pediatrician and later from child psychiatrists and psychologists. School social workers, psychologists, and special education teachers worked with him, but it wasn't until late in his adolescence that a correct diagnosis of his condition was made. Over the years, he has tried several medications and a wide variety of psychotherapy treatment approaches, but nothing has significantly or consistently relieved his symptoms.

Both of Larry's parents were anxious, somewhat obsessive people. They were deeply concerned about Larry and tried everything they could think of to help him. His father, a successful attorney, unfortunately tended to respond to Larry's problems with anger and frustration; he didn't believe that a punitive approach was the best, but that's the approach he most often took. Larry's mother, who took medication to deal with her own symptoms, tended to hover over Larry. She would remind him about things he might have forgotten and ask him, often several times, if he had done something or done it correctly.

The best time in Larry's life was several years right after high school. A high school counselor had steered him toward a career in accounting, and he successfully completed a two-year program at a community college. While there, he lived on campus, away from his parents. He felt more confident than he ever had. He developed a social life, went to movies, learned to play golf, discovered he had a sense of humor. During his second year, he met and married a fellow student, against his parents' advice and wishes.

His wife at first didn't realize the extent of his problems. Later, for a time, through her understanding and support, she was able to provide the first significant help and relief he had experienced. His symptoms diminished, only to reappear periodically, sometimes in response to an identifiable external life stress and sometimes in response to some mysterious internal process.

His wife stayed with him during some stressful times—when he graduated and was looking for work, then when he was fired, when he looked for work again, and was eventually fired again. She stayed with him until he was hired the third time, and then left. He knew that she would, and he understood why; working with him in couples therapy, she had been very clear that she couldn't live with his problems indefinitely. Nevertheless, he was devastated. His symptoms increased dramatically, leading to the loss of his third job in seven years. He is now 28.

Obsessive-Compulsive Disorder's Effect at Work

- Slow pace
- Poor stress tolerance
- Distractibility

Slow pace. It would take Larry five hours to get washed, dressed, out the door, and in to work in the morning, if he made it. Once there, he would approach his work with a level of perfectionism that seriously slowed his productivity. His most recent job was as a bank teller. No matter what time of day, the line behind his window was long and slow moving. Whether the bank was busy or slow, Larry's work was backed up. He checked and rechecked everything several times. He never found a mistake, but never gave up trying; he had no confidence in his own ability. Often, coworkers had to help him finish up at the end of the day so the bank could close on time.

Poor stress tolerance. Ordinary daily events—a handshake, a sneeze, the act of handling other people's money—were stressful for Larry and could send him into his pattern of obsessive thoughts. Sometimes a bit of news or a snatch of song on the radio would remind him of some worry or trigger some thought, and he would stand for long minutes counting dollar bills, counting the characters on his computer screen, or silently repeating a prayer, while people waited in front of his window until he could work again.

If he were experiencing stress outside of work, which he often did as a result of interactions with his parents or the difficulties in his marriage and the subsequent breakup, or just trying to manage on his own, he might be unable to get to work at all or to do his job if he did get there.

Distractibility. With so many demands on his attention, Larry has a hard time concentrating. He is inefficient in everything he does. When he makes mistakes, like missing his bus in the morning, it is usually because he is so distracted by the turmoil in his mind and the need to cope with it that he can't pay attention to the things that must get done. The external world becomes secondary to his internal struggles. His distractibility is compounded by the anxiety, the emotional pain, and the sense of shame that he experiences almost continually.

At work, he would be distracted by all his usual worries and by the people around him. He tried to focus on the work but often could not. He would resort to his ineffective coping techniques, such as counting or repeating phrases, and become even more distracted and inefficient. Recognizing that he was not concentrating, he would become very concerned about mistakes and take even more time to check and recheck his work.

Working with Obsessive-Compulsive Disorder

When his symptoms are at a minimum, Larry can be a productive and conscientious worker. He is detail oriented and persistent. He has high standards and he is capable of meeting them. He sticks with a task until it is done, and he takes pride in his work. He wants to do well and to please others. Unfortunately, his symptoms at their worst make all of this impossible.

Being a bank teller was a poor job choice for Larry. He knew it at the time, but the job was available, the bank was willing to hire him, and he thought that maybe he could salvage his marriage if he were working. But the time pressures and the constant stress of dealing with the public were too distracting. He could not stay focused on his work. He found thousands of things to worry about. His compulsive rituals become more obvious, though he tried hard to disguise them. He was frequently late in the morning and late from breaks.

After his wife left, his symptoms escalated dramatically. He was late nearly every day and could barely function when he came in. His boss didn't know about his disorder, but she suspected that something was wrong. She tried talking to him, but he felt too ashamed of himself to be open with her. She eventually imposed an ultimatum on his behavior, especially the lateness, which quickly led to his being fired.

Larry's first job had involved turning in cash reports at regular intervals throughout the day. Sometimes the workload was extremely heavy, and sometimes his report would show almost no activity. He never knew what to expect from day to day, or from hour to hour. He developed an elaborate system of rituals and silent repetition of words and phrases in an attempt to control the flow of work, but of course he never could. He began missing deadlines, and he was eventually fired from that job because his attempts to control the work interfered so dramatically with his ability to do it.

In his second job, he worked as a research assistant to a professor of statistics at a university. He had very little contact with people. He worked with numbers and formulas, compiling page after page of figures and statistics for the professor and his students to analyze. The job didn't require that he have or acquire any knowledge of the statistical research being done; it was very routine work and some might say boring. But Larry liked it. He lasted five years in that job; it was his longest stable period, with relatively mild symptoms.

Then things changed at the university. The easy pace and routine work of Larry's job were no longer enough. The professor was under pressure to publish more of his research more quickly and to teach more classes. He began to require more of Larry, even though he knew that Larry didn't have the necessary training. Larry became extremely anxious. He was obsessed with doing everything the professor wanted done, and doing it perfectly. He got to work early, and stayed late, but his efficiency and his work performance deteriorated. He became increasingly distracted. Soon he was engaged in compulsive rituals again, and absorbed by checking and rechecking for mistakes in his work. The professor eventually had to fire him.

After he lost each of his previous two jobs, Larry's wife had helped him get himself together to apply for a new job. She helped his emotional state, and she provided concrete help in finding job possibilities, revising his résumé, getting him to interviews, and so on. After losing his bank job, though, he was on his own. He felt anxious, discouraged, and ashamed. He felt completely at the mercy of his symptoms. He was afraid he might be unable to work at all and have to apply for disability benefits.

He had a psychotherapist, a psychologist named David, whom he saw regularly but infrequently—his insurance plan would cover no more than six sessions a year. His next scheduled appointment was a month away, but Larry called to see if he could get in to see David immediately. David had worked with Larry off and on for seven years, through good times and bad. He was convinced that Larry was fully capable of working, though his current condition was about as bad as David had seen him.

He began by referring Larry to a psychiatrist for medication. Larry was reluctant to go; he reminded David that no medication had worked for him in the past. But David had seen research suggesting that newer medications showed some promise in treating obsessive-compulsive symptoms, and he urged Larry to try. Larry found that the medication did not provide dramatic relief, but it did take the edge off; he was no longer completely absorbed by his symptoms, and he could function better.

Meanwhile, David had managed to convince the insurance company that Larry was in crisis, and they authorized five additional sessions. David intended to use the sessions to get Larry back to work. He believed, and Larry agreed, that structure and routine were very important to Larry's stability and mental health, and that a job was the best way to provide that—if they could find the right job.

They talked about Larry's previous jobs in light of his obsessive-compulsive disorder, trying to identify which work conditions helped him to function and which exacerbated his symptoms. They decided that the ideal work setting would be one that combined flexibility with structure and routine—flexible time frames, routine tasks, structured and predictable expectations.

Larry also recognized that he needs some control over his work environment; he is more at ease when he can arrange things the way he likes them. He needs few surprises and virtually no changes in expectations from day to day. He needs the option of coming in late and working late if necessary. He needs the option of working alone or access to private space when he wants it. He needs to avoid extremely high levels of stress. Working with demanding customers or supervisors, working under time pressures or deadlines, or working with unsympathetic or impatient coworkers would almost certainly exacerbate his symptoms.

David raised the issue of emotional support on the job, something Larry had never had because he always tried to keep his problems secret. David thought it would help Larry a great deal if coworkers and supervisors understood something about his disorder and its symptoms. They could then understand his behavior and be sympathetic to his needs. They could provide supportive feedback, with emphasis on the things he does well, instead of pressuring him or complaining about his slow work pace. Larry agreed in principle, but he wasn't sure how much about his difficulty he would be willing to disclose.

The next step was much more difficult—finding a job that met at least some of Larry's criteria. He liked working with numbers, and he thought back to his training as an accountant. He began looking for entry-level jobs in the accounting field. He found the job search very stressful, and several times he was late for interviews or missed them altogether. He was always scrupulous about his grooming and hygiene, and he became even more so, taking so much time at it that it interfered with his job search.

Larry was still seeing David weekly, but he felt he needed more support than that in order to continue. David knew of a drop-in center, staffed by mental health workers and psychiatric nurses. It offered regularly scheduled support groups as well as the opportunity to stop in and talk for a few minutes as needed. It also offered job-seeking resources and, sometimes, information about available jobs. Larry knew about the drop-in center; David had been trying to get him to make use of it for years. He began stopping in each afternoon to check the jobs bulletin board. He found the atmosphere relaxed and open, and he found at least some of the help and support he needed.

Eventually, Larry was hired to work in the accounting department of a large insurance company. The job offered many of the conditions Larry felt he needed—flexible scheduling, semi-private workspace, highly structured and routine work, no public contact. It wasn't perfect, though. He found that the workload, and consequently the stress level, could vary widely. Sometimes the variations seemed to be seasonal, and sometimes they seemed to have no pattern at all.

Larry became absorbed in trying to predict and control the workload, and he recognized this as a danger sign. With some coaching from David, he approached his supervisor and explained his problem. He asked if his workload could be kept more constant. He tried to make it clear that his intention wasn't to avoid the work, but to help ensure that he could get it done. His supervisor agreed to a compromise: he would allow Larry to work consistently at his own pace if Larry would agree to work extra hours during especially busy times. Larry felt that was a fair trade-off.

By identifying the workplace conditions he needed in order to succeed, Larry was able to find a job that provided most of them. His obsessive-compulsive symptoms will probably never leave him completely, and his ongoing success will depend on his ability to keep them at bay. He has a good chance if he can reduce the stress in his life by keeping things predictable and routine and maintain social support, both at work and outside of work.

Summary: Obsessive-Compulsive Disorder's Effect on Vocational Abilities

Level of Impairment

1. no impairment
2. mild—minimal impairment with little or no effect on ability to function
3. moderate—some impairment, which limits ability to function fully
4. serious—major impairment, which may at times preclude ability to function
5. severe—extreme impairment

Understanding and Memory

Remembers locations and basic work procedures

1____X____ 2_____ 3_____ 4_____ 5_____

Understands and remembers short, simple instructions

1____X____ 2_____ 3_____ 4_____ 5_____

Understands and remembers detailed instructions

1____X____ 2_____ 3_____ 4_____ 5_____

Concentration and Persistence

Carries out short, simple instructions

1____X____ 2_____ 3_____ 4_____ 5_____

Carries out detailed instructions

1____X____ 2_____ 3_____ 4_____ 5_____

Maintains attention and concentration for extended periods of time

1_____ 2_____ 3____X____ 4_____ 5_____

Can work within a schedule, maintain attendance, be punctual

1_____ 2_____ 3_____ 4____X____ 5_____

Sustains ordinary routine without special supervision

1____X____ 2_____ 3_____ 4_____ 5_____

Can work with or close to others without being distracted by them

1_____ 2____X____ 3_____ 4_____ 5_____

Makes simple work-related decisions

1_____ 2_____ 3____X____ 4_____ 5_____

Works quickly and efficiently, meets deadlines, even under stressful conditions

1_____ 2_____ 3_____ 4_____ 5____X____

Completes normal workday and workweek without interruptions due to symptoms

1_____ 2_____ 3____X____ 4_____ 5_____

Works at consistent pace without an unreasonable number or length of breaks

1_____ 2_____ 3_____ 4____X____ 5_____

Social Interaction

Interacts appropriately with general public

1_____ 2____X____ 3_____ 4_____ 5_____

Asks simple questions or requests assistance when necessary

1_____ 2___X___ 3_____ 4_____ 5_____

Accepts instruction and responds appropriately to criticism from supervisors

1_____ 2_____ 3___X___ 4_____ 5_____

Gets along with coworkers without distracting them

1_____ 2___X___ 3_____ 4_____ 5_____

Maintains socially appropriate behavior

1___X___ 2_____ 3_____ 4_____ 5_____

Maintains basic standards of cleanliness and grooming

1___X___ 2_____ 3_____ 4_____ 5_____

Adaptation

Responds appropriately to changes at work

1_____ 2_____ 3___X___ 4_____ 5_____

Is aware of normal work hazards and takes necessary precautions

1_____ 2___X___ 3_____ 4_____ 5_____

Can get around in unfamiliar places, can use public transportation

1_____ 2___X___ 3_____ 4_____ 5_____

Sets realistic goals, makes plans independently of others

1_____ 2___X___ 3_____ 4_____ 5_____

Summary: Vocational Strategies and Accommodations

To optimize the chances for vocational success, a person with obsessive-compulsive disorder needs:

- Flexible scheduling to accommodate fluctuations in symptoms.
- Routine, predictable work and consistent expectations from day to day, to minimize the need for ongoing decision making.
- To have the option of setting his or her own work pace to accommodate perfectionistic tendencies and behavior.
- To have the option of working alone if proximity of others is distracting or if rituals are disruptive to others.
- To be able to exercise some level of control of workspace in order to reduce anxiety and symptoms.
- Ongoing positive feedback about work well done; social support.

- To disclose as appropriate some information about his or her problems to a supervisor and coworkers, in order to bring about needed accommodations and support from them.

CHAPTER 3

Somatoform Disorders

Pain, fatigue, dizziness, fainting, paralysis, blindness, memory loss, seizures, weakness, nausea: surely a frightening list of symptoms, especially when no doctor can find a cause. People with somatoform disorders might go from physician to physician, medical center to medical center, and insurance company to insurance company, but medical findings, even a great many of them, cannot explain why they feel so bad.

The situation becomes even more frightening if, every time life gets hard, the symptoms get worse. Still, a doctor who suggests the obvious—that the physical condition has a psychological component—is likely to get short shrift from the affected person. "The doctor says it's all in my head" is a reason to change doctors, not to examine the psychological factors involved. A key feature of somatoform disorders is not only psychological naïveté, but an unwillingness to consider a psychological explanation and a tendency to minimize psychological features such as stress.

Somatoform symptoms vary widely; they could fill the entire index of a general medical textbook. Somatization disorder involves a variety of symptoms at several locations throughout the body, commonly including such things as chronic back pain, headaches, fatigue, weakness, and visual problems. Conversion disorder involves dysfunction of a specific organ system; it can include blindness, deafness, or paralysis. Pain disorder involves pain in one or more specific locations. Hypochondriasis is the fear of and preoccupation with having a serious illness.

Stress is a factor in all of the somatoform disorders, causing predictable exacerbation of symptoms. All of them cause grave difficulties in a workplace, interfering dramatically with steady and reliable work performance.

SOMATIZATION DISORDER

Prevalence rates for somatization disorder are less than 0.2% in men, but run as high as 2% in women. Variations in prevalence rates depend on demographic factors, on how the diagnosis was made, and by whom; physicians are much more likely to diagnose somatization disorder than are mental health professionals who might encounter such patients. It is a chronic disorder, with initial symptoms often appearing during adolescence, often in the form of menstrual problems. Symptoms may come and go and vary in intensity, but the disorder rarely goes away completely and usually results in visits to a medical professional at least once a year because of unexplained physical problems. Between 10% and 20% of close female relatives of women with somatization disorder also receive the diagnosis, while close male relatives are at increased risk for developing antisocial personality disorder or a substance-related disorder (American Psychiatric Association, 1994).

Marianne

The staircase loomed in front of Marianne, enormous and intimidating. She did not see how she could possibly climb to the top. The pain in the back of her neck nearly made her faint, her vision was acting up again—she could see two staircases when she looked up—and the pounding in her head wouldn't quit. She lifted her arm to grasp the hand railing, and even that small gesture took all the strength she had. She sat down in a chair at the foot of the stairs to wait for Don to come and help her up to bed. She was so tired.

The doctor had been no help. As usual, this one knew nothing, couldn't seem to grasp the seriousness of her condition, couldn't figure out what to do for her. He wanted her to see a psychologist. That's what they all say when they don't know what's wrong and don't want to bother finding out. She would have to convince her insurance company to send her to another doctor. How could it be that all those tests had found nothing wrong, when it was obvious she must have a brain tumor, or something worse? And why now, when things were so hard for her and Don? Don would just have to carry on without her help, because she couldn't do a thing.

What Somatization Disorder Is Like

- Physical symptoms not fully explained by medical findings
- Physical symptoms increase in times of stress

- Poor psychological insight
- Dramatic presentation
- Secondary problems

Physical symptoms not fully explained by medical findings. Marianne is 55 years old, married to Don for 30 years, the mother of three grown children. She has worked a variety of clerical jobs, most recently in the records department of the county administrative offices. She had to take a leave of absence because the computer work bothered her eyes. When the leave was nearly up, she developed other symptoms, including neck pain, headaches, weakness, and fatigue. She has been to two doctors so far. Based on what she told them, they developed slightly different theories about the cause of her problems, ran several different sets of tests, and came to the same conclusion: there was no medical basis for her symptoms.

Marianne has had similar problems before. Her headaches started when she was about 20 and became severe around the time of her wedding. She had problems with vomiting throughout each of her pregnancies. She felt weak and couldn't do her housework for a year or more after each child was born. She went back to work when her youngest child started school, but almost immediately developed back problems and had to quit.

She periodically has difficulty sleeping and becomes easily fatigued, to the point where she can do nothing but lie in bed. Two years ago, she suddenly became intolerant of almost all food. She could eat only ice cream and some fruits; everything else made her gag. She became so weak that she could barely lift her head from the pillow, and each time she did, the room spun around her. In each instance, she sought medical help—a great deal of medical help—but the doctors could never find a medical basis to explain the extent and severity of her symptoms.

Physical symptoms increase in times of stress. That this latest illness should strike her now seemed to Marianne the cruelest of blows. Don had just lost his job, their son was in trouble with the police, and now this. The last time Marianne was this sick was two years ago, right after her daughter got pregnant and ran away from home. The time before that was when she and Don were having marital problems, and he almost moved out. Other bouts with severe symptoms coincided with pressures she felt at work, financial troubles, her older brother's near-fatal car accident, and the time her parents sold her childhood home and moved to a condo in Arizona.

Poor psychological insight. When Marianne thinks about it, she can see that the ebb and flow of her symptoms follows the course of her life difficulties with remarkable accuracy, but she attributes this to bad luck and nothing more. Being sick is an added misfortune at times of trouble. Marianne sees no causal relationship.

Somatoform disorder symptoms are not consciously created, they are not under voluntary control, and they are not fictitious or made up. But they indicate a psychological, not a medical, disorder. To Marianne, however, the suggestion that her symptoms might be psychological in origin is like a slap in the face; it means that people don't believe her. She is unwilling to consider the role stress plays in exacerbating her symptoms, or to consider psychological methods of dealing with them.

Dramatic presentation. In seeking relief over the years, Marianne has received medical care from many sources, sometimes simultaneously, leading to the development of a complicated and confusing medical history with several diagnoses under consideration at any one time. She has a hard time remembering it all and often has a hard time accurately portraying her situation. She tries to be clear but is often vague or uncertain, because her history is so complex and so many of her symptoms defy description.

In her efforts to make people understand how sick she really is, Marianne is given to theatrical gestures and dramatic phrases to explain her plight. She doesn't have a headache, she has "a thousand jackhammers pounding" in her head. She doesn't have an occasional problem with double vision, "the world doubles itself" in front of her eyes. She doesn't feel a little weak, her "muscles have failed" her. At work, she would often turn and raise her hand to her forehead, breathing deeply, so her coworkers and supervisor could see for themselves how much the computer screen bothered her eyes. She didn't want them to think she was just complaining.

Secondary problems. Marianne often feels depressed. Even when things are going fairly well for her, she still has sleep problems and suffers from low energy and fatigue. She has trouble concentrating, and she tends to be irritable, especially when she isn't feeling well and especially with people who don't demonstrate a sympathetic attitude toward her. She has at times been addicted to sleeping pills, pain pills, and tranquilizers, so that some pharmacies she has used in the past will no longer fill those prescriptions for her, which is a great source of irritation.

Somatization Disorder's Effect at Work

- Poor persistence and reliability
- Very poor stress tolerance

• Questionable motivation
• Poor interpersonal functioning, irritability

Poor persistence and reliability. Marianne finds it extremely difficult to go to work, or to complete her tasks, when she is not feeling well. If her symptoms start to bother her when she is in the middle of something, she is likely to stop doing it. She needs a great deal of rest and often extends her break times or leaves work early. She feels strongly that her job is secondary to her health.

Very poor stress tolerance. Even a small increase in stress can result in a large increase in Marianne's symptoms. Time pressures, extra work, conflicts with coworkers, an upcoming performance review, and other routine workplace circumstances send her straight to the bottle of prescription pain medicine she keeps in her desk, and that often doesn't help. Large stressors, like her current problems at home, send her straight to bed, and then in search of new and better medical care.

Questionable motivation. Marianne is not consciously or intentionally creating her symptoms, but she is not above using them to get out of doing unpleasant tasks. She frequently cites her illness for purposes of secondary gain. She can't help Don deal with their son's legal problems because she's sick. Even though Don lost his job, she can't return from her leave of absence because she's sick. When she does go back, she will request extra break times, because she has such problems with her eyes. She leaves the main burden of work in her office to her coworkers, doing only what she feels she can do, because she gets so tired. She makes it clear that no one can expect much of her because of her symptoms.

Poor interpersonal functioning, irritability. Marianne is preoccupied with herself and her symptoms. She is largely unaware of the needs or feelings of others. She has difficulty functioning as part of a team, because she doesn't think she should be expected to do her share of the work. She has difficulty responding to routine requests or normal expectations without irritation.

Working with Somatization Disorder

The county human resources department doesn't know what to make of Marianne. They granted her leave of absence on the basis of one doctor's report, hoping that doing so would reduce her taking of sick time on her return. They extended the leave on the basis of another doctor's report, which advanced the hypothesis that she might have a neurological disorder and needed diagnostic testing. They studied her request for reduced workload and increased break times

on her return but, based on the latest medical reports, saw no justifi-
cation for granting it. What Marianne actually can and can't do is unclear, even to her.

In an effort to resolve the situation fairly, the human resources department consulted with Ted, a vocational rehabilitation specialist.
He reviewed all of the available records and interviewed Marianne,
who agreed to participate only when she was told that the county
would take steps to fire her if she didn't cooperate. Ted's first recommendation was strongly worded and clear: Marianne must be evaluated by a psychologist, preferably one who specializes in performing
psychological evaluations for vocational purposes.

Marianne actually had seen a psychologist several years ago, but
she had refused to allow the report to be released to her employer, so
it was not among the rest of her records. That psychologist had diagnosed her with somatization disorder, had explained the diagnosis to
her, and had suggested a psychological approach toward easing and
living with her symptoms. Marianne had felt angry and humiliated.
She rejected the diagnosis and the suggestions, concluded that the
psychologist was incompetent, continued to seek a medical cause,
and quickly put the incident out of her mind.

Marianne never objected to extensive and repeated medical tests,
but she was extremely resistant to the idea of submitting to another
psychological evaluation. On the day of the appointment, she felt too
ill to go and called to reschedule. She canceled two subsequent appointments for the same reason. When the psychologist informed
Ted that Marianne had canceled three appointments, Ted recommended that the county begin the process of firing her. Frightened of
losing her job, Marianne asked for one more chance and this time
managed to keep the appointment.

The psychological evaluation was thorough. It consisted of several
psychological tests and a lengthy interview. The psychologist took
the time to wade through Marianne's complicated medical history
and her family and employment troubles. Marianne knew that she
didn't have the option of withholding the report from her employer
this time, and she did her best to convince the psychologist that her
problems were not psychological but medical. The pattern of stress
exacerbating her physical symptoms was very clear, however, and a
diagnosis of somatization disorder was also consistent with psychological testing data.

The psychologist explained her findings to Marianne in a follow-up
interview. Her report included recommendations for workplace accommodations that would help Marianne keep her job and be a more

productive worker. The psychologist said she would work with Ted and with Marianne's supervisor as needed. Marianne appreciated the time the psychologist had spent with her. She liked the idea of workplace accommodations, if it meant the reduced workload and extra breaks she had requested. But she didn't like the implied expectation that she become a more productive worker, and in general she felt hurt, humiliated, and misunderstood. She remained convinced that she had a medical problem and angry that no one believed her.

Marianne felt especially annoyed and put off by the treatment the psychologist had recommended. It included psychological techniques such as relaxation training and stress management. It emphasized the idea that Marianne could change her attitude toward her symptoms, learn to minimize or ignore them, learn to live with them, so they wouldn't limit her activities to the extent they did. To her it sounded like she was being told not to take herself seriously. In order to keep her job, however, she completed the required six sessions of psychotherapy. She didn't practice or even try the techniques she was taught. She didn't change her attitude, either, and was angry at the notion that she should work, or do anything at all, when she felt ill.

Ted wanted to involve Marianne's medical doctors in the efforts to help her keep her job and be more productive. He saw that Marianne tended to keep separate the various people working with her, and even to hide their findings from each other, and he thought that wouldn't help her in the long run. With her reluctant permission, he sent the psychological report to the physician she had seen most recently. Then, with both Marianne and her supervisor present, he spoke with the doctor by telephone, asking specifically about medical limitations on Marianne's work activities. The doctor said that though her symptoms were certainly painful and difficult at times, they need not restrict her ability to work to the extent they had.

Finally, Ted talked with Marianne and her supervisor about how to restructure her job in order to increase her chances of success. He recommended against the idea of allowing her additional break times, suggesting flexible scheduling instead. She would still work the same number of hours as the other employees, but would have more control over when she worked them.

Ted also recommended against reducing her workload and suggested reducing her stress level instead. He asked that as much as possible she be given routine, predictable tasks without time pressures or deadlines, and that she work on her own, at her own pace, and not as part of a team. He thought that Marianne could probably work fairly consistently and reliably with these accommodations.

Ted also emphasized the need for clear and consistent expectations with regard both to the quality of her work and her reliability on the job. Emotional support from coworkers and supervisors might help, and might make working with her a little easier, but Marianne would benefit more from unambiguous standards of workplace behavior. She must be clear about what she has to do, and what she can't do. She needs an explicit understanding of the limits of workplace accommodations, and of the extent to which her problems will not be tolerated or allowed to interfere with the work to be done.

Marianne finally returned to work feeling frightened and angry. She felt betrayed by her supervisor, by Ted, by the psychologist, and by her doctor. She felt unable to perform at the level they expected of her. Her husband Don had also gone back to work, but their financial situation remained precarious, and she could not consider quitting. She was still bothered by neck pain, fatigue, and weakness, but she found with some surprise that flexible scheduling, routine tasks, and working alone at her own pace helped her do her job. Most days, she was able to work a full day and do the amount of work required.

After several months, however, Marianne's daughter returned home, with her two-year-old son. Marianne immediately began to notice a new symptom—pain in her joints. She had managed to earn three sick days, and she used them to consult first her own doctor and then a specialist in rheumatology. Tests and x-rays showed no evidence of arthritis or any other condition that would explain the joint pain.

The pain got worse, however, so that Marianne had difficulty driving, and again she began to miss days of work. Her supervisor called Ted. He met with Marianne and reminded her of the limits on the amount of time she could take off. She had already used all of the sick and vacation time she had coming; taking more would lead to her firing. She was not eligible for any more leaves of absence until she had worked steadily for a year.

Marianne explained her new symptoms to Ted, expecting sympathy and understanding. Instead, he asked her questions about stress in her home life, and then referred her back for six more sessions of pain management therapy. Marianne went, but she still could not make the connection between her psychological state and her aches and pains. She was unable to make use of therapy.

After several more months of Marianne pushing the limits and her supervisor giving her warnings, the county took steps to fire her. Marianne protested on the grounds that she was disabled and needed further accommodations. But, in addition to flexible scheduling, being allowed to work at her own pace, and having a predictable workload,

Marianne also had, at county expense, special lighting, a special ergonomically designed chair, a footstool, and a heating pad, as well as permission to make personal phone calls and eat snacks and lunch at her desk since moving around was hard for her. Her supervisor didn't see that much more could be done for Marianne, but she agreed to arrange another meeting with Ted.

Having worked with Marianne for as long as he had, Ted could offer just one suggestion: for the time being, Marianne should give up trying to work full-time and cut her hours to half-time. This was possible under the county's employment policies, but it meant that she would only be paid for hours she worked, and she could not accrue sick or vacation time. Still, it was at present Marianne's only alternative to being fired, and both she and her supervisor thought it was a good idea.

Her half-time job involved a slightly different set of tasks from those Marianne was used to, but she made the transition. She often had to change her schedule when her symptoms flared, but overall she was able to work 20 hours a week reliably. In time, as stress in her home life eased, her joint pain and other symptoms also diminished. Marianne wanted to improve her family's financial situation by increasing her hours again, but was afraid that her health would suffer if she went back to working full-time. She and her supervisor agreed on 30 hours a week, which Marianne was able to maintain.

Marianne may never understand the true cause of the physical symptoms she experiences and may always respond to stress and difficulty in her life by becoming ill. But by identifying useful workplace accommodations and finding a level of flexibility that both meets her needs and is acceptable to her employer, she may not have to lose her job because of it.

Summary: Somatization Disorder's Effect on Vocational Abilities

Level of Impairment

1. no impairment
2. mild—minimal impairment with little or no effect on ability to function
3. moderate—some impairment, which limits ability to function fully
4. serious—major impairment, which may at times preclude ability to function
5. severe—extreme impairment

Understanding and Memory

Remembers locations and basic work procedures

1___X___ 2_____ 3_____ 4_____ 5_____

Understands and remembers short, simple instructions

1___X___ 2_____ 3_____ 4_____ 5_____

Understands and remembers detailed instructions

1___X___ 2_____ 3_____ 4_____ 5_____

Concentration and Persistence

Carries out short, simple instructions

1_____ 2___X___ 3_____ 4_____ 5_____

Carries out detailed instructions

1_____ 2___X___ 3_____ 4_____ 5_____

Maintains attention and concentration for extended periods of time

1_____ 2_____ 3___X___ 4_____ 5_____

Can work within a schedule, maintain attendance, be punctual

1_____ 2_____ 3_____ 4___X___ 5_____

Sustains ordinary routine without special supervision

1_____ 2___X___ 3_____ 4_____ 5_____

Can work with or close to others without being distracted by them

1_____ 2___X___ 3_____ 4_____ 5_____

Makes simple work-related decisions

1___X___ 2_____ 3_____ 4_____ 5_____

Works quickly and efficiently, meets deadlines, even under stressful conditions

1_____ 2_____ 3_____ 4_____ 5___X___

Completes normal workday and workweek without interruptions due to symptoms

1_____ 2_____ 3_____ 4_____ 5___X___

Works at consistent pace without an unreasonable number or length of breaks

1_____ 2_____ 3_____ 4_____ 5___X___

Social Interaction

Interacts appropriately with general public

1_____ 2__X____ 3_____ 4_____ 5_____

Asks simple questions or requests assistance when necessary

1_____ 2__X____ 3_____ 4_____ 5_____

Accepts instruction and responds appropriately to criticism from supervisors

1_____ 2_____ 3__X____ 4_____ 5_____

Gets along with coworkers without distracting them

1_____ 2__X____ 3_____ 4_____ 5_____

Maintains socially appropriate behavior

1_____ 2__X____ 3_____ 4_____ 5_____

Maintains basic standards of cleanliness and grooming

1__X____ 2_____ 3_____ 4_____ 5_____

Adaptation

Responds appropriately to changes at work

1_____ 2__X____ 3_____ 4_____ 5_____

Is aware of normal work hazards and takes necessary precautions

1__X____ 2_____ 3_____ 4_____ 5_____

Can get around in unfamiliar places, can use public transportation

1__X____ 2_____ 3_____ 4_____ 5_____

Sets realistic goals, makes plans independently of others

1_____ 2__X____ 3_____ 4_____ 5_____

Summary: Vocational Strategies and Accommodations

To optimize the chances for vocational success, a person with somatization disorder needs

- Coordination among supervisor, physician, rehabilitation professional, and other involved professionals, due to the complexity of the disorder.

- Flexible scheduling to accommodate fluctuations in physical symptoms.
- Routine, predictable tasks to accommodate perceived physical limitations.
- As few deadlines and time pressures as possible to minimize stress-related symptom flare-ups.
- To work at his or her own pace, and not as part of a team, to accommodate irregular schedule.
- Enforcement of clearly expressed and agreed upon standards for quality and quantity of work.
- Enforcement of clearly expressed and agreed upon limits on extra breaks and time off.
- Enforcement of clearly defined and expressed limits of workplace accommodations.

PART II

Problems Getting Along

The way we understand the world and our place in it defines our personality. We all express this understanding by means of our personal style—our traits, mannerisms, habits, quirks, and idiosyncrasies. For better or for worse, we show our personalities in all facets of life, in our interactions with others, in family relationships, in social situations, and at work. If we are conscientious, self-confident, and ambitious, we stand a pretty good chance in life. But if we ratchet those traits up a notch or two, and become perfectionistic, arrogant, and exploitative, we might find that we have problems getting along with others.

A personality disorder consists of traits that deviate noticeably from the norm. The traits are pervasive; they show up and cause trouble in most life situations. They are rigid and not amenable to change. They influence the range, intensity, consistency, and appropriateness of emotional responses; they can lead to emotional pain and distress. They can affect impulse control and judgment. They are evident in the way a person thinks about self, others, and events. They can ruin interpersonal relationships, including those at work.

From the proliferation of "What Type Are You?" tests offered in popular magazines to the use of sophisticated psychological instruments, the need to understand personality traits and personality disorders is obvious. DSM-IV categorizes them into clusters, "odd," "dramatic," and "anxious." Adding a dimensional view, such as Costa and Widiger's Five-Factor Model (see below), helps us to see the traits on a continuum, which deepens and clarifies our understanding of them. Costa and Widiger (1994) have explained how personality disorders may be described in terms of a five-factor model of personality, which posits that personality is composed of permutations along five dimensions:

1. Neuroticism (N) refers to chronic high levels of emotional maladjustment and instability, such as anxiety, anger, depression, self-consciousness, impulsivity, and vulnerability (e.g., high in borderline, low in schizoid).
2. Extroversion (E) characteristics include sociability, talkativeness, activity, and expressions of affection (e.g., high in histrionic, low in avoidant).
3. Openness to experience (O) refers to the tendency to appreciate experiences for their own sake. Open individuals are curious, imaginative, creative, and unconventional (e.g., high in schizotypal, low in obsessive-compulsive).
4. Agreeableness (A) refers to the degree to which one is compassionate versus antagonistic. High A individuals tend to be softhearted, good-natured, trusting, helpful, forgiving, and altruistic (e.g., high in dependent, low in antisocial).
5. Conscientiousness (C) assesses the degree of organization, persistence, control, and motivation in goal-directed behavior (e.g., high in obsessive-compulsive, low in antisocial).

Wherever their characteristics may fall along these dimensions, employees with personality disorders are likely to be the source of problems in the workplace, problems that may range from subtle bad vibes to disorder and violence. They tend not to do well in various aspects of life, including work and relationships, though the cause of their difficulties may not be obvious. For vocational rehabilitation professionals, understanding the nature of personality disorders and their specific effects in the workplace can make the difference in the success or failure of efforts on behalf of the clients who manifest them.

CHAPTER 4

The "Odd" Cluster: Paranoid, Schizotypal, and Schizoid Personality Disorders

Among the more familiar members of this group we might find the shy, reclusive gardener, the eccentric professor, and the litigious, ever-watchful guy next door. On its outer edges lurk terrorists and political extremists, cult members, and hermits. The "odd" cluster of personality disorders is characterized by idiosyncratic thinking, social withdrawal, and suspiciousness.

Those with paranoid personality disorder misinterpret others' actions to such an extent and with such overt hostility that those around them may succumb to a self-fulfilling prophecy by becoming hostile in return. Paranoid people don't trust anyone, they are always vigilant for confirmation of their suspicions, and they react with a vengeance when they believe they have been wronged, which is often. These are the people who just might draw a gun and hold coworkers hostage after an unfavorable performance review.

People with schizotypal personality disorder tend to be seen by others as out of the ordinary, a little strange. Their thinking is peculiar, their behavior mysterious, and their responses to others may be unnerving. Their grasp of reality may be erratic and uncertain. Their understanding of ordinary events in daily life may differ greatly from that of others. Their interactions with others are likely to elicit a "Twilight Zone" feeling; they may be called "kooks," "oddballs," "weirdos," "freaks" behind their backs. They are very uncomfortable around other people, and most other people steer clear of them.

Greta Garbo's famous plea—"I want to be alone"—may not reflect a serious personality problem on her part, but it is the rallying cry of those with schizoid personality disorder, or it would be if they were likely to rally. People with schizoid personality disorder show a profound and enduring indifference to others. They are loners. They are reclusive, solitary, withdrawn, cold, distant, and aloof. They are motivated by nothing that has to do with other people, except to shut them out. Nothing, good or bad, excites them, and they may appear to others to be unmotivated by anything at all.

The interpersonal tension these disorders create in the workplace can be profound. The threat of physical danger is very real, especially with regard to people with paranoid personality disorder. Understanding the disorders and their vocational effects, and making appropriate adjustments where possible, is essential if the client is to succeed on the job and the workplace remain hospitable and safe for everyone.

PARANOID PERSONALITY DISORDER

Some characteristics of paranoid personality disorder, such as guardedness and defensiveness, or anger and hostility, may be the result of life circumstances, especially those experienced by minority groups, immigrants, or refugees. Such behaviors in context are not the same as paranoid personality disorder, and the diagnosis can only be made after evaluating the context. More men than women are diagnosed with paranoid personality disorder. It occurs in 0.5%–2.5% of the general population, 2%–10% of those in outpatient mental health clinics, and 10%–30% of those in inpatient psychiatric settings. It may first appear in childhood, with such characteristics as social anxiety, poor peer relationships, hypersensitivity, underachievement in school, tendency to be alone, idiosyncratic thoughts, or strange language. Some of these behaviors might make a child seem odd to other children, who might respond with teasing and ridicule, thus beginning what can become a lifelong, self-perpetuating cycle (American Psychiatric Association, 1994).

Martin

The meeting had begun when Martin arrived. He entered the room cautiously and stood just inside the door with his back to the wall. He looked around, taking his bearings, getting a sense of the place, of the people there. He noticed a few surreptitious glances in his direction, but no one spoke to him.

Someone came in after him; he recognized his neighbor from down the street. She smiled, greeted him by name, said how glad she was to see him there, and took his arm to lead him over to join the group. But Martin merely nodded curtly. He kept his hands in his pockets and stood where he was. His neighbor joined the others, and Martin watched her shrug her shoulders and whisper briefly to them.

No one told him about the meeting, which was for the purpose of discussing neighborhood crime prevention. He found a flier about it on his front porch, but he was sure it was left there by mistake. He believed that the real agenda of the "crime prevention" meeting had to do with him and his gun collection. He had long suspected that certain neighbors knew about the gun collection, though he took pains to keep it secret. He believed they wanted it, and him, out of the neighborhood. Martin was there to protect his rights.

He listened to the proceedings from his place near the door. Several times people asked his opinion on certain issues—additional lighting in alleys, neighborhood crime watch signs—but these issues didn't concern Martin, and he declined to express an opinion.

He stayed until the end of the meeting and continued to watch and listen as people left the room and walked outside. He did not hear his name, or the subject of guns, mentioned at all, but he knew that was only because he was present. He was no fool; he knew he had to be vigilant and act to protect himself all the time or other people would walk all over him. He considered that he had done a good evening's work.

What Paranoid Personality Disorder Is Like

- Misinterpretation of interpersonal situations
- Hostile and aloof
- Blaming and vindictive
- Overtly rational
- Litigious

Misinterpretation of interpersonal situations. Martin's distortion of his neighbors' motives and intentions is a fundamental feature of his personality. He believes that most people he encounters would take advantage of him in some way if they could. He believes he must be on guard at all times, or others will exploit his weakness. He is secretive and devious, believing that any information he gives others about himself is potential ammunition against him. He is constantly scheming, planning counterattacks in the event of success on the part of his adversaries, who are everywhere. In all of his interactions with others, he looks for, and finds in abundance, confirmation of his suspicions and proof of his beliefs.

Hostile and aloof. Martin believes not only that others want to harm him, but that he is in fact being treated unfairly almost all the time;

he can't get a fair shake in life. As a result, he tends to be touchy and argumentative, snapping back, demanding his rights, promising revenge, and generally letting people know he is someone to be reckoned with. Nobody can push him around, and those who try had better watch out.

Martin is 52 years old. He was married once, but the marriage was ill-fated. He blames his wife for its demise; he is certain she was cheating on him, though he never could prove it. He has lived alone, in the same house, for 20 years. His neighbors rarely see him and hardly know him. They were surprised that he came to the crime prevention meeting and baffled by his behavior there.

Martin's only hobby is hunting, which he does alone two or three times a year. He collects guns not so much to enhance his hunting experience, but to arm himself in the event of a serious confrontation with someone; he doesn't know who, but he believes such an event is inevitable and only a matter of time.

Blaming and vindictive. Martin sees the fact that he has not been successful in life as the fault of other people, not his own. It is evidence that his world view is correct; people are out to bring him down. Even back in high school, he never got what was coming to him. He was a bench player on the football team because the other guys conspired to make him look bad. Girls wouldn't go out with him because someone, and he knew who, told lies about him. Teachers ruined his chances for good grades and then mocked him with phony encouragement. Martin is an auto mechanic, and he's good at it. But on every job he's ever had, and he's had plenty, some jerk messes things up for him. The bosses just want to get rid of him and give his job to the undeserving punks who suck up to them.

For Martin, every criticism is an unfair assault, a call to battle, and further proof of other people's agenda against him. He never forgets. He bears grudges for years when he feels he has been treated poorly. He plots revenge against those who have cheated him, put him down, or wronged him in any way. And, far from suffering in silence, he complains loudly and frequently about others' attitudes toward him and the constant barrage of injustices against him.

As unhappy as he has been in his life, Martin has never thought of seeking help from a doctor or a psychotherapist, because he believes they're all quacks, and because he doesn't believe he has any problems that other people haven't caused. He sees his task as getting revenge on the world; the idea of changing his own behavior would strike him as ludicrous and foolhardy.

Against his better judgment he attended three sessions of couples counseling with his wife before she left. The counselor strongly implied that Martin's concerns about his wife's fidelity were paranoid in nature; as Martin put it, the guy thought he was some kind of nut. Martin could see that his wife and the couples counselor were working together to make him look bad and force him out of the marriage. He was sure his wife wanted the house and everything he had; he was surprised when she left quietly, taking only those belongings she had brought with her and allowing him to dictate the terms of the divorce. He saw it as evidence that she had indeed had extramarital affairs.

Overtly rational. Martin can lay out clear, logical, and coherent proof supporting his views. His thought system is internally consistent, and every experience he has confirms it. He can justify all of his vengeful belligerence on the basis of calmly reasoned, lucid assertions, which makes him seem more credible to others and more difficult simply to write off. But while each individual suspicion may seem reasonable on its own, the unrelenting pattern of suspicion, distrust, and secrecy reveals a distorted world view.

Litigious. A primary tool of revenge for Martin is the lawsuit. He doesn't trust lawyers any more than he trusts anyone else, but he believes that the court system is there to right wrongs, and it ought to serve him. The threat of legal action is often enough to make his point, but he is just as likely as not to follow through. Lawyers who tell him he doesn't have a case become targets of revenge themselves. He once sued a neighbor whose cottonwood tree annually scattered white fluffy seeds that got stuck in his window screens. The judge ordered the neighbor to trim the tree so no branches hung into Martin's yard, but that didn't solve the problem. Martin tried going back to court, but that time the case was thrown out.

On several occasions, he has sued over employment issues. His interpersonal difficulties have led to loss of promotions and raises and to three firings. In one instance, he won a settlement from a car dealership that had fired him without following its stated procedures to the letter. Martin is still planning his revenge on the other employers who've screwed him over, including the shop that recently denied him a supervisor's position and then forced him to quit.

Paranoid Personality Disorder's Effect at Work

- Profound interpersonal tensions
- Difficult to supervise
- Difficult to work with
- Workplace danger

Profound interpersonal tensions. Martin's relationships with supervisors and coworkers suffer constant strain. He trusts no one, gets along with no one, and is pleasant to no one. His complaints about the raw deal he's getting, his secrecy, his belligerence, and the current of hostility he puts forth keep others at a wary distance from him.

Difficult to supervise. In Martin's view, any criticism of him or his work is an attack—unwarranted, unfair, and requiring revenge. This view extends to supervisory attempts to give him direction, to manage his work, or to provide him with necessary feedback. He sees any supervisory input as gratuitous interference in his rightful domain. He is obstinate, stubborn, and inflexible. On his first job, in a small neighborhood garage when he was 19, he once punched the owner, who had asked him to redo a brake job. Martin rarely resorts to physical violence anymore, and never at work, but his attitude sends a clear enough message.

Difficult to work with. Martin doesn't hang around having a smoke and chatting with his coworkers at break times, because he thinks that would play into their plans to sabotage him. He sees them all as co-conspirators, none of whom can be trusted, and most of whom have it in for him. In many of the repair shops where he has worked, this has eventually turned out to be true. His own hostility comes back to him; coworkers do in fact ostracize him and begin looking for ways to get rid of him.

Workplace danger. Other than the one instance of slugging his boss in his youth, Martin has not engaged in physical violence at work, though he often threatens. His revenge planning focuses more on his gun collection. He is always ready to sue and received satisfaction that way once. But he is under no illusions about the reliability of legal means to compensate fully for the wrong done him by other people, and he is ready to blow them all away should he ever be pushed that far.

Working with Paranoid Personality Disorder

Martin is a good auto mechanic. He works hard, he works quickly, he attends to all aspects and details of any job he is doing. He is persistent in solving problems. He maintains his education to keep up with changes in the field. He is very concerned about safety factors in the cars he works on. He comes to work every day; keeps his work station, his tools, and his personal appearance clean, neat, and organized; and sometimes stays after hours to complete a job. These are the reasons he feels cheated when he is fired or denied promotions.

He acknowledges being suspicious, secretive, and quick to lash out at others. But, far from seeing these traits as flaws in his own character, he sees them as necessary to his survival and justified by the treatment he has received. Since he feels no responsibility for his interpersonal difficulties, he sees no reason to change his behavior. He blames others for all the problems he has had getting along with people on the job.

Martin quit his last job, but he believes he was in fact forced out. He was denied a promotion for which he was clearly qualified based on training and experience. He was then reassigned to work with a bunch of guys who already disliked him, doing routine maintenance work instead of the more challenging diagnostic and repair work he preferred. He was denied the option of working overtime, which he liked to do not only to earn extra money but because he enjoyed working alone in the shop after hours. He didn't see how he could continue to work there under those conditions. Amid threats of retaliation and lawsuits, he packed his tools and walked out.

He spoke with several lawyers about his case, but none of them could come up with a basis on which to sue. The person promoted over him was equally qualified and had more seniority, and the shop management had violated no aspect of employment law or its own policies. Martin put the situation, and specifically the shop manager, on his list of targets for future revenge.

He believed that someone ought to pay for the fact that he was now out of work. He applied for and was denied unemployment compensation. He researched the possibility of a lawsuit over that, but eventually decided against it. The way he saw it, they had all their big guns lined up against him, and he didn't stand a chance.

But Martin felt strongly that he'd been wronged, and that someone had to make it right. If he couldn't get satisfaction over the loss of his old job, then he was owed a new one, simple as that. With this attitude, he applied for services at his state Department of Rehabilitation Services. He held government agencies in particularly low regard and believed government employees were all flunkies who couldn't get hired elsewhere. But someone owed him a job, and, according to Martin's reasoning, it was up to the state to provide one.

He met with Andy, a young vocational counselor just out of graduate school. Andy had played college football, and he was big, bigger than Martin, who is six feet two inches tall. Martin, already on his guard, recognized the football player physique. He asked Andy if he'd played, not to make conversation, but to size up the situation; he still remembered his old rancor at not quite making it on his high school team. Andy smiled a big, relaxed, friendly smile. He loved football, loved talking about it, assumed Martin was being friendly, and responded in kind. Martin, however, regarded the friendly tone with nothing but suspicion. He watched Andy without smiling, trying to figure out his game plan.

Martin had come to his appointment expecting to be asked about his job history, and he was prepared to talk about it. In fact, he had several file folders full of evidence of his mistreatment as an employee. He showed Andy records of his successful lawsuit against the car dealership that had fired him. He described at length the circumstances leading him to leave his most recent job. His attitude toward Andy as well as toward all his former employers was hostile. Still, he presented his evidence in a reasonable, logical, coherent, consistent, and convincing manner.

Andy had no reason to disbelieve Martin's version of events, though the entire history struck him as strange. He couldn't understand how one person, seemingly a good employee, could have the misfortune of ending up in one bad work situation after another. Because he didn't share Martin's paranoid world view, he was baffled by the idea of so many malicious and vindictive employers, supervisors, and coworkers out there in the world of auto mechanics. He wasn't exactly sure what Martin wanted from him or from the agency or what kind of help he could provide. And he felt intimidated by and vaguely frightened of Martin, a feeling he wasn't used to having.

Andy brought the case to his supervisor, who identified the threads of paranoia running through Martin's story. She had enough experience to suspect that Martin would be difficult to work with—demanding, hostile, uncompromising, and litigious if he didn't get what he wanted. She advised Andy to be very careful, to follow all rules and procedures fully, to document everything, and to be as clear and direct as possible when communicating with Martin, especially about what the agency could and could not offer. She also suggested referring Martin for a psychological evaluation, both to provide needed information about his problems and to give Andy some back-up in working with him.

Martin's view of life includes the understanding that, because the world is a hostile and dangerous place and nothing comes easily, he is forced to jump through one hoop after another just to secure his basic rights. This is how he saw Andy's referral for a psychological evaluation. He angrily informed Andy that he needed a job, not a shrink. He demanded to know if such referrals were standard procedure for all agency clients. He hinted strongly that he would make trouble for

Andy if anything got in the way of his getting a good job, and made it clear that he had expected to be employed by now and didn't appreciate the delay.

Andy explained that the evaluation would help them understand Martin's needs and help clarify why so much had gone wrong for him in the past. Martin said that he already knew all that and didn't need some quack shrink to tell him about it. In the end, though, feeling tricked by Andy into jumping through another hoop, he went for the evaluation. He approached the psychological testing and interview in a characteristically hostile and defensive manner, deeply suspicious of the process and the uses to which it might be put, and prepared to counterattack whenever necessary.

The psychologist diagnosed paranoid personality disorder and included in the report the recommendation that it not be released to Martin because he would likely misinterpret the findings, possibly becoming upset and hostile. Martin believed he had a right to his own copy of the full psychological report and was furious when Andy told him he couldn't have it. He called the psychologist's office saying he knew his rights and they could expect to hear from his attorney. In response, the psychologist sent him a letter, summarizing the findings of the evaluation in lay terms. But that wasn't enough.

Martin called the summary letter bogus and continued demanding to see the full report, threatening all forms of retaliation if he didn't get satisfaction. Feeling that he was in over his head, and unsure how to proceed, Andy nevertheless held his ground on the issue and tried to redirect Martin's energy back to his need for a job. Martin indicated that he wasn't giving up; "I never forget a jerk who jacks me around," he said of the psychologist, hinting that he meant Andy, too. But he turned his attention to what Andy could do for him.

Martin wanted Andy simply to find him a job, and he was suspicious of what he saw as extraneous steps along the way—more hoops to jump through. He was impatient and annoyed. He continually wanted to know if Andy was following standard procedures in working with him, and how other clients in similar circumstances would be treated. He thought, and said as much to Andy, that he would have been better off finding a job on his own, rather than having quacks and do-gooders snooping around in his life and trying to tell him what was good for him.

Andy nodded sympathetically, acknowledged Martin's feelings, and refocused the discussion onto his work needs. Martin liked being an auto mechanic and wanted another job in that field; the only question was what sorts of workplace conditions would help him succeed.

To Martin, it all depended on how many jerks he had to work with, and how many ways they would find to harass him. He did not see his own role in creating his interpersonal problems and had trouble thinking of anything he could do to prevent them. He could, however, with some help from Andy, envision a setting that would help him focus on work, which he did well, and not on coworkers, with whom he couldn't get along.

First of all, Martin is better off working alone. He has worked in repair shops that group the mechanics into teams, but he hasn't lasted long. He does far better in shops organized by individual work stations with individual work assignments and individual responsibility for accomplishing them. Interactions with others are stressful for him. If he can work on his own, separate from others and undistracted by interpersonal concerns, he has a better chance of succeeding. Unfortunately, as Andy pointed out, unless Martin opened his own solo shop, he would still have to deal with supervisors and coworkers, and would sometimes need their cooperation in order to do his work.

Andy thought, but did not say to Martin, that if supervisors and coworkers understood something about the nature of his interpersonal problems, the workplace would be safer and more pleasant for them, as well as more conducive to Martin's ongoing success. He knew that Martin deeply resented being labeled paranoid and would never agree to any kind of disclosure of his personal business at work. But thinking about some of the recommendations in the psychological report, and talking it over with his supervisor, Andy thought that maybe, once Martin found a job, his supervisors and coworkers could somehow be alerted to his "interpersonal oversensitivity" and given some techniques for handling it. But he couldn't think how he could bring that about.

Using some leads that Andy supplied for him from his employment resources, Martin eventually found a job in a small but very busy general purpose auto repair shop. It had the necessary condition of independent work stations and individual responsibility for tasks. Andy congratulated him on getting the job and said he wanted to help him keep it. Martin said the only way to do that was to keep the jerks away from him. This was the opening Andy had hoped for. He offered to meet with Martin's new supervisor, to let him know about Martin's workplace needs.

Martin is exquisitely attuned to the subtlest of nuances and the merest hint of duplicity. Predictably, he reacted defensively to Andy's idea. He immediately suspected a hidden agenda, a secret purpose, a devious plot of some kind. He didn't want Andy messing around in his business. He accused him of interfering and meddling, and said he didn't need that kind of help. But Andy was ready for this response. He said that Martin would be included in the meeting, and that he wouldn't say anything Martin didn't want said; they would work together to plan the content.

Martin was still suspicious, but he did offer some input as Andy tried to come up with some ideas that might help him get along better. First, his supervisor and his coworkers should leave him alone as much as possible and let him do his work. When interaction is necessary, a direct and straightforward approach is valuable. Even if Martin doesn't like what he hears, he says he can tell the difference between an honest, candid, and forthright telling and some attempt to soften or rearrange the truth.

Martin needs to be included in decisions that involve him, from work assignments to break time rotation, to planned overtime, to anything else that goes on. No one should talk behind his back or give the impression that they might be. Taking care to include him in issues that concern him will help alleviate his sense of alienation to some extent.

Performance evaluations and routine feedback and criticism are especially touchy areas for Martin, yet they are a necessary part of any work setting, which Andy made a point of emphasizing to him. Again, a direct, open, plain-talk approach is best, in a neutral or slightly upbeat tone of voice, with an emphasis on strengths and abilities. Martin is especially alert to, and likely to react to, implications of personal shortcomings. If his supervisor focused on the work itself and the specific tasks necessary to get the job done right, not on Martin's approach to it or his decisions about it, Martin might be more able to accept supervision.

Martin still didn't like the idea of a formal meeting, even if it included him. He agreed only to a telephone conversation, only if he were present when Andy made the call, and only because he knew his supervisor was aware that he was working with a rehabilitation counselor. The conversation was short and to the point; Andy explained that people sometimes took a dislike to Martin and then offered his recommendations to help avoid conflict. The supervisor was glad for the information; he said that he knew Martin's work was good and hoped things worked out.

Martin will never win any popularity contests, and he is unlikely to change significantly the world view and the attitudes that keep him separate from and suspicious of others. He is unlikely ever to see his own role in his interpersonal difficulties or to change his behavior. But if he can accept that interaction with others, including feedback and criticism, is inevitable in the workplace, and if supervisors and coworkers can learn effective ways to approach him, he might be able to get along well enough to keep his job.

Summary: Paranoid Personality Disorder's Effect on Vocational Abilities

Level of Impairment

1. no impairment
2. mild—minimal impairment with little or no effect on ability to function
3. moderate—some impairment, which limits ability to function fully
4. serious—major impairment, which may at times preclude ability to function
5. severe—extreme impairment

Understanding and Memory

Remembers locations and basic work procedures

1____X____ 2_____ 3_____ 4_____ 5_____

Understands and remembers short, simple instructions

1____X____ 2_____ 3_____ 4_____ 5_____

Understands and remembers detailed instructions

1____X____ 2_____ 3_____ 4_____ 5_____

Concentration and Persistence

Carries out short, simple instructions

1____X____ 2_____ 3_____ 4_____ 5_____

Carries out detailed instructions

1____X____ 2_____ 3_____ 4_____ 5_____

Maintains attention and concentration for extended periods of time

1____X____ 2_____ 3_____ 4_____ 5_____

Can work within a schedule, maintain attendance, be punctual

1____X____ 2_____ 3_____ 4_____ 5_____

Sustains ordinary routine without special supervision

1____X____ 2_____ 3_____ 4_____ 5_____

Can work with or close to others without being distracted by them

1_____ 2_____ 3____X____ 4_____ 5_____

Makes simple work-related decisions

1____X____ 2_____ 3_____ 4_____ 5_____

Works quickly and efficiently, meets deadlines, even under stressful conditions

1____X____ 2_____ 3_____ 4_____ 5_____

Completes normal workday and workweek without interruptions due to symptoms

1____X____ 2_____ 3_____ 4_____ 5_____

Works at consistent pace without an unreasonable number or length of breaks

1____X____ 2_____ 3_____ 4_____ 5_____

Social Interaction

Interacts appropriately with general public

1_____ 2_____ 3_____ 4_____ 5____X____

Asks simple questions or requests assistance when necessary

1_____ 2_____ 3____X____ 4_____ 5_____

Accepts instruction and responds appropriately to criticism from supervisors

1_____ 2_____ 3_____ 4_____ 5____X____

Gets along with coworkers without distracting them

1_____ 2_____ 3____X____ 4_____ 5_____

Maintains socially appropriate behavior

1_____ 2_____ 3____X____ 4_____ 5_____

Maintains basic standards of cleanliness and grooming

1____X____ 2_____ 3_____ 4_____ 5_____

Adaptation

Responds appropriately to changes at work

1_____ 2_____ 3____X____ 4_____ 5_____

Is aware of normal work hazards and takes necessary precautions

1____X____ 2_____ 3_____ 4_____ 5_____

Can get around in unfamiliar places, can use public transportation

1____X____ 2_____ 3_____ 4_____ 5_____

Sets realistic goals, makes plans independently of others

1____X____ 2_____ 3_____ 4_____ 5_____

Summary: Vocational Strategies and Accommodations

To optimize the chances for vocational success, a person with paranoid personality disorder needs:

- To work alone, or as independently as possible, and not as part of a team, in order to reduce anxiety and suspiciousness.
- To have all interactions conducted in a direct, straightforward manner.
- To be included to the extent possible in decisions involving or concerning him or her.
- To be free of the impression that others are withholding information.
- To be free of the impression that others talk behind his or her back.
- To have the emphasis placed on specific tasks when receiving feedback or instructions in order to avoid feelings of being personally attacked.
- To have emphasis placed on strengths, abilities, and work well done.
- Help from a rehabilitation professional in providing information regarding his or her interpersonal oversensitivity to supervisor and coworkers to maximize likelihood of a positive interpersonal work environment.

SCHIZOTYPAL PERSONALITY DISORDER

Certain cultural beliefs, especially those regarding religious traditions, can appear to be the characteristic symptoms of schizotypal personality disorder to those uninformed as to their nature; for this reason, the evaluation of cognitive and perceptual distortions must be made in the context of the person's cultural background. Thirty percent to 50% of those diagnosed with schizotypal personality disorder also experience major depressive episodes. Schizotypal personality disorder co-occurs frequently with schizoid, paranoid, avoidant, and borderline personality disorders. Its occurrence in the general population is about 3%, and it is more common among close biological relatives of people with schizophrenia. While some people with schizotypal personality disorder might experience short psychotic episodes, especially in response to stress, the course of the disorder is generally stable over a lifetime, and few actually develop schizophrenia or another psychotic disorder (American Psychiatric Association, 1994).

Shelly

The auras were strong; Shelly felt them as soon as she stepped outside. Fingering the scarab talisman she wore on a long silver chain, she pulled her cape closer around her shoulders and walked briskly toward the campus. Her hair, long and graying and wild, slipped from its clasp as she walked, but she was too concerned about the meaning of the signs to pay attention. The clasp was heavy brass, in the shape of a Celtic cross; it clinked on the sidewalk when it fell, but Shelly didn't notice. The strength of the auras confirmed the premonition she had had last night at midnight.

She reached the corner and stopped to wait for traffic to clear so she could cross the street. She felt a tap on her shoulder and turned to face a young man. He was unfamiliar to her. She eyed him coldly and turned away. At the same time, she sensed that someone was trying to reach her. She moved back from the young man, so he wouldn't interfere with her communication channels, but he approached again.

Shelly extended her arms toward him. Her cape fell open, revealing the crystals and charms hanging from her belt. She was staring at a place just over the top of his head. The young man thrust the hair clasp toward her and quickly crossed the street, hardly daring to look back. Shelly took the clasp and held it high over her head. The young man's aura was now clear to her, as was the meaning of the signs.

What Schizotypal Personality Disorder Is Like

- Unusual interpretation of ordinary events
- Aloof and disinterested, or oddly intense and excited

- Odd and eccentric thoughts
- Unusual dress or behavior

Unusual interpretation of ordinary events. Shelly believes that supernatural forces swirl around her and are manifest in the actions of other people. She sees interconnected patterns everywhere. She feels herself to be the target of magical interventions—some beneficial and some malevolent. She believes that such things happen to everyone, though few are open to the experience, which is why hardly anyone understands or can relate to her. She feels that those who are not on her wavelength, who are not "kindred spirits," are unworthy of her time and attention.

She has never married. She is 46 and lives alone in an apartment near the campus of a large university. She attended classes there off and on for 10 years and accumulated a large number of credits but no degree. As a student, she began working part-time shelving books in the back stacks of the library, and she stayed on even after she stopped taking classes. Unfortunately, she recently had to quit because of pressure she felt from the books in a certain section of the stacks. It was a rather large group of books, whose "essence" she believed disliked her from the beginning, and whose negative influence spread throughout the section and eventually throughout the stacks.

As early as high school, Shelly was aware that others did not share her reality and considered her weird. She didn't dress like they did, didn't talk like they did, and had her own interests, which didn't fit in with theirs. On one or two occasions, before she learned to say nothing to the ignorant, she revealed the source of her good grades in history class as the spirits of the historical figures the class was studying, who visited her the night before a test. The other girls giggled and made the sign of the cross, as though warding off a vampire, when they passed her in the halls. It never bothered her. She was uninvolved in school activities and had no interest in dates or parties. She never questioned her own interpretation of reality.

Aloof and disinterested, or oddly intense and excited. Shelly is uncomfortable and ill at ease around most people. She is deeply absorbed in her private world, and she resents intrusion, especially by people or "forces" antithetical to it. She is largely indifferent to events outside the realm of her characteristic interpretations and to people who doubt her experiences.

Still, she is lonely at times and feels a desire to share her wisdom with those capable of understanding it. She becomes animated and excited when talking about her telepathic abilities, her out-of-body experiences, her knowledge of auras, and so on, to someone she believes is a sympathetic and trustworthy listener, such as the psychics she regularly consults. She is otherwise cold, aloof, and self-absorbed.

Odd and eccentric thoughts. Shelly believes she can sense others' thoughts, and that certain outside forces read her own thoughts. She believes she has access to the astral plane, an experience denied to most mortals. She senses the presence of ghosts and apparitions, though she has never seen one. She has strong premonitions and believes she can predict the future. She regularly communicates with extraterrestrial beings, from whom she derives emotional sustenance and who occasionally spirit her away for sexual purposes.

For a while, she was intrigued by the New Age movement, and in the past has attempted to participate in groups organized to explore phenomena that interest her, such as ESP and seances. But she has always been disappointed by what she sees as the shallowness and limited nature of these explorations and by the narrow-mindedness of the other participants. She feels that they lack her depth and don't truly believe her experiences.

She does not trust medical doctors and would never voluntarily go to one; their auras cause her pain. She takes her occasional sore throats, ear infections, and turned ankles to faith healers, aroma therapists, transcendental meditationists, and other alternative practitioners as the mood strikes her. Her oddness has prompted several people she has known—family members, coworkers, neighbors—to suggest psychiatric care. Shelly believes that such suggestions are the result of hostile forces working against her, a view confirmed by her psychic consultant.

Unusual dress or behavior. Shelly wears a collection of charms, talismans, crystals, amulets, and assorted symbols at all times. In doing so, she is not attempting to control the forces at work around her but to communicate with them, so they will know who she is and where she stands. She wears the India prints and crushed velvets she's had since 1969, when her attire and her long flowing hair did not attract the attention they do now. She is indifferent to fashion trends and to ordinary good grooming, though she is scrupulously clean because uncleanliness disrupts her communication channels. She behaves in response to her inner directives and her belief system, not to societal norms. She doesn't care if she appears odd to others or if they back off from her; in fact, she prefers to be left undisturbed.

Schizotypal Personality Disorder's Effect at Work

- Strained interpersonal relationships
- Vague or absent goals

- Ostracized by others
- Unusual ways of processing information

Strained interpersonal relationships. Shelly's discomfort with other people and her indifference to ordinary responsibilities make work relationships difficult to sustain. Feedback or instructions from supervisors have little impact on her behavior or her performance. The library where she worked had recently established a new protocol for the reshelving of books; shelvers were to work together in organizing the books on carts, then certain high-use categories were to be shelved first, followed by a prioritized list. Shelly followed the system halfheartedly if at all.

Instead, she picked up piles of returned books at random and organized them on her own cart without regard to the other shelvers. Especially after she started having trouble with the "essence" of the books in some categories, she used her own priority system, so a returned book might languish on her cart for hours or days before being properly shelved, and the librarians had no way of knowing where it was. She had little interest in the fact that she was disrupting the smooth functioning of the library, that her coworkers resented her, and that her supervisor wanted her fired.

Vague or absent goals. Shelly's goals have to do with the private world she inhabits, and she doesn't talk about them. Otherwise, she doesn't much care what she does. She has no plans, no particular sense of direction about her life, and no desires related to achievement. She is not interested in financial gain beyond her simple needs for food and rent. She is not interested in personal fulfillment, in work, or in leisure activities other than those related to her perceptions of reality. She is not interested in social involvements or motivated by interactions with others.

Ostracized by others. When she first started college, in the late sixties, Shelly had a few friends, or at least people in her life who tolerated her odd ways and even thought she was cool and far out. However, she did nothing to maintain those relationships, and everyone she knew eventually moved on. Since then, most people she knows or encounters have been leery of her and tended to keep their distance.

At the library, her coworkers formed a tight team designed to exclude her. They tried to maintain the prescribed reshelving schedule and would take books from her cart behind her back to shelve in the proper order. Shelly interpreted her coworkers' ostracism and interference as the manifestation of negative energy from the books themselves, which eventually forced her to quit.

Unusual ways of processing information. Shelly filters all information through her belief system, leading to her strange interpretations of everyday events. She makes mistakes not only with regard to reality and interpersonal situations, but also in concrete ways. If left to her own devices and not watched carefully, she sometimes shelved books incorrectly, following some inner directive about where the books wanted to be, rather than the external directive about where other people could find them.

Working with Schizotypal Personality Disorder

After quitting her job, Shelly thought she might make some money by reading tarot cards or offering telepathic consultations. But she found few takers, and even fewer who took her skills seriously. She began spending much of her time wandering the campus or sitting for long periods in certain locations she considered especially open to channels.

With no structure in her life and virtually no interaction with other people, her already tenuous grasp of reality slipped further. Her odd behavior soon caught the attention of the campus police. They watched her and monitored her activities, largely out of concern for her safety, but also because she seemed unpredictable and they couldn't rule out the possibility that she might be a danger to others as well. They spoke to her occasionally, in a friendly way, but she rarely responded.

One of the places Shelly liked to sit was on a large rock located near the intersection of two alleys, near the backyard of a rooming house. She felt that the rock anchored her to Earth, and the crossroads greatly increased and enhanced the channels open to her. The alleys were little used, and the place was quiet. Shelly spent more and more time there, sometimes long into the night. The people who lived in the rooming house noticed her but were unconcerned. They watched her meditating or performing her rituals and found her amusing. Her presence became a source of jokes among them.

Residents of the other houses backing on the alley also became aware of her, and the story spread. People began walking past to get a look at her. They sometimes spoke to her, just to see what kind of odd response they would get. Usually she ignored them or stared at them coldly until they left. But sometimes they were rewarded. "Breath is life," she might say, "thoughts are words, your life breathes your thoughts." Her voice was foreboding and her manner portentous. She became quite a source of entertainment.

But Shelly felt as though her sacred place had been tainted and de-filed. More people were walking or biking through her alley, and they spoke to her more often. She was annoyed by the intrusions. They made her nervous and distracted her. She tried to gather friendly forces around her to ward them off, resulting in her performing ever more strange rituals and delighting her audience even more. She sometimes snapped angrily at them and adopted an intimidating and threatening attitude, but the sense of defilement and the intrusions continued.

She thought of abandoning the rock but decided to try a purifica-tion ritual first. She often burned incense there and sometimes made small fires of dry leaves and sticks. But one night, the night of a full moon, she gathered a large bundle of oak branches, and brought them to her rock, together with incense and a collection of powders she had bought at a New Age store; the powders had special attributes that she felt would work to her advantage.

Unfortunately, the night was windy, and the fire Shelly built was soon out of her control. It expanded to a pile of brush and leaves near the rock and ignited the garage next door. Someone called 911, and a fire truck arrived, accompanied by the campus police; they knew Shelly's habits and suspected she might be involved. Shelly did not leave the spot. She wasn't sure how to interpret the conflagration and was trying to open herself to communications and signs. This is what she told the police, who took her to the psychiatric unit of the uni-versity hospital. The fire was quickly controlled and did little damage to the garage.

Shelly was placed on 72-hour hold, and commitment proceedings were begun. She was evaluated by a psychiatrist, who diagnosed schizotypal personality disorder. Though clearly troubled and out of touch, she was not disoriented and not psychotic. The psychiatrist did not think she represented a significant danger to others.

The county attorney thought differently, however, and pushed for involuntary hospitalization. Eventually, a legal compromise was reached; the judge stayed the commitment order with the stipulation that Shelly agree to attend a psychiatric day-treatment program, run by the university hospital, in order to structure her life, bring her more in touch with reality, and stabilize her mental health.

Shelly was badly shaken by the whole experience. She knew she had committed arson, though she thought it was unfair that no one took the trouble to understand why. She had no intention of damag-ing property or hurting anyone. It wasn't her fault that her special place had been invaded and defiled by outsiders. She thought the hospital staff, though they made an effort to be nice to her, were patronizing, condescending, and narrow-minded. She believed, but by this time knew enough not to say, that her being in the hospital was the work of negative energy and malevolent forces at large in the universe.

She saw the referral to day treatment as a kind of punishment, something she must endure until the friendly forces returned to her. She did not believe she could be helped there. She did not believe she needed to be helped at all; she had only to wait for her benevolent forces to return, do what she could to summon them, and be open to their arrival. Clearly, attending day treatment was a hindrance in this regard, but she intended to comply fully and to complete the program, because she understood the consequences for doing otherwise. Being picked up by the police, being brought before the judge, being involuntarily committed to a hospital would be much worse. Her only goal was to get back to her occult studies, to reestablish her positive ties with the universe, and to get away from people who interfered with her.

Shelly's case manager in the day-treatment program was Jane, a middle-aged social worker. Shelly tried to get in touch with Jane's aura, to get a reading on her, but felt blocked and attributed that to the hospital atmosphere. Unclear which side Jane came from, and distrustful of her friendly, maternal style, Shelly felt anxious and distressed. Having recently experienced the penalty for revealing too much about her life view to outsiders, she was reluctant to tell Jane anything.

Each day Jane commented on some item among the chains and amulets that Shelly continued to wear. She expressed interest in the brass Celtic-cross hair clasp, the scarab talisman, a crystal, a charm, a woven bracelet. Suspicious and reticent at first, Shelly soon began deliberately wearing pieces that she thought Jane might like: a pair of earrings made of bird feathers, an amber pendant with strange dark markings, a velvet vest embroidered with druid symbols. Jane noticed and commented on them all. Eventually, Shelly brought in a few objects from home. She showed Jane a candle holder, a piece of driftwood, an hourglass, a painted ceramic lion, but said little about what they meant to her.

Jane brought in a book on mandala symbolism from home. It was an art book, with large, lush, colorful plates and little text. She left it on a small table in her office, and noticed Shelly looking through it whenever she had an opportunity. She took to wearing a few of her own relics from the sixties—a pair of gypsy-style earrings, strings of colored beads. She never directly asked Shelly about her beliefs or her perception of reality, and never challenged or contradicted any of the small bits she gathered from the little Shelly told her. She merely expressed mild interest.

The day-treatment program required Shelly to spend some individual time with Jane each day, to work on personal issues and goals. Shelly began expanding on the required time and seemed to seek Jane out whenever she could. Jane understood that the reason had to do partly with Shelly's discomfort in the group-oriented aspects of the program, but she also hoped it meant that Shelly was developing some trust in her.

Shelly had been unable to articulate any goals for herself in the program, but she allowed Jane to set some for her. One of these was getting a job again. Jane had no illusions about the likelihood of significantly changing Shelly's personality or her view of life. But she did believe that some of Shelly's traits and behaviors could be modified enough to make her employable, if Shelly were willing to work, and if the right work setting could be found. Jane recognized that as a lot of "ifs."

Shelly realized that she had to work, and she was not averse to it, though she was not excited by it either. She didn't know what kind of work she could do, or wanted to do, and found it difficult to think about or discuss. She hadn't liked or disliked the job in the library. She was able to keep it as long as she did only because the bureaucracy at the university never got around to firing her. She is reasonably intelligent and fully capable of attending to details and organizing information, which she does in pursuit of her occult interests. But she has no goals and no ambition in the world of work, and she is unmotivated by money or by interpersonal success or failure.

Before considering what kind of work and work setting would be best for Shelly, Jane wanted to concentrate on work readiness. In day treatment, Shelly practiced such skills as making eye contact, responding appropriately when spoken to, and staying on the subject in a conversation. She worked on being punctual, staying all day, and staying on task. She had no difficulty doing any of these things when she made the effort. She understood their relationship to work skills. But she was generally uninterested in doing them, finding her private reality and her desire to be open to the return of her benevolent forces much more compelling. Much of the time, Shelly remained self-absorbed and withdrawn.

Shelly continued to be reticent about her views and interests, but Jane spoke to her openly and without judgment about various occult matters, sometimes asking Shelly to explain a concept or a symbol to her. Shelly was confused as to how to respond; she knew Jane didn't fully share her views or believe her experiences, yet the interest she showed, though mild, seemed genuine and was gratifying.

At the same time, Jane wanted to make a distinction between Shelly's reality and the reality most people experience. She wanted to convince Shelly to exercise greater control over her comings and goings from the world of shared reality, so she could get a job. Gradually, Shelly began to respond to the idea that there is a time and a place for everything, and she made more of an effort to participate in the program.

Jane next turned to Shelly's appearance. She didn't want to suggest radical changes, or insist that Shelly give up her trinkets and capes entirely, but she did think that some significant modifications were necessary. She began with the idea of a haircut, which Shelly accepted with surprising enthusiasm. They talked at some length about what hairstyles might be attractive, and Shelly came in a few days later with a nice-looking short cut that showed her naturally curly hair to its best advantage. She also accepted the mild advice on styles and grooming that Jane offered and toned down her aging-hippie look somewhat.

Finally, Jane began to think about a job for Shelly. She knew she would do better in a solitary work situation, one in which there was no expectation to function as a team member. Shelly's apathy toward work and her odd behavior only antagonize others, and the team atmosphere does nothing to enhance her performance. Much of her unusual interpretation of events hinges on the behavior of those around her, and if she can be largely free of the distraction and stress of having to relate to others, she might be able to focus to a greater extent on the work.

On the other hand, an unstructured and minimally supervised job setting could be disastrous, especially in situations where misinterpretation of reality is seriously problematic. At her library job, Shelly could ignore the structure provided because the shelvers in the back stacks were not closely supervised; they were expected to work together and check each other's work. While her insistence on following her own interpretation of reality rather than the prescribed procedure did cause problems for the efficient running of the library, her coworkers often compensated for her mistakes. For Shelly to succeed, Jane knew she would need a job that struck a delicate balance, one that would allow her to work alone but under close supervision.

The day-treatment program did not include a vocational counseling component, but Jane consulted with a vocational rehabilitation counselor with whom she often worked. They came up with a short list of job possibilities for Shelly, and the vocational counselor helped arrange some interviews. Shelly showed no particular interest in one job over another; the nature of the work or the tasks involved held no meaning for her. Jane knew that the nature of the work setting, the relationships, and the expectations were much more important for Shelly's success.

Eventually, Shelly was hired by a commercial laundry. Her job was to press shirts, specifically those that were unusually large or small or for some other reason didn't fit on the standard pressing machines. Her work area was apart from, but in view of, the main work area and her supervisor. Shelly showed her characteristic indifference. Jane, however, was delighted; the setting was perfect, and the need to relate to others was low. She figured that Shelly would eventually discover some sort of supernatural activity going on among the shirts for which she was responsible, and could only hope she'd be able to cope with it when the time came.

Jane recognized Shelly's indifference to emotional support, encouragement, and other interpersonal incentives. Still, she thought if her supervisors and coworkers understood something about her personality disorder, her behavior would seem less mysterious and bizarre to them, they would be more comfortable leaving her alone to do her work, and there would be less tension among them. Shelly gave her permission for Jane to call the supervisor. Jane offered a brief and straightforward explanation of Shelly's personality and of her particular idiosyncrasies. She framed it in a way that invited cooperation and acceptance from the supervisor, who was glad to have the information.

Jane went on to describe Shelly's need for unambiguous expectations and clear instructions, reviewed often and thoroughly. She suggested that the supervisor regularly check her work for accuracy and completeness, and point out mistakes so Shelly could correct them. She emphasized that Shelly needs clear guidelines, and she needs them enforced, if she is to succeed. Dress codes, behavioral expectations, and performance expectations that are explicit and unequivocal will help her stay on track.

Shelly had formed a minimal connection with Jane, but enough that it seemed helpful to her. Hoping to preserve that, and hoping that Shelly would tell her what she was experiencing at work so Jane could help with effective coping skills, Jane offered her follow-up visits over the next several months.

At best, Shelly is an indifferent worker. To a large extent, her employability may always depend on the nature of the work setting in which she finds herself, and on the understanding and goodwill of her employers. But having learned some appropriate workplace behaviors, and having an informed supervisor and coworkers, may help her stay employed.

Summary: Schizotypal Personality Disorder's Effect on Vocational Abilities

Level of Impairment
1. no impairment
2. mild—minimal impairment with little or no effect on ability to function
3. moderate—some impairment, which limits ability to function fully
4. serious—major impairment, which may at times preclude ability to function
5. severe—extreme impairment

Understanding and Memory

Remembers locations and basic work procedures

1___X___ 2_____ 3_____ 4_____ 5_____

Understands and remembers short, simple instructions

1___X___ 2_____ 3_____ 4_____ 5_____

Understands and remembers detailed instructions

1___X___ 2_____ 3_____ 4_____ 5_____

Concentration and Persistence

Carries out short, simple instructions

1___X___ 2_____ 3_____ 4_____ 5_____

Carries out detailed instructions

1___X___ 2_____ 3_____ 4_____ 5_____

Maintains attention and concentration for extended periods of time

1_____ 2_____ 3___X___ 4_____ 5_____

Can work within a schedule, maintain attendance, be punctual

1___X___ 2_____ 3_____ 4_____ 5_____

Sustains ordinary routine without special supervision

1_____ 2_____ 3___X___ 4_____ 5_____

Can work with or close to others without being distracted by them

1___X___ 2_____ 3_____ 4_____ 5_____

Makes simple work-related decisions

1___X___ 2_____ 3_____ 4_____ 5_____

Works quickly and efficiently, meets deadlines, even under stressful conditions

1_____ 2_____ 3_____ 4___X___ 5_____

Completes normal workday and workweek without interruptions due to symptoms

1___X___ 2_____ 3_____ 4_____ 5_____

Works at consistent pace without an unreasonable number or length of breaks

1_____ 2___X___ 3_____ 4_____ 5_____

Social Interaction

Interacts appropriately with general public

1_____ 2_____ 3_____ 4_____ 5___X___

Asks simple questions or requests assistance when necessary

1_____ 2_____ 3_____ 4_____ 5___X___

Accepts instruction and responds appropriately to criticism from supervisors

1_____ 2_____ 3_____ 4_____ 5___X___

Gets along with coworkers without distracting them

1_____ 2_____ 3_____ 4_____ 5___X___

Maintains socially appropriate behavior

1_____ 2_____ 3_____ 4_____ 5___X___

Maintains basic standards of cleanliness and grooming

1_____ 2_____ 3___X___ 4_____ 5_____

Adaptation

Responds appropriately to changes at work

1_____ 2_____ 3__X__ 4_____ 5_____

Is aware of normal work hazards and takes necessary precautions

1_____ 2_____ 3__X__ 4_____ 5_____

Can get around in unfamiliar places, can use public transportation

1__X__ 2_____ 3_____ 4_____ 5_____

Sets realistic goals, makes plans independently of others

1_____ 2_____ 3__X__ 4_____ 5 _____

Summary: Vocational Strategies and Accommodations

To optimize the chances for vocational success, a person with schizotypal personality disorder needs:

- To work alone, not as part of a team, to accommodate poor social skills.
- To work under close supervision and consistent levels of accountability, in order to prevent inappropriate "creativity" or unusual interpretations of reality applied to work tasks.
- Clear expectations with regard to work performance, behavior, and appearance, in order to maximize marginal levels of motivation.
- Unambiguous instructions, reviewed often and thoroughly.
- Frequent checks for accuracy and completeness of work.
- To have mistakes pointed out in a direct manner, in order to correct them.
- Help from a rehabilitation professional in discussing personal idiosyncrasies with supervisor and coworkers in order to engender a degree of acceptance and provide assistance in managing employee's behavior and motivation.

SCHIZOID PERSONALITY DISORDER

Schizoid personality disorder is rare in clinical settings, though it may appear as an antecedent to delusional disorder or schizophrenia or to a major depressive episode. It is diagnosed slightly more often in men than in women and may cause more impairment in men. It may appear more often in the relatives of people with schizophrenia or schizotypal personality disorder. It may show up in childhood or adolescence as poor peer relationships, underachievement in school, solitariness, or other behaviors that set the child apart and cause teasing. The characteristics of schizoid personality disorder, such as constricted emotions and lack of expression, desire to be alone, passivity in response to adverse circumstances, or tendency to seem cold, hostile, or indifferent may appear in the interpersonal styles of people from a variety of cultural backgrounds or people in difficult life situations. Someone who grew up in a rural setting and moved to a big city or a recent immigrant, for example, may mistakenly be labeled with schizoid personality disorder (American Psychiatric Association, 1994).

Ed

Ed heard someone call his name, but he didn't look up. He felt a hand on his shoulder, but he didn't turn around.

"Ed! I can't believe it's you!"

He saw a vaguely familiar face, but he didn't respond.

"Hey, don't you remember me? It's me, Billy." Billy slid in across from Ed in the booth. Ed stirred his coffee.

"Long way from the old neighborhood, isn't it?" Billy said. "I haven't seen you in years, Ed. How long has it been, you figure?"

Ed stirred his coffee. "Don't know," he said.

"I went back a few years ago, ran into your mother, had a nice talk. How is she?"

"She's dead," Ed said. His tone of voice was flat and noncommittal. His expression communicated nothing.

"Sorry," Billy said, removing his hat. He was silent for a few minutes, waiting for Ed to say more, but Ed just sipped his coffee. "So, what are you up to, Ed?" Billy finally asked.

"Working," Ed said.

"Yeah? What do you do?"

"Computers," Ed said.

"Computers, great. You like it?"

"Not much," Ed said. He finished his coffee and stood up. He dropped some money on the table and left the cafe without looking at Billy.

What Schizoid Personality Disorder Is Like

- Aloof and disinterested
- Flat affect, bland expression
- Low motivation, vague or absent goals

Aloof and disinterested. Ed is a loner. He has no interest at all in other people. Their presence is meaningless to him. He feels no need to communicate with them or respond to them. His emotional withdrawal is so complete that he appears to have no emotions. He holds himself aloof, he distances himself from others as much as possible, and his behavior toward them appears cold.

Ed has never married. He has no friends, apparently by choice. He lives alone in an efficiency apartment in a large building, and he never talks to his neighbors. His conversation with Billy, whom he knew as a teenager, is the longest social encounter he has experienced in some time, and neither their long acquaintance with each other nor the coincidence of meeting again in a big city meant anything to him. By all appearances, he was more annoyed by it than anything, although he showed not a trace of feeling.

Flat affect, bland expression. Ed does not replace friendships and social interactions with other interests; he has no interests. Few things give him pleasure, and he rarely seeks or finds it. The expression on his face doesn't change, nor does his tone of voice. His boss once commented on his apparent lack of interest in life, and Ed concurred. In a burst of chattiness, he once confided to his boss that he felt "low"; but he doesn't look sad, only blank. He has a vague sense that other people don't care much about him, but he's just as glad—dealing with people who cared about him would be an unwelcome burden.

Despite the mild dissatisfaction with his life that he occasionally expresses, Ed does not feel that he has any problems, and he wouldn't talk about them if he did. He goes to the dentist when he has a toothache, but he would never in a million years go to a psychotherapist to talk about feeling "low," and any suggestion that he do so would bring no response from him.

Low motivation, vague or absent goals. Ed is 34. He has always been a loner. Billy was his only friend in high school, and that was because they lived across the alley from each other, and Billy waited for him every day to walk home from school together. Ed didn't work very hard in school. Based on his math scores on standardized tests, a guidance counselor directed him toward computer programming. Ed never considered any other field. He took the minimum training at a technical college and went to work for a small start-up company.

At the beginning, the company employed only six other people, including the boss, who owned it. All of them had more interest in numbers and computers than in each other, and things went fine for Ed for a few years. But the company grew. New employees came on, new opportunities opened up, new responsibilities developed, and Ed never changed the way he did things or the way he related to others. Growth and opportunity didn't interest him. Eventually, the company was bought out by a large corporation. The new organization had no place for Ed, and he was let go with a little severance pay and an offer of outplacement services. He left with no plans and no goals.

Schizoid Personality Disorder's Effect at Work

- Deeply constricted interpersonal relationships
- Supervision largely ineffective
- Inability to work as a "team member"
- Disinterest in achievement or promotions

Deeply constricted interpersonal relationships. Ed can relate to computers but not to people. His coldness, his obvious desire to distance himself from others, his avoidance of any social contact, his stiff, awkward behavior when forced to respond, all contribute to extremely poor working relationships.

Supervision largely ineffective. Feedback from his boss had virtually no impact on Ed's behavior. Efforts to include him in the sort of limited social interaction that took place in the early days of the company—"Hey, Ed, we're ordering take-out, you want some?" No response from Ed—failed miserably. Efforts to engage him in discussions or decision making about the company's work also failed, as did efforts to motivate him, no matter how they were presented; juicy incentives or threats of firing were all one to Ed. He was passive in the face of changing performance requirements, and he refused to do anything but what he had always done or to do it any differently from the way he had always done it. He avoided contact with his boss, and he avoided demands for more or better work.

Inability to work as a "team member." For the most part, Ed ignored his coworkers. Sometimes they tolerated his isolation, and sometimes they needled him about it; either way, Ed was indifferent. They were scrupulous about inviting him to all work-related social gatherings, which became more numerous as the company grew, but Ed never responded, even to refuse. Several strong, work-based friendships developed in the company over the years, but not for Ed. Growth, expansion, and more and bigger projects often required teamwork among the employees, but Ed avoided all demands to work with others. One coworker tagged him the Lone Wolf, and several of them created a suitable graphic, which they hung at his work station. Ed didn't even seem to see it, and it hung there untouched for five years, until Ed was laid off.

Disinterest in achievement or promotions. Ed does what he has to do. He has never shown himself to be especially motivated to do well. He doesn't care what people think of him, and he doesn't care about achievement for its own sake. He avoided chances for promotion, because pursuing them would mean increased contact with others and increased responsibilities. He was content to sit at his computer and do his work and then go home.

Working with Schizoid Personality Disorder

Unfortunately for Ed, the days of the lone cowboy riding the trail are gone. Other employment options open to earlier generations of schizoid men, such as hermit, monk, mountain man, or lighthouse keeper, have likewise gone by the wayside. Ed is forced to earn a living in a highly social society, which relies increasingly on the concept of teamwork in employment settings. His personality is ill suited to the task.

He waited several weeks before taking advantage of the outplacement services his company offered. Using the want ads, he looked for work on his own. He made a few phone calls, and sent one or two résumés, but received no offers. After a while, he quit checking the want ads and spent his time watching TV or sitting in coffee shops. When his severance pay was nearly gone, he contacted Sara, the outplacement counselor.

Sara was used to working with ambitious, career-minded people. Her first inkling of what it would be like to work with Ed came when she looked at his résumé. It consisted of three lines: his name and telephone number, the name of the technical college he had attended and the date he graduated, and the name of the company he had worked for with his dates of employment. He made no mention of the nature of projects he had worked on or completed, areas of particular interest or expertise, skills and abilities, or continuing education.

Sara also examined Ed's performance reviews over his 12 years at the company. The early reviews were quite informal and mildly complimentary about Ed's work. His training and skills were adequate and up-to-date; he was a decent, if uninspired, computer programmer. He was reliable and conscientious in his work, though he did nothing more than required and made no effort to excel.

Later performance reviews expressed increasing concern over Ed's lack of interpersonal skills. Reading through them, Sara got the impression of a misfit in the growing and successful company. His work was still satisfactory, but his inability to relate to supervisors and coworkers, or to clients and customers, set him apart and created tension and distrust. Sara was curious about Ed's apparent unconcern and his unwillingness or inability to change, in spite of being informed of the complaints against him and the danger to his continued employment.

Having read through these materials, Sara felt as though she knew quite a lot about Ed, but she wasn't prepared for the experience of meeting him. Usually relaxed and confident with new clients, Sara felt ill at ease and off balance with Ed. Her naturally bubbly style and friendly conversation seemed overdone and out of place in the face of his expressionless gaze and monosyllabic responses. He merely shrugged when she asked him what kind of position he hoped to find and what he saw himself doing in 10 years' time. She could detect no interest at all on his part in the process ahead of them.

Imagining him with a prospective employer, Sara knew a major part of her work with Ed would include teaching and practicing interviewing skills. But she wanted to start with his résumé. She thought that would be less threatening to him and might be a way to establish a relationship. Before beginning to work on the résumé, however, Sara needed more information from Ed about his education, his continued training, his role in the company, the kinds of tasks he preferred and was good at, his goals.

Getting Ed to discuss these things turned out to be much more difficult than Sara had anticipated. His sparse responses conveyed only the vaguest idea of what he had done, what he could do, what he might strive for, or find satisfying. He hinted that he didn't much like computer work, but he had done it for 12 years, and he could name nothing else that he might like better.

Still, Sara thought that working with him to discover areas of interest would increase his chances for success. She arranged for some interest and aptitude testing for him. The tests did not yield strong results, but did seem to indicate that being a computer programmer was as good a job as any for Ed to have. Ed expressed no opinion when Sara explained the testing results to him.

Feeling frustrated by her inability to establish any kind of rapport with Ed, Sara began to wonder if he had a medical or psychological problem of some kind that had never been identified. She consulted with a psychologist she knew, who specialized in evaluations for vocational purposes. She explained to Ed that in order to help give him the best shot for vocational success, they both needed to understand things about him that he himself may not understand—what motivates him, for example. Ed shrugged. He agreed to a psychological evaluation, or, more accurately, he didn't object, and he kept the appointment.

After administering several psychological tests and interviewing Ed, the psychologist diagnosed schizoid personality disorder. He explained the disorder at length to Sara and sent her a detailed report. He included a nontechnical version of the report for Ed's benefit. Ed glanced at it and left it on Sara's desk when their session was over that day. The information may have held no interest for him, but it was vital for Sara. She could stop blaming herself for the difficulty she experienced in working with Ed, and she had some insight into his behavior and his vocational needs.

Sara now recognized that Ed would need a great deal more help constructing a résumé than she was used to providing to her more articulate and motivated clients. She showed him several examples of well-constructed and well-written résumés, and asked him to choose one and use it as a model in describing his own vocational experiences. He chose the one with the fewest categories, and at their next meeting he brought in his own version of it, minimally completed and spare, but, Sara figured, a start.

She worked with him to flesh out his descriptions of his education, training, work experience, and responsibilities. She gave him a list of positive, active words to enliven his presentation; she told him to memorize these, because he would also need them when the time came to interview for jobs.

After a long struggle to create a usable résumé, Sara was almost giddy in expressing her pleasure with the finished product. She felt that it described Ed to his best advantage and at the same time was concise, readable, and informative. She was by now used to Ed's terse and uninterested replies and no longer felt put off by his laconic style. She hoped her enthusiasm for their efforts would be infectious, but Ed never caught it.

When she was honest with herself, Sara had to admit that she wished she could end her work with Ed right then and send him on his way. But she knew that the hardest part of her job with him still remained: teaching him interviewing skills. She had hoped that some kind of relationship and rapport would evolve over time, but he was every bit as cold and distant toward her as he had been at the beginning. Working on interviewing skills under such circumstances would be difficult.

She set up some role plays. In the first one, she had Ed play the interviewer, while she played a job-seeker. She modeled and demonstrated effective interviewing techniques. She made eye contact, she smiled, she offered a firm, warm handshake, she used Ed's name, she sat forward in her chair to show interest and enthusiasm, she demonstrated a knowledge of the job and of the company, she described her experience clearly and concisely showing confidence but stopping short of bragging, she described her special skills and her long-term work goals and pointed out how well they fit this job and this company. When she finished, she told Ed that they would switch roles.

Ed's first effort was less than stellar, but no worse than Sara had anticipated. She worked on each interview element separately until Ed could perform it. He never managed a convincingly interested facial expression, but he learned to make eye contact and to offer a firm handshake. They worked the longest on content. One-word answers were unacceptable. Positive, active words were essential, words like create, lead, innovate, solve. In subsequent role plays, Sara insisted that Ed respond fully to all questions and that he initiate conversation, ask questions, and volunteer information. Finally, she was satisfied that he wouldn't damage his chances of being hired for lack of interview skills.

Ed met with Sara a few more times as he began applying for jobs. His training and his 12 years of experience qualified him for higher level jobs than the ones he chose to apply for. Sara recognized that his ideal working conditions probably involved the graveyard shift in an empty building, not the opportunity to use or expand his abilities, and she made no comment. She helped him understand his options but did not pressure him to choose one over another. Eventually, he was hired as a computer programmer for a large corporation, working with others primarily by means of e-mail.

Sara's final effort on Ed's behalf was to request his permission to talk to his new boss. She thought it was important that supervisors and coworkers understood something about Ed's personality so they didn't take his cold, aloof manner personally, and so they could give him the space he needed to function as an employee. She told Ed that she wanted to make sure his supervisor knew about his preference for working mostly alone. Ed said it was unnecessary, but he had no objection to her making the call.

She explained to the supervisor that Ed is uncomfortable around other people. She said that he experiences most interpersonal interaction as stress. An expectation that he function as part of a team would be detrimental both to him and the team. A requirement that he interact on a regular basis with the public would be very difficult for him to fulfill. He would probably react to either situation by withdrawing further and appearing more cold and aloof. The supervisor said that Ed sounded like the perfect guy for this particular job, since it involved almost no face-to-face contact with anyone.

Allowing him to be only as ambitious as he chooses to be is essential to his success; efforts to push him toward higher goals or greater achievement will likely backfire. He seems to need a sense of self-direction and independence—a sense of freedom from entanglements with others—in order to feel comfortable. With solitary working conditions, a minimum of interaction, and little pressure to achieve new things or to "grow as a person," Ed should be able to perform his job adequately for years to come.

Summary: Schizoid Personality Disorder's Effect on Vocational Abilities

Level of Impairment

1. no impairment
2. mild—minimal impairment with little or no effect on ability to function
3. moderate—some impairment, which limits ability to function fully
4. serious—major impairment, which may at times preclude ability to function
5. severe—extreme impairment

Understanding and Memory

Remembers locations and basic work procedures

1___X___ 2_____ 3_____ 4_____ 5_____

Understands and remembers short, simple instructions

1___X___ 2_____ 3_____ 4_____ 5_____

Understands and remembers detailed instructions

1___X___ 2_____ 3_____ 4_____ 5_____

Concentration and Persistence

Carries out short, simple instructions

1___X___ 2_____ 3_____ 4_____ 5_____

Carries out detailed instructions

1_____ 2___X___ 3_____ 4_____ 5_____

Maintains attention and concentration for extended periods of time

1_____ 2___X____ 3_____ 4_____ 5_____

Can work within a schedule, maintain attendance, be punctual

1___X____ 2_____ 3_____ 4_____ 5_____

Sustains ordinary routine without special supervision

1___X____ 2_____ 3_____ 4_____ 5_____

Can work with or close to others without being distracted by them

1_____ 2_____ 3___X____ 4_____ 5_____

Makes simple work-related decisions

1___X____ 2_____ 3_____ 4_____ 5_____

Works quickly and efficiently, meets deadlines, even under stressful conditions

1_____ 2_____ 3___X____ 4_____ 5_____

Completes normal workday and workweek without interruptions due to symptoms

1_____ 2___X____ 3_____ 4_____ 5_____

Works at consistent pace without an unreasonable number or length of breaks

1___X____ 2_____ 3_____ 4_____ 5_____

Social Interaction

Interacts appropriately with general public

1_____ 2_____ 3_____ 4_____ 5___X____

Asks simple questions or requests assistance when necessary

1_____ 2_____ 3_____ 4_____ 5___X____

Accepts instruction and responds appropriately to criticism from supervisors

1_____ 2_____ 3_____ 4_____ 5___X____

Gets along with coworkers without distracting them

1_____ 2_____ 3_____ 4___X____ 5_____

Maintains socially appropriate behavior

1_____ 2_____ 3_____ 4_____ 5___X____

Maintains basic standards of cleanliness and grooming

1_____ 2_____ 3___X___ 4_____ 5_____

Adaptation

Responds appropriately to changes at work

1_____ 2_____ 3___X___ 4_____ 5_____

Is aware of normal work hazards and takes necessary precautions

1___X___ 2_____ 3_____ 4_____ 5_____

Can get around in unfamiliar places, can use public transportation

1___X___ 2_____ 3_____ 4_____ 5_____

Sets realistic goals, makes plans independently of others

1_____ 2_____ 3_____ 4___X___ 5_____

Summary: Vocational Strategies and Accommodations

To optimize the chances for vocational success, a person with schizoid personality disorder needs:

- Solitary working conditions with no expectation to work as part of a team, in order to accommodate poor social skills.
- As little face-to-face interaction as possible with supervisors, coworkers, or the public.
- Options with regard to setting goals, with little pressure to choose one over another.
- No expectation to excel or achieve high goals, due to low motivation.
- Help in identifying skills and abilities, due to low level of interest and insight.
- Help from a rehabilitation professional in explaining personality traits to a supervisor, in order to ensure acceptance and prevent misinterpretation of cold, aloof behavior.

CHAPTER 5

The "Dramatic" Cluster: Borderline, Antisocial, Histrionic, and Narcissistic Personality Disorders

Inflated ego, swaggering, braggadocio, and capricious shifts in attitudes and loyalties characterize the "dramatic" cluster of personality disorders. Its hallmarks are intense emotional expression, sudden mood swings, low frustration tolerance, poor impulse control, and volatile interpersonal relationships.

Instability is the key feature of borderline personality disorder. Those who manifest it ride a rough sea of dangerous waves; mood, self-definition, and close relationships are all subject to mercurial shifts that occur with dizzying speed, staggering intensity, and behavior to match. Self-destructive acts and cruelty to others are as likely as obsequious displays of dependency and devotion, all of which can instantly give way to biting sarcasm or raging tantrums.

Those with antisocial personality disorder act as though laws are for other people. They disregard rules, standards, and accepted social customs. Deception, ill-will, and brutality are their frequent companions. Thuggish intimidation and cool manipulation are the cornerstones of their relationship skills. They are never too far from violence and can be a source of danger in the workplace.

Often attractive in appearance, extroverted, gregarious, witty, charming, and entertaining, people with histrionic personality disorder might be welcomed and admired—at first. Unfortunately, their interpersonal interactions quickly betray them. They lack emotional depth and come across as phony, affected, duplicitous, insincere, and shallow. They find relationships difficult to sustain and are likely to blame others for the difficulty.

People with narcissistic personality disorder act like they are the only people in the world who matter; others exist only to endorse and amplify this fact. They feel exempt from the normal constraints of interpersonal interaction, entitled to special privileges and extra advantages, and they behave accordingly. They believe that they have unique talents and abilities, magnificent in scope and patently evident, but mysteriously unacknowledged by others.

People in the "dramatic" cluster are rarely capable of empathy. They are often self-centered and prone to temper tantrums. They tend to be irresponsible, impulsive, and remarkably free of remorse. Deceit, superficiality, and arrogance cloud all of their relationships. They have great power to create confusion, disruption, and violence in the workplace; their presence there is a stick of dynamite waiting for a match.

BORDERLINE PERSONALITY DISORDER

People with borderline personality disorder report a relatively high level of abuse, neglect, conflict, and early loss or separation from parents in their childhood histories. They are likely to experience mood disorders, substance-related disorders, eating disorders, or posttraumatic stress disorder. The risk of successful suicide increases in those with concurrent mood or substance-related disorders. About 75% of people diagnosed with borderline personality disorder are women. It occurs in about 2% of the general population, 10% in outpatient mental health settings, and 20% among psychiatric patients. It is about five times more common among close biological relatives of those who have the disorder than in the general population. The greatest impairment, instability, and risk of suicide is in the young adult years. The disorder tends to wane as the person ages; during their thirties and forties, most people who have it experience greater stability in both relationship and vocational functioning (American Psychiatric Association, 1994).

Carol

Carol lined up the pill bottles on her kitchen counter. She had about two weeks' worth of antidepressants, 15 sleeping pills, two different prescriptions for pain, and an unopened economy-size bottle of Tylenol caplets. She wasn't sure if it was enough to really do the job, but it should get the message across to John, her boyfriend.

She opened all the bottles and poured herself a glass of wine. She took the sleeping pills, one pill at a time, until they were gone. She refilled her wineglass and went to the phone. She dialed John's and heard him answer. She didn't say anything. He said, "Hello? Hello?

Who is this?" She let the hint of a sob escape her throat, then a sigh. John said, "Carol? Carol? Is this you? Is something wrong?"

"You did this," Carol said, letting her words slur together and her voice sound weak and far away. "I'm going to die because of you."

What Borderline Personality Disorder Is Like

- Instability in relationships, sense of self, and mood
- Lack of empathy and remorse
- Impulsivity, irresponsibility, unreliability
- Inappropriate expression of anger
- Self-destructiveness
- Fear of abandonment; hypersensitivity to rejection

Instability in relationships, sense of self, and mood. Earlier that evening, John and Carol had dinner together. She nestled close to him in the restaurant, stroked his back, and told him he was the most wonderful man she had ever met. He said gently that their relationship was moving a little fast for him. He had accepted a chance to attend a month-long training session in another city. He looked forward to starting fresh with her on his return, perhaps at a slower pace. Carol threw a drink at him, screamed that he was a no-good son-of-a-bitch, that she hoped his plane went up in flames, and that he'd better not dare ever to call her again. Then she left the restaurant.

In the three weeks since they'd begun dating, Carol had twice before become enraged at John, once when he wanted to spend an evening alone at his own apartment, and once when he invited a friend to join them for dinner. On both occasions, he responded to her tears and anger with caring and equanimity. Both times, she quickly reversed herself, saying she was no good, she didn't deserve him, she didn't deserve anything good in life, and she wondered how could he put up with her. In response to his comforting words, she became playful and seductive, insisting that they just laugh and have a good time.

John was understandably confused. When Carol called him after taking her pills, he was packing for his trip; he had a plane to catch at six the next morning. Still, he rushed to her apartment, very worried about her condition. He bundled her into his car and raced to the hospital emergency room. He stayed until he was sure she would be all right. Carol was contrite and expressed gratitude. But as he was leaving, barely in time to make his flight, she said sarcastically, "I can see how much you care about me."

Instability is the basis of Carol's personality. Her treatment of John is typical of the way she treats anyone close to her. Everyone in her life is either wonderful or horrible; her assessment of them is ongoing, and it flips dramatically back and forth. Likewise, her sense of self also changes quickly, depending, in part, on others' responses to her. She has no inner core of self-understanding; her self-concept rests on constantly shifting sands. Her moods, from rage to grief to joy to shame to passion, are intense, unpredictable, and capable of doing great damage to her and to those around her.

Lack of empathy and remorse. That her behavior toward John might cause him distress never occurred to Carol. That he, or anyone, has feelings or needs as valid as her own is an alien idea to her. That he, or anyone she depends on, has or deserves a life separate from her involvement in it, is something she has never considered. She does not experience empathy for other people because she finds her own feelings and needs overwhelming and all-consuming.

While she is prone to brief attacks of intense guilt, Carol does not experience true remorse in the sense of moral anguish over pain caused to others. This is partly because she can't conceive of others' pain, and partly because she does not take responsibility for her own behavior. Her actions, mistakes, and misdeeds are not her fault because someone else provoked her or otherwise caused her to act as she did. To her way of thinking, John's mistreatment of her forced her to take drastic measures. The emotional turmoil and disruption of his life that she caused mean little to her.

Impulsivity, irresponsibility, unreliability; inappropriate expression of anger. Carol's behavior is ruled by her emotions. She acts on impulse, without thinking and without considering consequences. She says whatever comes into her head, regardless of her motivation or of the circumstances. She makes commitments she doesn't honor and promises she doesn't keep. She refuses to be held accountable for anything she says or does; nothing is her responsibility or her fault. Her anger is intense and easily ignited. She doesn't feel a need to hold back in expressing it. Bitter sarcasm and violent rages are her frequent responses to ordinary, daily interactions with others.

Self-destructiveness. Carol's suicide "attempt" is not her first. She has twice before been hospitalized under similar circumstances, but on none of these occasions did she fully intend to die. Her primary intent was to communicate her anger toward someone else. Endangering her life in doing so is characteristic of her tendency to be self-destructive.

It shows up in other ways, too. She developed an eating disorder as an adolescent and routinely starves herself or binges on junk food.

She is a reckless driver, sometimes intentionally. She likes to go to bars alone and stay until closing. When she was 18, she allowed herself to be the "guest of honor" at a fraternity stag party, and her treatment there resulted in her first overdose and hospitalization. She drinks too much and experiments freely with drugs. Once, when angry at a boyfriend, she burned his initial in her arm with a cigarette.

As a result of her self-destructive behavior and unstable moods, Carol has had years of psychotherapy and has tried many medications, all to no avail. She is either furious at or in love with her therapists, and her goal in therapy is to get attention and support. Toward this end, she pays lip service to the stated goal of understanding and working on changing her own behavior, but she makes little attempt to do so. Her mood swings are the result of her personality structure, and so far no medication has had any effect on controlling them. She is likely to misuse prescribed medication, taking too much or too little, taking it haphazardly, and sometimes stockpiling pills for future suicide gestures.

Fear of abandonment; hypersensitivity to rejection. The precipitant for much of Carol's self-destructive behavior and her treatment of others is a fear of being alone. She is terrified of being abandoned, of having no one. To her, it is imperative to control others so they don't leave her, and she is willing to go to great lengths to do so. She experiences the mildest put-off as complete rejection, which she sees as life-threatening, and responds accordingly.

Borderline Personality Disorder's Effect at Work

- Tense, unstable relationships
- Frequent changes in career and training plans
- Poor stress tolerance
- Workplace danger

Tense, unstable relationships. Carol's relationships with her supervisors and coworkers are unsettled and turbulent, marked by intense and unpredictable ups and downs. The wonderful boss becomes a tyrant from hell in a matter of minutes. The friendly group in the lunchroom becomes a target for spite in the space of a break time. She experiences supervisory input as a threat to her fragile sense of self and is unlikely to accept it without argument.

She disputes decisions and assignments, bickers over perceived mistreatment, and demands that unfavorable performance reviews be changed. She agitates her coworkers against management and against each other, only to switch sides when her mood changes. She picks fights, and she is quick to cry abuse, harassment, or discrimination when such charges are far from warranted.

She once succeeded in getting a male supervisor fired for sexual harassment. She initially liked him and tried hard to impress him, but he treated her the same way he treated the other employees; he was enthusiastic and encouraging, but he showed no special interest in her. This infuriated her, and she complained to the division director that he looked at her in a sexual way. They were never alone together, and no coworker corroborated her story, but the supervisor was fired, largely due to the disturbance Carol caused and her threats to go to the press or take legal action.

Frequent changes in career and training plans. Carol is 26 years old. She has attended college and various technical schools off and on, but she has no career plans. She worked for the last six months as an assistant manager at a discount shoe store, but quit over a dispute about her hours. She has had a fairly consistent dream of becoming an actress but has done nothing to make the dream a reality. She finds the process of setting goals difficult, and she lacks the self-discipline to follow through on plans.

Few things hold her interest for long, and boredom is not a condition Carol tolerates well. She has impulsively quit jobs and training programs, often when the training is nearly complete or her probationary period nearly over, to pursue something else that strikes her as more interesting. The ups and downs of her moods and her constantly shifting self-image have led her to start and then abandon seven different career paths since she graduated from high school. Her judgment is poor, and she does not plan ahead. Each time she quits a job, she creates a financial crisis for herself as well as staffing problems for her employer.

Poor stress tolerance. Carol leads a very stressful life. The constant turmoil of her emotional state and the continual conflicts with others take a great deal of time and energy. Work pressures and demands can increase her level of stress to a point she finds overwhelming, and she may respond by lashing out in anger, becoming self-destructive, or impulsively walking out.

Workplace danger. Carol's temper tantrums can include breaking and throwing things and lashing out physically as well as verbally. She has at times slapped, kicked, spit on, and pushed family members, boyfriends, roommates, and others. She has never done so at work, but the possibility exists that she might. Even in the absence of violent behavior on her part, her unpredictable and frequently unpleasant interactions with others set up dangerous and potentially explosive interpersonal situations at work.

Working with Borderline Personality Disorder

Carol's most recent suicide gesture and subsequent hospitalization occurred about a week after she impulsively quit her job in the shoe store. It was a stressful time for her, since she had no money saved and no idea what she would do next. She was pretty sure she had not taken enough of an overdose to cause her death but was characteristically careless and unconcerned about the outcome. On a conscious though unarticulated level, she hoped that John, her boyfriend of three weeks, would rescue her by offering her marriage or at least financial support. She felt that her neediness obligated him to care for her. Part of her fury at his leaving came from fear about how she would survive, pay her rent, and buy groceries, as well as fear of being abandoned.

At the time, Carol had not been in psychotherapy for about a year. She fired her last therapist in a snit over his refusal to engage in extended telephone conversations about her needs, outside of regularly scheduled appointments. She was a sporadic member of several support groups and periodically made use of crisis hot lines and drop-in counseling centers but had no ongoing therapeutic involvement.

She was released from the emergency room to the psychiatric unit. The social worker there knew Carol from her two previous suicide gestures. He knew that these were primarily cries for help rather than actual attempts to end her life, but he also knew how close to the line she came and how easily that line could be crossed. Though Carol insisted she was ready to go home, he was unwilling to consider discharge planning until she was established in a therapy relationship. Carol herself believed that she needed to go back into therapy, but something about the social worker's attitude rubbed her the wrong way. She refused to accept his referral, made a scene about being held prisoner on the psychiatric unit, and left the hospital against medical advice.

Each of her previous therapy relationships had started out with warm feelings and high hopes on Carol's part and had ended in deep dissatisfaction, with a rocky trail of alternating idealization and demonization of the therapist in between. She entered therapy not with the intention of gaining insight or of changing her behavior, but with the expectation that the therapist would relieve her unhappiness and make her life better.

She quickly came to resent what she saw as the therapist's refusal to act on her behalf. She rejected most interventions a therapist might attempt. She usually ended the relationship at the point at which a therapist began to confront her behavior and hold her accountable. Regardless of whether this point came sooner or later, or was expressed gently and subtly or directly and pointedly, it meant to Carol that the gig was up and it was time to move on. She left feeling that the therapist didn't care about her, didn't listen to her, didn't understand her, didn't do enough for her, asked too much of her, and tried to control her.

One of the support groups that Carol sometimes attended met at a women's resource center, which provided basic medical care, job resources, support groups, AA and Al-anon groups, and psychotherapy for women. Carol had been involved there for several months. She had her conflicts with staff and with other participants, but the casual, relaxed atmosphere suited her mood at the moment. She arranged an initial psychotherapy appointment with the director of the center, a psychologist named Georgia.

Carol had heard good things about Georgia's warmth, her caring style, and her skill as a therapist. At their first meeting, however, she had strong doubts about the relationship. Georgia had been around for a long time. She had worked with many women with a wide variety of backgrounds, problems, and issues. She recognized borderline personality disorder in the history Carol gave her, as well as in Carol's approach to the interview and her attitude toward the therapy relationship. Georgia was unlikely to allow herself to be manipulated, and she made that clear from the outset. Rather than starting out with her usual warm and fuzzy idealization of the therapist, Carol started out mad.

Several days after their first meeting, Carol called Georgia to say that she didn't think it was a good match. She wanted to cancel their next appointment. Georgia said she was sorry that Carol felt that way and wished her luck. She was not surprised, however, when looking at her schedule for the following week, to see that Carol had rescheduled the appointment.

The night before the appointment, Carol called Georgia's answering service. When Georgia returned the call, Carol was in tears. She said she felt hopeless, alone, and suicidal. She had enough medication for an overdose, and she planned to take it. Georgia said she was sorry Carol felt that way. She would be happy to arrange for hospitalization, and she would send a squad car to pick her up to make sure she got to the hospital. After a pause, Carol said she thought she could probably make it until morning.

She began the next day's session by saying she wanted to express her anger about Georgia's lack of concern about her. Georgia listened without comment. When Carol finished, Georgia said she was sorry Carol felt that way. She suggested that they move on and set some goals and priorities for dealing with the immediate problems Carol faced, since living with such stress obviously made her life much more difficult than it needed to be.

Carol was annoyed at Georgia's reply; she craved an emotional response and was used to getting one from most people she had relationships with. Still, the invitation to talk about her current woes was compelling, and she launched into a description of her pain and her needs. To Carol, her worst current problem was what she saw as John's defection. He was back in town, and although she had called him several times, he didn't want to see her. He had betrayed and abandoned her, left her to die, left her at the mercy of her landlord and her credit card companies. Georgia nodded sympathetically and ended the session.

Again Carol called in the middle of the week, angry, tearful, and accusatory, threatening suicide, threatening to leave therapy. Georgia responded in the same way she had to the previous call. She was sorry Carol felt that way. Carol could leave therapy if she wanted to. If Carol felt suicidal, she could go to the hospital. Georgia cut the call short with a brief "Good luck."

Carol kept their next appointment. Georgia took charge of it from the beginning. She thought it was time to get serious about Carol's only solvable problem—lack of a job and lack of the necessary interpersonal skills to keep a job if she had one. She knew from experience that it would be useless to get bogged down in Carol's issues with men in general and John in particular. Likewise, she knew that Carol would try to keep the focus of therapy on the therapeutic relationship, and that this also would be a fruitless pursuit. She wanted Carol to understand her own behavior enough to see that it hurt her in the work world, though she knew how difficult a task that would be.

Georgia set a limit on the number of sessions that she and Carol would have. She set a limit on the topics open for discussion. She set a limit on the number of between-session telephone calls that Carol could make and on their nature. She said she would no longer return late evening calls to her answering service from Carol. She said that as far as she was concerned, the best way to deal with Carol's pain was to focus on her need for a job and on her workplace behavior once she got a job.

Carol was dumbfounded, then furious. She was holding an empty paper coffee cup, which she threw at Georgia. The cup landed harmlessly on the floor between them, but Georgia stood up, said that at no time would she tolerate such behavior, and ended the session.

Georgia didn't hear from Carol for several weeks. One day Carol called, appropriately during business hours, and asked if she could come back to therapy. She had been hired, and then quickly fired, from a waitress position, and she said she realized that she needed to deal with work issues. Georgia said that her limits and expectations had not changed, but that Carol was welcome back if she thought she could work within them.

Carol seemed like a different person at their next appointment. She was pleasant, appropriate, and on task. She knew she had an anger problem, she knew she needed to be a cooperative team player to keep a job, she knew she needed the kind of help that Georgia had offered to provide. Would Georgia please help her? Because of her years of experience, Georgia recognized that this transformation, while not false, was not permanent either. It was simply the side of her personality that Carol chose to show at present, for reasons unknown perhaps even to her.

The balance of their work together was far from smooth. Carol continually pushed the limits. She had no more temper tantrums and made no more suicide threats, but she wanted extra sessions, she wanted to put aside the work issues because she felt sad and lonely, she became tearful and disarmingly remorseful when admitting that she knew she had personality problems. She often said that Georgia wasn't helping her and she was going to leave therapy. But Georgia stayed the course.

Carol is at her worst in close, ongoing relationships with people who matter to her. She can appear friendly and vivacious in less significant, short-term interactions. She interviews well. Her experiences in retail, which include the shoe store, a women's clothing store, and a large kitchen-supply store, were her most successful. She is good at dealing with the public, she likes it, and it tends to hold her interest. It is her inability to deal with ordinary, day-to-day relationships with coworkers and supervisors that causes her problems, and this is what Georgia focused on.

Carol began applying for jobs before Georgia thought she was ready. By listing her experiences selectively, and by employing creative phrasing on her résumé, she looked like a strong candidate for entry-level retail management positions. She was soon hired in the designer fashions department of a large department store. Her confidence was buoyed by what she considered a prestigious position, exactly the kind of job she wanted. She dismissed Georgia's misgivings and warnings and left therapy.

Unfortunately, the environment in the designer fashions department turned out to be quite stressful, with much expected and little support provided—just the setting in which Carol is likely to become unstable, unreliable, and hostile. Within a few weeks, she had a serious run-in with a coworker and was confronted by the department manager about several aspects of her behavior. Shaken and uncharacteristically concerned about keeping the job, she called Georgia for help.

Georgia agreed to work with her for a few more sessions, maintaining the focus on workplace behaviors. Carol continued to blame those around her for her interpersonal problems, and Georgia saw trying to change that point of view as a waste of time. Instead, she tried to redirect Carol's attention to those things she could control, such as whether she exploded in anger in front of customers or chose to contain herself until she could express her concern in a way that wouldn't be self-destructive.

Georgia came up with the idea of explaining some of Carol's workplace needs to the department manager, and Carol almost begged her to do so. With Carol's written permission, Georgia called the department manager. She explained a little about Carol's hypersensitivity to rejection, her moodiness, and her hostility. She noted that Carol tends to respond positively to efforts on the part of those around her to be supportive. She said that Carol would be more likely to succeed with some accommodations designed to meet her need for unusual interpersonal flexibility. Confronting her interpersonal problems would likely make things worse, while pointing out and supporting her strengths might help. In addition, flexible scheduling might give her a sense of self-direction and autonomy and help her cope with her mood swings.

Georgia went on to say that as important as a supportive attitude is in helping Carol succeed, firm supervision with clear expectations, boundaries, and methods of evaluation, is essential. Carol needs to know in no uncertain terms what kinds of behavior will not be tolerated, what level of performance is required, what the limits of her role are, and how her work will be assessed. She needs concrete consequences for misbehavior. Being sent home for the day, or being docked pay, for example, might be useful tools to deal with less than acceptable behavior.

Because of her instability and unpredictability and her propensity for acting out toward herself and others, monitoring her behavior and insisting on behavioral standards are important not only to help her succeed but to ensure her safety and the safety of the entire workplace. A direct and straightforward approach on the part of a supervisor, firm but supportive, focused on her work and her behavior rather than on her as a person, could help.

Borderline personality disorder can cause such severe and intractable interpersonal problems that a competitive work setting may not be possible. Carol is able to work, and even to experience success at work, to the extent that she can maintain her sources of emotional and social support, exercise self-control when necessary, and make an effort to keep her job, rather than throwing it away over a perceived slight or because her mood changes. Unfortunately, given her unstable history with regard to career planning and long-term vocational goals, significant longevity, even at a job she likes and is successful at, is unlikely.

If she continues to work in therapy with Georgia, and if she talks about her plans before acting impulsively on them, Georgia will have a chance to encourage her to reflect, consider her options, and consider her long-term self-interest. If Carol slows down enough, the impulse to quit and move on to something else might pass. On the other hand, Carol is unlikely to stay in a stable therapy relationship either. In the end, her chances of long-term vocational success are subject to the dictates of her personality problems.

Summary: Borderline Personality Disorder's Effect on Vocational Abilities

Level of Impairment

1. no impairment
2. mild—minimal impairment with little or no effect on ability to function
3. moderate—some impairment, which limits ability to function fully
4. serious—major impairment, which may at times preclude ability to function
5. severe—extreme impairment

Understanding and Memory

Remembers locations and basic work procedures

1____X____ 2_____ 3_____ 4_____ 5_____

Understands and remembers short, simple instructions

1_____X_____2_____3_____4_____5_____

Understands and remembers detailed instructions

1_____X_____2_____3_____4_____5_____

Concentration and Persistence

Carries out short, simple instructions

1_____X_____2_____3_____4_____5_____

Carries out detailed instructions

1_____X_____2_____3_____4_____5_____

Maintains attention and concentration for extended periods of time

1_____2_____X_____3_____4_____5_____

Can work within a schedule, maintain attendance, be punctual

1_____2_____3_____X_____4_____5_____

Sustains ordinary routine without special supervision

1_____2_____3_____X_____4_____5_____

Can work with or close to others without being distracted by them

1_____2_____3_____4_____5_____X_____

Makes simple work-related decisions

1_____X_____2_____3_____4_____5_____

Works quickly and efficiently, meets deadlines, even under stressful conditions

1_____2_____3_____X_____4_____5_____

Completes normal workday and workweek without interruptions due to symptoms

1_____2_____3_____4_____X_____5_____

Works at consistent pace without an unreasonable number or length of breaks

1_____2_____3_____X_____4_____5_____

Social Interaction

Interacts appropriately with general public

1_____ 2_____ 3____X____ 4_____ 5_____

Asks simple questions or requests assistance when necessary

1_____ 2_____ 3____X____ 4_____ 5_____

Accepts instruction and responds appropriately to criticism from supervisors

1_____ 2_____ 3_____ 4_____ 5____X____

Gets along with coworkers without distracting them

1_____ 2_____ 3_____ 4____X____ 5_____

Maintains socially appropriate behavior

1_____ 2_____ 3_____ 4____X____ 5_____

Maintains basic standards of cleanliness and grooming

1_____ 2____X____ 3_____ 4_____ 5_____

Adaptation

Responds appropriately to changes at work

1_____ 2_____ 3____X____ 4_____ 5_____

Is aware of normal work hazards and takes necessary precautions

1_____ 2_____ 3____X____ 4_____ 5_____

Can get around in unfamiliar places, can use public transportation

1____X____ 2_____ 3_____ 4_____ 5_____

Sets realistic goals, makes plans independently of others

1_____ 2_____ 3____X____ 4_____ 5_____

Summary: Vocational Strategies and Accommodations

To optimize the chances for vocational success, a person with borderline personality disorder needs:

- Help from a rehabilitation or mental health professional in explaining to a supervisor the need for unusual interpersonal flexi-

bility, in order to reduce tensions and receive necessary accommodations.
- Strong support for vocational strengths, rather than constant emphasis on inappropriate interpersonal behaviors.
- Flexible scheduling to accommodate mood swings.
- Clearly spelled out behavioral and work expectations, unambiguous interpersonal and job-related boundaries, and unambiguous methods of evaluation, to help reduce arguments and disagreements.
- Firm supervision with concrete consequences for misbehavior, to help control potential danger to self or others.
- A direct and straightforward approach on the part of the supervisor, firm but supportive, focused on work and on concrete behaviors.
- Social support both within and outside of the workplace to help reduce attention-seeking and self-destructive behaviors.

ANTISOCIAL PERSONALITY DISORDER

Antisocial personality disorder is diagnosed much more often in men than in women. It seems to be associated with low socioeconomic status and urban settings, raising the concern that the diagnosis may be mistakenly applied to people engaging in protective survival strategies that look like antisocial behaviors. For this reason, assessing the context in which the behaviors occur is essential to an accurate diagnosis. The overall prevalence of antisocial personality disorder is about 3% in men and 1% in women. In clinical settings, it ranges from 3%–30%, depending on the nature of the population being studied. In substance-abuse treatment settings or prisons, the prevalence is even higher. It is much more common among first-degree biological relatives of those who have it; such relatives are also at increased risk for somatization disorder and substance-related disorders. Antisocial personality disorder is a chronic disorder but may become milder over time, with a noticeable reduction in criminal behaviors by around age 40 (American Psychiatric Association, 1994).

Rocky

Rocky dropped his cigarette on the linoleum floor and ground it out with his boot heel. He took another from a crumpled pack. He worked his hand into the front pocket of his jeans and pulled out a lighter. He leaned back against the "no smoking" sign and lit up. Two people sitting at the counter in the tiny donut shop threw disapproving looks at him. He grinned back and turned slightly away from them, displaying the knife in his back pocket.

He could hear sounds from the back room but the counter person didn't appear. He was getting impatient. "Hey," he shouted, but still no one came. "This is bullshit," he said to the people sitting at the counter. "I don't have to put up with this." He stuck his cigarette in the corner of his mouth, walked around the display case, and filled two bakery bags with donuts and jelly bismarcks.

The counter person hurried out from the back room, wiping her hands on a towel. "You're too late," Rocky said. "I already helped myself." He showed her the full bags and walked out.

What Antisocial Personality Disorder Is Like

- Disregard for rules, norms, and laws
- Frequent alcohol and drug abuse
- Lack of empathy and remorse
- Impulsivity, irresponsibility, unreliability; physical and verbal aggression
- Poor relationships with authority figures

Disregard for rules, norms, and laws. "No smoking" signs and laws about paying for donuts in the donut shop don't bother Rocky. He does what he wants. If having things his way means lying, cheating, threatening, or manipulating, that's OK with him. Just like his old man always told him, rules are for chumps. The only rule is, don't get caught.

Rocky is 28 years old. He lives with a girlfriend and their four-year-old son, when he feels like it. He comes and goes as he pleases, pays something for household expenses if he's employed and in a good mood, and knocks his girlfriend around if she gives him a hard time. He was kicked out of school in the sixth grade for hitting a teacher. He helped rob a gas station at 14. He did several stints in juvenile detention, where he learned to fight.

He dropped out of high school and passed an equivalency program by cheating on the exams. He joined the military, decided immediately he didn't like it, and concocted a mysterious array of psychotic symptoms to get himself discharged. He is currently on probation for his part in a bar fight. He spends most of his time with his buddies, a group of small-time drug dealers.

Frequent alcohol and drug abuse. Rocky and his friends deal in marijuana, crack, speed, and anything else they happen to run across. They enjoy sampling their product almost as much as ripping off the people they sell to. Rocky has used drugs and alcohol since junior high. He prefers alcohol and isn't fussy about the drugs he chooses to go with it. He often drinks as much as a case of beer a day.

Lack of empathy and remorse. The problems faced by the people he harms do not interest Rocky. He figures that people who get in his way or don't do what he wants deserve what they get. If someone gets hurt, hey, too bad. It's not Rocky's fault. His girlfriend's feelings and their son's needs, for instance, are not among his concerns. He expects them to be there when he wants them and leave him alone when he doesn't; otherwise, he rarely thinks about them.

His girlfriend once kicked him out of her house and filed abuse charges against him. Rocky turned on the charm, which is one of many manipulative techniques he employs as needed. He sweet-talked and wheedled until she dropped the charges and let him move back in. He didn't feel bad about hitting her, but he felt terrible about not having a place to live and about the possibility of going to jail.

Rocky sees all of his problems in life—his inability to hold a job, his jail time, his bad temper, his propensity for violence, his volatile relationships—as someone else's fault. Other people let him down, they steer him wrong, they mess him over. He feels perfectly justified in doing whatever he can to get what he wants or to have a little fun. He has had plenty of opportunities, some forced and some voluntary, to receive support and psychotherapy to help him change his ways, learn a trade, hold a job, stay out of jail, be a better father, and so on. He sees these as additional chances to manipulate people for his own gain. He can demonstrate a convincing level of sincerity, appearing to be serious and committed, in order to finish a program or a class as quickly as possible and please those in charge, while having no intention of following through in any way.

Impulsivity, irresponsibility, unreliability; physical and verbal aggression. Once, on the spur of the moment, Rocky bought a Doberman pinscher puppy from a friend who breeds them. He brought the puppy to his girlfriend's place, against her strongly expressed wishes. He cared for it for about a week, then decided to take off for a few days with a buddy, leaving the puppy behind. He returned six weeks later. His girlfriend kicked him and the dog out, and he lived in his van until he once again persuaded her to take him back.

He never trained the dog in any way. He became impatient when it wasn't the obedient companion he had imagined, and he began to abuse it. When the dog was about a year old, Rocky took it to a motorcycle rally. He had it on a leash, but he couldn't control it, and it bolted. It ran out onto the highway, was hit by a pick-up truck, and died. Rocky was furious. He blamed the driver of the pick-up truck, started a fist fight, and threatened to kill the driver's German shepherd. Only his buddies' intervention prevented him from acting on the threat.

Poor relationships with authority figures. When informed by his probation officer that he has an antisocial personality disorder, Rocky said, "The hell I do. I'm not antisocial, I like people." Still, his relationships, especially those with authority figures, are deeply troubled. His father was cold, authoritarian, and abusive. He taught Rocky by word and example to fight hard, to get away with as much as possible, and to "take no bullshit from no one." Rocky's mother was passive and alcoholic. She did her best to protect Rocky from the consequences of his behavior. Rocky is resentful and contemptuous of anyone in a position of authority, and he is highly successful in demonstrating his attitude.

Antisocial Personality Disorder's Effect at Work

- Superficial, troubled relationships with supervisors and coworkers
- Easily bored, poor judgment
- Danger in the workplace
- Can be charming and persuasive

Superficial, troubled relationships with supervisors and coworkers. Rocky has worked as a laborer, a roofer, and a machinist, among other things. He has worked for many different employers in a variety of settings. He once was self-employed for a short time; he started a window-washing business and was awarded a large contract to help with the clean-up of a newly rehabilitated warehouse. The owners of the building were anxious to make it ready for tenants. They liked Rocky's low bid, but they quickly became dissatisfied with his progress. Rocky thought he was his own boss; he didn't like being told he had to show up and work every day. He strung the job along for a while, but the owners fired him less than halfway through the project. He didn't bother trying to get other contracts, and soon his new van, with his business logo painted on the side, was repossessed.

Rocky doesn't like anyone telling him what to do. He talks back to supervisors and argues with coworkers. He is good at finding ways to get out of his responsibilities and often shows up late or not at all for no good reason and without prior approval. He believes himself to be exempt from normal workplace expectations and entitled to get what he can while contributing as little as possible.

Easily bored, poor judgment. Rocky makes no commitments. When he gets sick of something, he moves on. He craves a certain level of excitement or stimulation and quickly loses interest when it's not present. He might get bored with the work, or "pissed off about the bullshit," and quit a job impulsively. He does not plan ahead and often leaves himself in a financial bind, from which he counts on his girlfriend, his mother, or his buddies to rescue him.

When his girlfriend became pregnant with their child, Rocky, in an uncharacteristic burst of fatherly responsibility, managed to snag a well-paying machinist job at a large, highly regarded heavy equipment plant. He wore the company uniform, went to work every day, and even brought his girlfriend to the annual employee picnic. But, about a month before the baby was born, he started oversleeping, going in late, missing a day here and there, getting in arguments with the foreman, and feeling bored with the exacting and uncompromising requirements of the work. A buddy stopped by one evening, and Rocky left town with him; he never went back to the plant. His girlfriend went on welfare until she could go back to her waitress job. Since then, Rocky has not worked for longer than six months at a time.

Danger in the workplace. Rocky is short-tempered, argumentative, impulsive, and prone to theft. He sees no reason to avoid violence, and his behavior often encourages it. He provokes fist fights and instigates chaos. He steals from his employers or his coworkers if he thinks he can get away with it, and vehemently denies any involvement if accused. He made up symptoms of mental illness to get out of the military and has feigned physical injuries to get out of work and collect benefits.

Can be charming and persuasive. In spite of all this, Rocky is not without his appeal; he understands social norms well enough to manipulate them to his benefit, and he has a pleasant, amiable streak tucked in among his bluster and brawl. He is popular among his group of friends and often among coworkers, because of his sense of humor and his fun-loving approach to life. He has a terrific smile, and he can assume a very convincing attitude of sincere goodwill. He genuinely likes social contact; he enjoys meeting new people, engaging in light conversation, and sharing a good laugh. He can be positive and enthusiastic. He is good at drawing people in and persuading them to like him.

Working with Antisocial Personality Disorder

Rocky is not a bad worker; his problems on the job have been the result of impulsivity and irresponsibility, not laziness. He is strong, energetic, and willing to face danger. In another era, he might have been a knight or an explorer, helped in either endeavor by his superficial charm and his ability to get others to give him what he wants.

Work that is fast-paced, exciting, outdoors, and dangerous appeals to him. He once volunteered to join a group fighting a forest fire burning out of control in the mountains of Idaho; he enjoyed the thrill, he worked hard, and he did well. He stayed until the blaze was under control, long after most volunteers had left in exhaustion. Such opportunities are not available every day, and they often come at a price Rocky is not willing to pay; he couldn't stick it out in the military, for instance, despite the potential for excitement that he believed it held.

The conditions of Rocky's current probation require him to be employed. He is expected to turn in current pay stubs to Mike, his probation officer, at their weekly meetings. After quitting his last job as a warehouse laborer, he avoided meetings with Mike for several weeks in a row, calling in and offering excuses for why he couldn't appear in person. Mike finally told him he had to show up within two days or he would have him arrested. Rocky scrambled to find a job in that time but did not succeed.

He tried to convince Mike that he still worked at the warehouse, but Mike had called his former boss, and he knew better. He told Rocky he could send him straight to jail right then, but would rather help him get his life turned around and get working again, at a job he would be likely to keep. Seizing on this evidence of sympathy, which he saw as weakness on Mike's part, Rocky adopted his most sincere expression and tone of voice and expressed his desire to change his ways. He flashed his brilliant smile, shook Mike's hand, thanked him for his confidence, and promised to get a job that very day.

But Mike had heard it all before. He knew that the idea of Rocky turning his life around held little meaning. But he also thought that sending Rocky back to jail would produce no particular benefit either. He wanted to use his current authority and the ongoing threat of jail time to force Rocky to improve his options. He wanted Rocky to undergo interest and ability testing, to take part in an appropriate training program as indicated by the results of the testing, and to find a job in that field. Rocky's probation would last another eight months, which Mike hoped would give him sufficient time.

Rocky was agreeable to the idea of a training program, but he said he didn't need any testing; he already knew what interested him. He wanted to be a fire-fighter. He likes danger and adventure, he said, and he likes to help people. Mike pointed out that the idea was commendable, but, unfortunately, few people would want to put their personal or household safety in the hands of someone with Rocky's history of violence, petty theft, and arrests.

Similar jobs that might interest him, such as rescue worker or police officer, were likewise out of the question. In addition, Mike went on, many such jobs require a psychological evaluation, which Rocky was unlikely to pass. In characteristically crude language, Rocky expressed his displeasure with the unfairness of a system that would impose such restrictions on his freedom to choose a line of work. Ending the conversation, Mike informed Rocky that he had no choice in the matter of vocational testing; Mike would arrange an appointment with a vocational counselor, and Rocky would go.

Rocky had taken part in vocational training programs in the past. The only one he completed was machinist training, and he completed that only because he was on probation at that time too. He could do the work, but his frustration tolerance is low enough to prevent him from doing well at anything exacting and detail-oriented, and he always hated it. Not wanting to find himself in a similar situation, he approached the vocational testing with the intention of figuring out how he could manipulate it to his advantage.

Nevertheless, the results showed a fairly accurate picture of his abilities and preferences. Looking them over and discussing them with the vocational counselor, Mike saw that vocational possibilities clearly existed for Rocky, more numerous possibilities, in fact, than Mike had anticipated. But each option seemed to be precluded by some aspect of Rocky's personality problem.

Rocky would be good at working with the public, for instance, but he couldn't be employed in any occupation that would allow him the opportunity to exploit others or that would offer the temptation to behave dishonestly. The availability of cash or merchandise or the chance to slip away while still on the time clock is beyond the scope of his will power. He might enjoy being an over-the-road trucker, but the long hauls would give him too much time outside the reach of supervision. He showed an aptitude for being a forest ranger, but not the necessary level of responsibility and reliability. He could learn to be a heavy equipment operator, but Mike doubted that he would stick with it long enough to justify the training.

From the testing results, Mike was surprised that Rocky had chosen to start a window-washing business and not surprised that it had failed. He asked Rocky why he had done it. It turns out that Rocky had embarked on the venture after learning mountain-climbing techniques from a friend. He worked with the friend for several months, using mountain-climbing equipment to hang from the sides of skyscrapers and wash the outside windows. He loved it; he loved being outdoors, being up high, being only a rope away from certain death, and seeing pedestrians far below look up and point. He even loved seeing the windows sparkle when he was done.

As Rocky explained it, his own enterprise failed because of the jerks who gave him his first contract and then, for no reason Rocky could figure out, refused to honor it. It soured him on the whole deal, he said. Mike concluded that the project wasn't exciting enough for Rocky, and that he lacked the self-discipline and self-direction to be successfully self-employed. But, since Rocky had enjoyed the work so much, Mike wondered why he hadn't continued to do it. Rocky said that he wasn't one to look back; when he was done with something, he was done.

Actually, he had forgotten about washing windows on skyscrapers; the five years since he had done it represented a long time in his fast-paced and chaotic life. He was by now bored with vocational testing and all the talk about it, and he was no longer interested in any kind of training program. The friend who taught him mountain-climbing and window-washing techniques had long since moved on, but Rocky looked in the Yellow Pages, and found several companies who offered high-rise window cleaning. Wearing clean work clothes, displaying his most convincing workplace attitude, and prepared with creative responses to explain his spotty work history, he presented himself as a job applicant at one of the companies. He had to visit two more, but by the time of his next visit with Mike, Rocky already had a pay stub to give him.

Rocky knew that Mike would need to contact his supervisor to discuss his situation and to keep tabs on him, but he tried to talk him out of it. He told Mike that things were finally going well for him, he had a good job, he liked it, he would stick with it, his supervisor knew nothing about his past, he was better off not knowing, and Rocky was a new person, fully reformed. Mike congratulated Rocky on his efforts and his resourcefulness, but reminded him that noncompliance with the terms of his probation could still send him back to jail. Rocky gave him the supervisor's name and phone number.

Rocky's supervisor, having hired and fired a lot of employees over the years, was not surprised to learn that Rocky was on probation, and he was glad to be in contact with Mike. He understood Rocky's need to be supervised closely, persistently, and at times forcefully. He had already explained how his work would be evaluated, what would happen if it was inadequate, and what would happen if Rocky took liberties with hours or scheduling. He wasn't too worried about Rocky's propensity for violence, since he would usually be working alone.

Mike told him to expect the possibility of resistance, complaints, manipulation, threats, and other expressions of hostility from Rocky, and urged him to call right away if such behavior occurred. He said that Rocky needed to be reminded clearly, explicitly, and often about limits, job expectations, rules, and consequences for noncompliance. He needed concrete consequences, such as docked pay, suspension, or firing, and needed them carried out quickly and firmly if necessary. The supervisor said that lately he had more work than he could handle, and he had been having some difficulty staying fully staffed. He would be reluctant to fire someone who already had skill and experience, but he would if he had to.

Rocky may or may not keep his job when his probation is up in a few months. Chances are by then he will have created some new trouble for himself or become bored and found a reason to move on. But the fact that he has an identifiable skill and work experience that he enjoys and takes pride in may well help him in the future. In general, the longer he is under external pressure, such as probation, the longer he is likely to be functional in the workplace.

Summary: Antisocial Personality Disorder's Effect on Vocational Abilities

Level of Impairment

1. no impairment
2. mild—minimal impairment with little or no effect on ability to function
3. moderate—some impairment, which limits ability to function fully
4. serious—major impairment, which may at times preclude ability to function
5. severe—extreme impairment

Understanding and Memory

Remembers locations and basic work procedures

1____X____2_____3_____4_____5_____

Understands and remembers short, simple instructions

1____X____2_____3_____4_____5_____

Understands and remembers detailed instructions

1____X____2_____3_____4_____5_____

Concentration and Persistence

Carries out short, simple instructions

1____X____2_____3_____4_____5_____

Carries out detailed instructions

1____X____2_____3_____4_____5_____

Maintains attention and concentration for extended periods of time

1_____2_____3____X____4_____5_____

Can work within a schedule, maintain attendance, be punctual

1_____2_____3_____4____X____5_____

Sustains ordinary routine without special supervision

1_____2_____3____X____4_____5_____

Can work with or close to others without being distracted by them

1_____2____X____3_____4_____5_____

Makes simple work-related decisions

1____X____2_____3_____4_____5_____

Works quickly and efficiently, meets deadlines, even under stressful conditions

1____X____2_____3_____4_____5_____

Completes normal workday and workweek without interruptions due to symptoms

1_____2_____3_____4____X____5_____

Works at consistent pace without an unreasonable number or length of breaks

1_____2____X____3_____4_____5_____

Social Interaction

Interacts appropriately with general public

1_____ 2____X____3_____ 4_____ 5_____

Asks simple questions or requests assistance when necessary

1_____ 2____X____3_____ 4_____ 5_____

Accepts instruction and responds appropriately to criticism from supervisors

1_____ 2_____ 3_____ 4____X____5_____

Gets along with coworkers without distracting them

1_____ 2____X____3_____ 4_____ 5_____

Maintains socially appropriate behavior

1_____ 2_____ 3____X____4_____ 5_____

Maintains basic standards of cleanliness and grooming

1_____ 2_____ 3____X____4_____ 5_____

Adaptation

Responds appropriately to changes at work

1_____ 2____X____3_____ 4_____ 5_____

Is aware of normal work hazards and takes necessary precautions

1_____ 2____X____3_____ 4_____ 5_____

Can get around in unfamiliar places, can use public transportation

1____X____2_____ 3_____ 4_____ 5_____

Sets realistic goals, makes plans independently of others

1_____ 2____X____3_____ 4_____ 5_____

Summary: Vocational Strategies and Accommodations

To optimize the chances for vocational success, a person with antisocial personality disorder needs:

- To be supervised closely, persistently, and at times forcefully, to help prevent violent, illegal, or unethical behavior.
- Frequent reminders about limits, expectations, and job requirements, to help ensure compliance with workplace needs and procedures.

- Very little flexibility with regard to hours, scheduling, and other requirements, to avoid manipulation and exploitation of policies perceived as lenient.
- To understand clearly the consequences for noncompliance or misbehavior; to have such consequences be concrete, such as docked pay, suspension, or firing; and to have them carried out quickly.
- Extended periods of external monitoring, such as court supervision, to help enforce consequences and maintain workplace stability.
- Monitoring with regard to drug or alcohol use, including periodic drug tests if necessary.
- Work that involves physical activity or is in some way fast-paced and exciting to help prevent boredom.

HISTRIONIC PERSONALITY DISORDER

Because interpersonal styles and norms vary widely in different cultures and age groups, the dramatic style, emotionality, seductiveness, novelty seeking, and other characteristics of histrionic personality disorder must be seen to cause clinically significant impairment or distress before the diagnosis can be made. In clinical settings, it has been diagnosed more often in women than in men. Other studies, however, suggest that prevalence is similar for men and women in the general population, with overall rates of 2%–3%. Rates as high as 10%–15% have been reported in outpatient and inpatient mental health settings. Sex role stereotypes may influence the expression of histrionic personality disorder behaviors. A man with the disorder, for example, may seek to be the center of attention by bragging about his business dealings, while a woman might seek attention by appearing extremely feminine (American Psychiatric Association, 1994).

Peggy

Peggy paused in the doorway long enough to give everyone in the room a chance to see her entrance. She wore a shimmering purple dress. Her coiffure was impeccable. Iridescent earrings nestled among her curls. Her fingers, encrusted with large, brilliant rings, were tipped with bright fuchsia on each perfectly shaped nail. Bracelets dripped from her wrists, making a musical sound as she floated forward on her high-heeled shoes. She was aware that her appearance set her apart rather dramatically from the other women present, a fact that gave her great satisfaction.

Her eyes swept the room. She saw Dale, her husband, standing toward the back with a small group of business colleagues, all of them looking at her. She waved gaily and blew kisses, jingling her bracelets and wafting vapors of a powerful fragrance all around. "How wonderful to see you all," she said, bestowing affectionate squeezes on arms and shoulders as she passed.

"I was worried," Dale said, taking her elbow and leading her away from the group. "I thought you'd be here an hour ago."

Peggy yanked her arm away from him. "Don't criticize me," she hissed. "You're lucky I came at all."

What Histrionic Personality Disorder Is Like

- Attention-seeking, excessively emotional and dramatic, self-centered
- Overly concerned with appearance
- Outgoing, extroverted
- Hypersensitive to rejection, inappropriate expression of anger

Attention-seeking, excessively emotional and dramatic, self-centered. Peggy's personality is structured around the need for attention from others and the belief that intense emotional expression is the way to get it. Her interpersonal style is dramatic and demanding. Her gestures, her voice, her facial expressions, and the words she chooses are all designed to give the impression that she has deep feelings and important opinions. The cumulative effect, however, rings a little hollow. She is more concerned with style than content, she frequently contradicts herself, and she tends to appear phony and duplicitous.

Peggy is at pains not only to keep the focus of attention on herself, but to control conversation so that most of it has to do with her. She is otherwise bored; she has little tolerance for situations that don't concern her and finds little of interest outside of herself. So strong is her belief that her feelings, her opinions, her experiences, and her desires are more interesting than any other topic, that she freely interrupts ongoing conversations to redirect them toward herself.

Peggy has been married to Dale for three months. She is 43 years old, and this is her third marriage. She has no children. Her first husband left after a year; he jumped at a chance for a job in what was then the Soviet Union, even after Peggy told him she would never go there. She found herself continually angry at her second husband because he was inconsiderate of her needs and feelings and criticized her habit of coming home from work and spending the evening in bed watching TV, even though he knew how tired her job made her. He left in response to her accusations of emotional abuse.

In between marriages, she had many brief affairs, including two with married men, which she justified on the basis of their wives being less attractive than she. She married Dale after they had known each other for a month. He seemed to understand and appreciate her, he was attentive to her needs, and he worked in advertising, a field she had always wanted to get into.

Overly concerned with appearance. To Peggy, few things in life are more important than her looks. She spends a great deal of time and money on her clothes, her hair, and her make-up. Despite a passion for food, she eats little and keeps her weight down. She dislikes sweat and physical exertion, but she nevertheless works out regularly five times a week, under the direction of a personal trainer. She consults color experts, she seeks professional advice on such issues as neckline shape and shoulder width, she spends weekends at beauty spas whenever she can. She never leaves the privacy of her home without every hair in place, her make-up expertly applied, and her clothing and accessories impeccable.

Outgoing, extroverted. Peggy is bored and troubled when she is alone; she craves contact with other people, preferably in groups of which she is the center. She is skilled at keeping other people's attention on her and frequently does so in entertaining ways. She maintains a constant stream of jokes and banter and pulls in stragglers by feigning a personal interest in them.

She loves to flirt, and much of her repartee consists of off-color or suggestive material, with matching body language. Far from shy about revealing her most intimate and private experiences, she will regale a crowd with the details of her emotional life, her diet, her physical condition, her deepest desires, and facts she has garnered from TV or magazines, in the sincere belief that these things are of crucial interest to everyone.

Hypersensitive to rejection, inappropriate expression of anger. Peggy has experienced her share of rejection, a fact that mystifies and frustrates her, given all the trouble she takes to prevent it. She is overly sensitive to any sign of possible loss of interest on the part of others. She perceives the smallest hint of disapproval as a brutal rebuff and reacts accordingly. Attention and admiration from others is to her like the oxygen in the air to most people.

Feeling criticized, rejected, or thwarted triggers Peggy's anger, which she expresses with all the vehemence and self-righteous fury she can muster, often out of proportion to the nature of the offense. Fiery though they are, her temper tantrums share the generally shallow sense of the other emotions she expresses; they are inappropriate and seem calculated for effect, and they belie sincerity.

At times in her life, Peggy has been unhappy enough to seek mental health help. She brought her second husband in for marital therapy, for instance, with the agenda of making both him and the therapist understand her suffering, in the hopes that he would then improve his behavior toward her. The therapy was unsuccessful.

Several times, usually after bitter endings of relationships, Peggy sought individual psychotherapy. Her primary agenda was to impress the therapist, to convey how unhappy she was and how unfairly others treated her, and to garner sympathy. Her self-centered preoccupation precluded a therapeutic connection. She responded to interventions designed to help her see her own role in her interpersonal difficulties with cold contempt. The therapist who discussed her diagnosis of histrionic personality disorder with her received the full force of her angry indignation.

Histrionic Personality Disorder's Effect at Work

- Quality of relationships dependent on emotional state
- Others react to self-centeredness
- Initial enthusiasm, poor follow-through

Quality of relationships dependent on emotional state. To the extent that she feels valued and appreciated, Peggy's relationships with coworkers and supervisors can be smooth and positive. On the other hand, should the required level of esteem and admiration flag, should Peggy begin to feel unsupported or neglected, her work relationships could quickly turn ugly. She can become hostile and malicious, subject to temper tantrums and exaggerated displays of her aggrieved condition.

Peggy was a child model. Unfortunately, adolescence brought bad skin and orthodontics, and Peggy was unable to get modeling work despite her mother's aggressive efforts on her behalf. Upset by her father's ridicule of her developing body and of her hopes of someday becoming a top model, she enrolled in "charm school," where she was taught concepts such as poise, grace, and glamour. She also attended classes in acting and dramatics, where she learned the importance of body language and voice inflection. She took the lessons to heart, and by the time she graduated from high school, she knew how to get herself noticed.

At age 18 Peggy was a runner-up in a beauty contest, but she was still unsuccessful in restarting her modeling career. She lacked the necessary self-discipline and determination to follow through and could not overcome the inevitable rejections. She took a job as a receptionist for a local TV station, hoping she could somehow get on the air, but it didn't happen. She began to feel unappreciated there, she lost interest in the routine details of her job, and she was eventually let go in a restructuring of the station's staff.

She worked at a variety of jobs for several years, always hoping to get back into modeling, or into acting, TV, or advertising. Finally, she was hired as a product demonstrator for a manufacturer of gourmet kitchen equipment. She appeared in promotional videotapes and television ads, and she traveled with a sales rep to show the products to retail executives. She went to trade shows and supermarket and mall openings, and she staffed the company's booth at fairs and festivals.

She liked the work and did well at it. She began to fancy herself a sort of celebrity within the company, and the sales manager encouraged her in that view. So she was stunned and humiliated when, after 10 years, her role as product spokesperson was inexplicably diminished, and she was asked to do more routine and clerical work for the company. She didn't hold back in making her displeasure known, and one day her boss fired her on the spot. After that, she did other demo work here and there, but she never quite recovered from her loss of esteem.

Others react to self-centeredness. Peggy took her job at the kitchen equipment company very seriously—so seriously, in fact, that she acted as though hers was the only valuable role. She played the prima donna, expecting others to take care of ordinary details, such as making sure she had the materials she needed and verifying her schedule. Should mistakes occur, her fury knew no bounds. Should things go smoothly, she never thanked anyone.

She graciously accepted the praise and acclaim of the sales staff and the marketing department, never noticing that their comments became increasingly sarcastic as the years went on. The entire clerical staff hated her for her self-centered arrogance, and after a while they didn't trouble themselves to hide it. Her presence was the direct cause of interpersonal tension, low morale, and frequent bickering throughout the company. In reducing her "celebrity" role, the company management hoped to make her more of a team player in order to ease these tensions, but Peggy was unable to accept the changes, and the plan backfired.

Initial enthusiasm, poor follow-through. On several occasions, Peggy's boss gave her special projects to do. He wanted her to organize and maintain a library of the company's promotional videos. He wanted her to prepare a demonstration, with a script on file, for each of the company's current products. He wanted her to work with the marketing director to develop new demonstration ideas. Peggy responded to each of these requests enthusiastically; she saw them as an enhancement of her role and as proof of her importance. She got started on each in a flurry of activity—much of it other people's activity at her direction—but somehow never completed the task. She got bored with the details and didn't bother to follow through.

Working with Histrionic Personality Disorder

Peggy comes on strong. She is fun and likable on first impression. People tolerate her preoccupation with herself in exchange for her attractive and entertaining presence, until they realize just how self-centered she is, how insincere her show of friendliness is, and how vindictive she can become. Being around her can be compared to experiencing the first snowfall of the season: novel and exhilarating at first, with the promise of fun and recreation ahead, but over time becoming pure drudgery, the initial sparkle no longer a delight to the senses.

When she met Dale she had a job as a salesclerk in an upscale gift shop. She quit when they got married but quickly became bored and lonely. She told everyone that the life of leisure was simply not for her, but joked that she was too old to take any old boring job anymore. She wanted a good job, one, that is, that would showcase her. She had head shots taken and registered with several modeling agencies. She was offered some opportunities to pose for department store inserts and print ads, but she generally found the experience not to her liking. She considered most of the clothes she was asked to wear dowdy, and she didn't like anyone telling her how to do her hair or her make-up. She thought the agencies were inadequate; they did not seem sufficiently impressed with her, and they were not aggressive in finding her the kinds of modeling jobs for which she felt she was suited.

She decided that what she really wanted was a job in television or advertising, and she began to lean on Dale to find her something.

Dale knew a lot of people in advertising, public relations, television, and production. Wary of the consequences to his marriage and his home life if he didn't, he actively sought out friends, friends of friends, business associates, and acquaintances who could arrange interviews for Peggy.

Peggy wanted a certain star quality in a job but was otherwise vague about her career goals. She didn't think that her lack of training or experience in the fields she wanted to join should be a hindrance. She didn't prepare much for her interviews, other than to attend to her personal appearance. She was sometimes unclear about whom she was meeting with, what his or her role was, or what kind of job possibility existed. She was unable to articulate exactly what she had to offer and felt miffed and put out if she were asked. She left a powerful first impression, but received no offers.

Finally, one of the people she interviewed with, the head of a production company, gave her some suggestions. She had the impression that he was attracted to her, which enhanced her willingness to listen. First, he told her, learn something about the field. Second, figure out how you can fit into it.

The idea of adapting herself to someone else's needs was unfamiliar to Peggy, but she thought it over. At the suggestion of one of Dale's coworkers, she called Lisa, a career consultant who specialized in advertising and public relations and who had helped the coworker get her job. Over the phone, Peggy thought that Lisa sounded young and inexperienced, but energetic, enthusiastic, and eager to get to know Peggy and meet her needs.

Lisa turned out to be not at all like Peggy had pictured her. She was not young, not inexperienced, and not interested in Peggy's need for special treatment. She was all business and she showed little patience for Peggy's chatty, gregarious style. After introductions and initial pleasantries, she told Peggy straight out that no one would hire her just because she's attractive and extroverted, and she added that it wouldn't help that she was over 40 with no relevant experience. It was a standard technique of Lisa's to burst the bubble and then build from the ground up, but Peggy was stunned. She felt betrayed and angry.

Lisa went on to explain that she herself was only a catalyst in the process of finding a good employment fit. She believed in placing most of the responsibility for vocational success on her clients, which is the exact opposite of where Peggy believed the responsibility should lie. Peggy fumed through about 20 minutes of the session, then stood up and announced with a condescending smile that she was sorry for taking Lisa's time, but it was obvious that Lisa lacked the skills necessary to be helpful to someone looking for the caliber of work that Peggy sought.

Lisa didn't react, except to ask pointedly how successful Peggy had been so far. Uncharacteristically at a loss for words, Peggy paused. Lisa waited, but Peggy could not come up with a suitable rejoinder. She didn't want to leave without having the last word, so she just stood there. Having made her point, Lisa invited her to sit down again. She softened her tone, and asked Peggy to talk some about herself, her experience, her hopes, her plans for the future, her understanding of what she could contribute to an employer. Feeling that finally they were getting somewhere, Peggy complied. At the end of the session, she still disliked Lisa but thought that she knew her business and might be useful to her.

One of Lisa's suggestions was that Peggy conduct a series of informational interviews as a way to learn about the field, get a sense of how she might fit in to it, and at the same time develop some contacts with people who might help her when the time came to apply for jobs. Together, they developed a format and a set of interview questions. Peggy preferred to be the one doing the talking, but she could get into the role of interviewer, and she played it quite well. She went back to see some of the people she had already met with, as well as others to whom Lisa referred her.

The informational interviews were very helpful, but not in the way Peggy had anticipated. She learned that her chosen fields offered little in the way of glamour careers. She learned that few star roles exist in television, advertising, or public relations, that teamwork and not individual glory is the norm, and that the work is often tedious and demanding with long hours and little recognition.

Peggy tearfully related her findings to Lisa, saying that there was no place for her in such a competitive world, that this was the loss of a dream for her, that she didn't know what she could do now. Lisa began to suspect that Peggy's real interest was in herself, not in finding an interesting and challenging career. She changed her tactics and began to think of ways to redirect Peggy's efforts.

Lisa knew that dealing with the public was easy and pleasurable for Peggy, and she thought that a job involving lots of public contact might meet her need to be the center of attention without requiring her to actually relate to others. A job that took advantage of the excellent first impression Peggy was capable of creating, and didn't rely on the quality of ongoing relationships, might suit her. She saw that Peggy was better at the big picture than at detail-oriented work, and more likely to be successful on a superficial level than in a pursuit involving depth of effort. She also understood from Peggy's history that her vocational problems had more to do with work relationships than with work performance. She was concerned that no matter what Peggy did, her interpersonal limitations would interfere.

With all this in mind, she met with Peggy again. In imagining her ideal career, Peggy always pictured herself involved in a great deal of fast-paced, exciting public contact, which was why she was so disappointed to learn that such scenarios were unlikely in her chosen fields. She was open to considering other lines of work. With Lisa's help, she put together a résumé that emphasized her interest and ability in working with the public, her vivacious and extroverted nature, and her enthusiasm for and comfort with all kinds of public interaction. Though it was outside her area of expertise, Lisa worked with colleagues to help Peggy come up with leads and options. Meanwhile, she coached Peggy in basic interviewing techniques, such as knowing the company, understanding the nature of the job possibility, understanding the role of the person conducting the interview, and being prepared with a response to the question about what she had to offer.

Eventually, through one of Lisa's contacts, she was hired by a national distributor of fashion and costume jewelry. The job was in many ways similar to her old job at the kitchen equipment company. It involved a great deal of travel, demonstrating and modeling the products, helping with presentations to retailers, and setting up short-term displays and shows in malls, trade meetings, and convention centers. It wasn't her ideal job, since it lacked the large crowds of fascinated and attentive people that Peggy wanted to see herself among, but it was close enough.

Lisa thought the job was an exceptionally good fit, but she had concerns about Peggy's longevity, given her interpersonal difficulties. She offered to call the district manager to help ease Peggy's transition back to full-time work and to explain some of Peggy's workplace needs. Peggy, who had never come to like Lisa and continued to feel underestimated by her, was surprised and flattered by such attentiveness and consideration on Lisa's part, and she readily agreed.

Lisa explained Peggy's oversensitivity to rejection and criticism, saying that while this made her a challenge to supervise, an understanding of it on the part of her manager and coworkers would help create tolerance for her behavior and prevent tensions from developing. She went on to say that while Peggy responds well to support and encouragement, she also needs a firm hand and clear boundaries. She warned about flirting, showing off, excessive time spent on personal grooming, excessive displays of emotion, and other forms of drawing attention to herself that are inappropriate in the workplace but that Peggy regularly indulged in. She urged that job requirements be made very clear, along with the understanding that Peggy could not expect coworkers to take care of her or pick up the slack while she's busy being the star of the show.

The manager said that she had already observed some of these tendencies, and she was grateful for the pointers. She thought Peggy would do all right, because most of her interactions and relationships would be time-limited and short, or sporadic with several months or even years passing between encounters. She would work closely and routinely with only a few coworkers, who could probably handle her behavior after being given appropriate information about it.

Otherwise, the manager said, she found Peggy delightful, and thought her energy and her attitude were perfect for her role. How long such enthusiasm can last is an open question, given Peggy's history. But as long as she receives the attention she craves and enough support from coworkers and management, she will probably be able to do her job well and enjoy it.

Summary: Histrionic Personality Disorder's Effect on Vocational Abilities

Level of Impairment

1. no impairment
2. mild—minimal impairment with little or no effect on ability to function
3. moderate—some impairment, which limits ability to function fully
4. serious—major impairment, which may at times preclude ability to function
5. severe—extreme impairment

Understanding and Memory

Remembers locations and basic work procedures

1____X____2_____3_____4_____5_____

Understands and remembers short, simple instructions

1____X____2_____3_____4_____5_____

Understands and remembers detailed instructions

1____X____2_____3_____4_____5_____

Concentration and Persistence

Carries out short, simple instructions

1____X____2_____3_____4_____5_____

Carries out detailed instructions

1_____2____X____3_____4_____5_____

Maintains attention and concentration for extended periods of time

1_____2_____3____X____4_____5_____

Can work within a schedule, maintain attendance, be punctual

1_____2____X____3_____4_____5_____

Sustains ordinary routine without special supervision

1_____2_____3____X____4_____5_____

Can work with or close to others without being distracted by them

1_____2____X____3_____4_____5_____

Makes simple work-related decisions

1____X____2_____3_____4_____5_____

Works quickly and efficiently, meets deadlines, even under stressful
conditions

1_____2____X____3_____4_____5_____

Completes normal workday and workweek without interruptions due
to symptoms

1____X____2_____3_____4_____5_____

Works at consistent pace without an unreasonable number or length
of breaks

1_____2____X____3_____4_____5_____

Social Interaction

Interacts appropriately with general public

1_____2____X____3_____4_____5_____

Asks simple questions or requests assistance when necessary

1____X____2_____3_____4_____5_____

Accepts instruction and responds appropriately to criticism from supervisors

1_____ 2_____ 3_____ 4___X___ 5_____

Gets along with coworkers without distracting them

1_____ 2_____ 3_____ 4___X___ 5_____

Maintains socially appropriate behavior

1_____ 2_____ 3___X___ 4_____ 5_____

Maintains basic standards of cleanliness and grooming

1___X___ 2_____ 3_____ 4_____ 5_____

Adaptation

Responds appropriately to changes at work

1___X___ 2_____ 3_____ 4_____ 5_____

Is aware of normal work hazards and takes necessary precautions

1___X___ 2_____ 3_____ 4_____ 5_____

Can get around in unfamiliar places, can use public transportation

1___X___ 2_____ 3_____ 4_____ 5_____

Sets realistic goals, makes plans independently of others

1___X___ 2_____ 3_____ 4_____ 5_____

Summary: Vocational Strategies and Accommodations

To optimize the chances for vocational success, a person with histrionic personality disorder needs:

- Public contact, in order to make use of extroverted nature and accommodate the need for ongoing attention from others.
- Help from a vocational rehabilitation or mental health professional in explaining oversensitivity to criticism and rejection to supervisor and coworkers, in order to help prevent interpersonal tensions from developing and create a level of tolerance.
- Ongoing support and encouragement, in order to respond to the need to be recognized and appreciated.
- Limited requirement to work as part of a team or to respond to coworkers' needs, in order to accommodate interpersonal difficulties.

- Clearly explained duties and job requirements, in order to prevent avoidance of certain tasks or passing them off on coworkers due to boredom.
- Limits placed on inappropriate attention-seeking and other unacceptable workplace behaviors, if needed.

NARCISSISTIC PERSONALITY DISORDER

Of those diagnosed with narcissistic personality disorder, 50%–75% are male. The kinds of narcissistic traits that are particularly common among adolescents do not necessarily indicate the development of narcissistic personality disorder in adulthood. Those who have the disorder, however, may have a great deal of difficulty adjusting to the realities and limitations that occur as they grow up and age. Estimates of its prevalence indicate that narcissistic personality occurs in 2%–16% of the clinical population and in less than 1% of the general population (American Psychiatric Association, 1994).

Gerald

Gerald elbowed his way to the front of the check-out line, with a smile and a polite "excuse me" to each person he nudged out of the way. He placed his loaded basket on the counter ahead of the single package of cold capsules belonging to a sniffling young man whose turn was next. "Excuse me," Gerald said. "I need to go ahead of you." He began to unload his basket, which contained a supply of personal hygiene items—hair care, shaving and dental products, lotions, colognes, deodorants.

"I'm sorry, sir," the clerk said. "This is the express line. Ten items or less."

Gerald smiled at her. "I know, but I'm very busy," he said.

The clerk hesitated, looking around for a manager. The other people in line muttered angrily. Gerald stopped smiling. "You're wasting my time," he said. "Ring me up so I can get out of here."

What Narcissistic Personality Disorder Is Like

- Pattern of grandiose, attention-seeking, and self-centered behavior
- Exploitation of others, lack of empathy
- Hypersensitivity to criticism and rejection
- Sense of entitlement

Pattern of grandiose, attention-seeking, and self-centered behavior. Gerald's belief that he is superior to and more important than other people is at the core of his personality. It is not exactly a belief, in the sense that he has thought it through or analyzed evidence and reached a conclusion. It is an article of unexamined faith; he doesn't question the truth of it any more than he questions his belief that he is a human being and not a cockroach.

He doesn't understand why others fail to see that his needs and desires take precedence over those of anyone else, and this failure on their part is a source of constant irritation to him. His attempts to rectify the situation more often than not fall on deaf ears. No matter how eloquently he explains his requirements, others persist in expecting him to comply with restraints and conditions intended for ordinary people.

He accepts the responsibility that he feels his superiority imposes on him, and he tries to educate others, though he finds it a thankless task. He holds forth at every opportunity on his ideas, his insights, his perceptions, his opinions, and his plans. He generously takes the trouble to share with others his incisive judgment as to their flaws and shortcomings. He welcomes and actively creates opportunities to display his acumen and intelligence. Some may call him affected, conceited, pompous, condescending, demanding, and a shameless show-off, but Gerald claims unconditional adulation as his birthright.

Gerald is 40. He has a master's degree in sociology. He finished course work for a PhD in the field, but never completed the research for his dissertation and never earned the doctorate. He taught at the university for seven years, but left in a huff when told that he must meet a deadline for the dissertation or lose the opportunity to complete it.

He felt that he had already demonstrated his value to the institution and was astounded at such lack of appreciation. He thought it criminal that the university steadfastly refused to grant his PhD, and that they pressured him so mercilessly about the dissertation. He maintained that the research was nearly complete, and that the data showed clear trends. He blamed his undergraduate research assistants for failing to perform the statistical analysis and failing to write up the results. His view of the matter did not prevail, however. His chance to earn a doctorate was rescinded, unless he started a new dissertation topic with a new research project.

After appearing unannounced in the office of the head of the department to express his opinion of his treatment there, and after writing a bitter and angry letter to the president of the university, Gerald left. He considered a lawsuit, but decided it wasn't worth his while. Instead, he took an instructor position at a small community college to help pay the bills while he worked on a book he intended to write. This book would be the definitive work in the field of sociology, and it would be acclaimed far beyond the academic community. It would be an innovative and transformative work, a work to amaze all the full professors who had humiliated him and cause them deep regret for allowing him to leave the university. Unfortunately, the time requirements for working on it cut rather drastically into Gerald's classroom schedule, a fact that bothered the community college administrators enough to fire him eventually.

Exploitation of others, lack of empathy. Gerald's career in the master's program at the university actually had been brilliant—or at least it appeared so due to the research skills and fresh ideas of an elite group of undergraduates to whom Gerald served as teaching assistant and informal advisor. He freely incorporated their work into his master's thesis and claimed it as his own. He assigned them research projects on the basis of his needs in the master's program, not on the basis of their needs for meeting graduation requirements. He never learned basic skills such as using media resources or analyzing statistics, and he forced those tasks onto his undergraduates. Further, he sometimes felt attracted to the young women he encountered in his classes, and he made it clear that their grades were contingent on supplying him with sexual favors as needed; the possibility that they might not wish to comply didn't occur to him.

Gerald was married briefly during that time. His wife was a graduate student in astrophysics. She was very busy with her own studies. Gerald felt that she ignored his needs, a fact that infuriated him, especially since he saw his work as more relevant and important than hers. She wouldn't go to the library for him, she wouldn't solve computer problems for him, she wouldn't cook him dinner, she wouldn't take his phone calls, and she wouldn't stay home and play hostess for his evening senior seminar; all because, as Gerald put it, she had some illusions about the significance of her research. He took little interest in her work or in her interpersonal needs and feelings. He didn't bother listening to her never-ending litany of complaints about their marriage, so he was truly bewildered when she left.

Hypersensitivity to criticism and rejection. Gerald was devastated by the break-up of his marriage. He felt as though his world had literally come to an end. His wife's leaving was a powerful and direct blow to his sense of self. He has difficulty withstanding any hint of criticism, and he could not tolerate a complete and total rejection. His belief in his superiority, invulnerability, and exemption from normal relationship responsibilities was badly shaken. He became deeply depressed, he cried real tears, and he was moved to take a colleague's suggestion that he see a psychotherapist.

He made an appointment with the director of the mental health clinic. The session went well at first. Gerald was able to explain in detail all of his wife's shortcomings, and he felt the therapist's sympathy. Things took a nasty turn, however, when the therapist's line of questioning seemed to imply that Gerald himself could have done something different to make the marriage work. He felt criticized, and it made him furious. He stomped out of the office railing loudly against the therapist's ignorance, insensitivity, stupidity, and incompetence, and that of the entire psychotherapy profession.

His response to the mildest of snubs, real or perceived, is hardly less dramatic. He repairs the psychological damage done by these blows to his ego by reminding himself, and others, of his conquests and triumphs, and by debasing as thoroughly as possible those who criticize or reject him.

Sense of entitlement. Gerald expects no more than his due. His sense of what he deserves, however, from other people and from life, is nearly limitless. He believes he should be given advanced degrees, full professorships, and lucrative publishing contracts on the strength of his personal presence alone; he sees the requirement of concrete evidence of ability as an annoyance, degrading to someone of his special brilliance. He believes that those close to him should anticipate and meet his every need, at the expense of their own needs if necessary. He believes that social rules and expectations of common courtesy do not apply to him.

Narcissistic Personality Disorder's Effect at Work

- Quality of relationships depends on feelings
- Others resent manipulations and self-centeredness
- Unwilling to take risks or branch out

Quality of relationships depends on feelings. When Gerald feels suitably appreciated, he can be a pleasure to work with. He is energetic, animated, and vivacious, and his enthusiasm is catching. People who see him this way—from department heads to clerical staff, from colleagues to freshmen—enjoy his presence and benefit from his dynamic spirit. Unfortunately, the conditions required to sustain this side of Gerald are precarious and short-lived. His friendly and cooperative persona is subject to sudden and complete reversal should he experience a momentary lapse in respect or support.

Sarcasm, hostility, and temper tantrums also characterize Gerald's long-term working relationships. He rarely feels the level of support he needs or the kind of respect he craves. Since he feels entitled to acclaim without producing anything and since he cannot tolerate criticism, normal workplace expectations put enormous strain on his relationships.

Others resent manipulations and self-centeredness. Gerald's principal means of healing the psychological injuries he sustains at the hands of insensitive others is to inflate his abilities and demean everyone else. He does so automatically and instinctively. The resulting behavior is manipulative and self-centered in the extreme, designed to control others so Gerald can feel good. It wears thin very quickly.

The community college that hired him as an instructor tolerated it for a year. Gerald assumed that what he thought of as a low-rate, back-water operation would be so thrilled to have someone of his caliber on the faculty that he could virtually do what he liked. He thought that just having his name in the course listing would be enough to justify his salary. He figured he could turn his classes over to teaching assistants and devote his time to writing his landmark book, which he had not yet found the time to begin. He was genuinely shocked to learn that the college expected him to teach his own classes, hold office hours, and perform other tasks routinely expected of instructors.

The administrative staff and the faculty showed so little understanding of Gerald's stature in the field or his innate ability that he was forced to demean himself by demanding the special treatment to which he felt entitled. Everyone referred to him as "His Highness" or "Lord Gerald" behind his back, but even levity and the camaraderie generated by universal irritation toward him were not enough to combat the resentment and bitterness that his behavior created. After he was fired, the college hired a consultant and held an all-staff retreat to help resolve the strife caused by his presence.

Unwilling to take risks or branch out. The arrogance and braggadocio that are characteristic of narcissistic personality disorder often develop as a defense against underlying feelings of inadequacy and low self-esteem. For this reason, Gerald is truly afraid to take risks. It accounts for his unfinished dissertation and his reluctance to start actually writing his book. The possibility of opening himself up to the judgment of others is simply too threatening. He would rather talk than do, rather insist on his worth than demonstrate it, rather demean others than allow himself to be scrutinized. He will not put himself in a position where he might fail, where he might experience his vulnerability, or where others might see his limitations.

Working with Narcissistic Personality Disorder

Gerald knows how to make a good first impression. He is articulate and expressive. He can be smooth and gracious, witty and outgoing, scattering goodwill and beneficence in his wake. He can appear friendly and open if he feels that his sense of superiority is unthreatened. Unfortunately, to know Gerald over time is to learn to dislike him.

Except for his habit of exploiting students, he was a reasonably good teacher. He was popular, especially among those who were not sociology majors and who took only one or two courses from him. He was known as a fun guy and an easy grader. He, in turn, liked teaching; it provided a perfect forum for his personality, students naturally looked up to him, they laughed at his jokes, and they rarely challenged his authority or his projected self-image. He could do well at teaching if it weren't for the requirements inherent in it, such as keeping up with the material, following administrative rules, refraining from exploitative behavior, and getting along with colleagues.

In fact, Gerald never considered a career outside of academia, and he would be unwilling to take the risks necessary to seek one. On being fired from the community college, he revamped his curriculum vitae, being careful though not strictly honest about what he included and what he left out, and about which personal references he listed. He sent it out to colleges and universities all over the country and was eventually hired by a small liberal arts college in a remote rural area. He moved there in largely the same arrogant and self-satisfied frame of mind with which he had started work at the community college, having learned little from his experience there.

He started the academic year on a positive and upbeat note. He understood that the college administrators, being so remote and, he assumed, ignorant, might not be familiar with his work or his reputation. He was willing to give them time to realize what a prize they had hired, and then he was sure he would be free to do whatever he wanted and to have all the support and assistance he needed to work on his book.

He talked at length and with great enthusiasm about his book in his classes, although he still had not started writing. He led classroom discussions and assigned reading and research projects intended to help him develop ideas for the book. He told the students they would all be his co-authors. His classes were loosely run and his grading system was far from rigorous. He once again became a popular instructor among the students, and he enjoyed it a great deal.

Early in its history, the college had adopted an egalitarian approach to its academic staff, so that instructors, regardless of what academic degree they had achieved, how much they had published, or how long they had served, were not differentiated according to full, assistant, or associate professorships. All were addressed as Mr. or Ms, or by their first names, by students. Gerald found this practice ludicrous, but it served his needs; his lack of a doctorate no longer rankled on a daily basis in such an atmosphere. He felt relaxed and accepted among his colleagues, though he didn't feel the level of esteem to which he believed he was entitled. He let a general understanding circulate that he in fact had a PhD.

Even before the end of his first semester, however, the college community began to see Gerald's unpleasant side. Librarians, computer lab technicians, and administrative staff began to mutter among themselves about his arrogance. His fellow instructors, both within and outside of the social sciences department, found his self-serving conversation tedious. They began to suspect that the accomplishments he described and the connections to well-known sociologists that he claimed were at best exaggerations of the truth.

But, for the most part, Gerald found the required level of attention and admiration among his students. He spent as much of his free time as possible with them, shooting pool in the student union, having a beer or two in town, playing softball, holding impromptu seminars at his home, regaling them with his wit and what he thought of as his infectious enthusiasm for learning, by which he meant his tendency to show off his knowledge and expose their ignorance of any topic under discussion. Many students disliked him, but many found him fun and entertaining.

Gerald's sense of self-importance expanded. By his own estimation, he single-handedly raised both the visibility and the reputation of the college, though he conducted no research of his own and had published no papers since joining the faculty. With the help of student ideas and student research papers, he eventually started his book, though his concept of its form and content remained vague. He wrote an introduction, which he used as a model for the dynamic writing style he wanted his students to adopt.

He continued to expect sexual favors from certain female students, though he made an effort to be discreet because he understood what the effect would otherwise be in such a small community; everyone, he thought, would want to have sex with him if word got out. One young woman, under the illusion that she was his only partner, was deeply hurt to learn otherwise. She was disillusioned and disgusted, and she was not one to suffer in silence. She went to the Dean of Students. She made no claims of abuse or coercion, but she did expose Gerald's pattern of exploitation, supported by two other women who also came forward.

Amid general outrage and calls for his resignation, Gerald attempted to discredit the young women. The family of one of them threatened a lawsuit against the college if Gerald did not step down. But Gerald had worked out a comfortable niche for himself, and he didn't want to leave. In addition, the college, though far from enthusiastic about his continued presence there, experienced chronic difficulty maintaining a full faculty. Gerald was at that moment one of only four members of the Social Sciences Department. His sociology courses, as well as a history course he taught, would have to be canceled if he left.

A compromise was struck whereby Gerald was placed on probation. He could remain on faculty only if he would refrain from any contact with the young women in question, and from any similar entanglements in the future, and if he would undergo psychotherapy and training in ethical behavior.

Gerald went to the nearest mental health center, which was a three-hour drive from the college, for an initial psychological evaluation. He would be required to return there monthly for 10 psychotherapy sessions. He would complete the ethics training part of his probation with Karen, a human resources specialist. She worked for a small human resources firm in town, which served the college as well as two nearby manufacturing plants and several local businesses.

Gerald was deeply angered by the situation. He felt humiliated. He believed he had been unjustly maligned, his reputation damaged, his career placed in jeopardy, and all for no reason. He could not understand all the fuss about the young women, and he did not see that they had been damaged by his behavior. Karen received the full fury of his feelings at their first meeting. She had the psychological report, which offered a diagnosis of narcissistic personality disorder with some recommendations for working with it. Because theirs was a small community, she already knew Gerald's reputation. She was prepared.

She understood that trying to change Gerald's personality would be a futile enterprise, as would any attempt to engender empathy on his part or to develop his level of insight into the damaging aspects of his behavior. Her task was to teach him ethical behavior, which she believed was possible, not to make him an ethical person, which she believed was not.

After his initial outburst of anger in her presence, Gerald treated Karen with a combination of condescension and ingratiating familiarity. He attempted to enlist her on his side, to make her an ally. He tried to involve her in sarcastic joking and derisive banter about his colleagues and the college administration. He implied that she, with her background and training, was surely on a level above the petty politics of a small town college. He indicated with a conspiratorial wink that they shared an understanding about the rules and behavioral expectations they discussed: of course these did not apply to him.

As Gerald saw it, and as he outlined to Karen, they would meet for the required amount of time, maybe at a bar or at his place rather than in her office, and, once the time was up, she would give him her stamp of approval, get paid by the college for her efforts, and he would go back to business as usual. A win-win, as he put it.

Karen, however, was not taken in. She maintained a professional distance and responded to his manipulations and flattery with cool detachment. Her response was the same when, frustrated by her attitude, he turned his derision, sarcasm, and occasional outbursts of anger toward her. She explained that part of her work with him was to demonstrate appropriate workplace behaviors and boundaries, and she stayed consistently on task. She said she would not give her "stamp of approval" until he showed an understanding of these concepts and a willingness to comply with behavioral expectations.

Karen's primary focus was on Gerald's sexual exploitation of young women students, on the power differential and boundary issues inherent in it, and on the likelihood of his inflicting psychological damage and seriously compromising their educational experience. Staying away from the language of empathy and personal responsibility, she stuck to concepts Gerald could relate to, like lawsuits. If the college was sued, Gerald could be personally sued as well. He would be fired, and his career would be over. Whether he understood that his own behavior caused his downfall, or whether he blamed it on others, the result would be the same.

Taking a similar tone, she forced him to explore issues of academic exploitation, performance of job requirements, and relationships with colleagues and other staff members. Gerald settled into an attitude of ironic detachment, as though he found the exercise humorous and couldn't quite believe that Karen took it seriously. Eventually, he was able to identify the ethical versus the unethical approach to a variety of interpersonal dimensions that she presented to him, though his responses were often mocking and cynical.

Karen believed that Gerald had an intellectual understanding of the ethical concepts she had tried to address, though she doubted that he fully accepted their applicability to himself. But she thought that he was motivated enough to keep his current job to comply, or at least to pay considerable attention to the appearance of complying, with the conditions for doing so.

She wanted to pass on to the college administrators what she had learned about working with Gerald and about his workplace needs, in order to improve the relationships and the quality of workplace life. Because of his status on probation and because of the nature of her relationship with the college, she didn't need his permission to do so. But she wanted to reinforce the idea of ethical treatment of others, so she informed him that she intended to discuss issues related to improved workplace relationships with the college administrators and invited him to attend the meeting. He declined.

The administrators had already seen the psychological report and spoken to the psychologist about Gerald's progress in therapy. Karen added to the psychological information by offering ideas about how to get along with him. She thought that frequent recognition of his abilities, accomplishments, and achievements could help keep his pleasant side predominant. Unfortunately, should such recognition be accompanied by ongoing expectations or by occasional criticisms, its benefit would be limited. Because of his oversensitivity to rejection, he needs an unusually high level of praise, support, and respect. Expectations and criticisms offered with due attention to this need might be accepted.

Karen pointed out that Gerald's grandiosity and his tendency to exploit or belittle others make him an unlikely team member; both he and the team are better off if he works independently. Likewise, he is a poor candidate for any position of authority unless his behavior is closely monitored. His oversensitivity to rejection and his unwillingness to take risks reduce his effectiveness in competitive situations and limit his chances for success. His inflated self-image leads him to reject work he thinks is unworthy of him. His sense of entitlement leads him to assume benefits and take advantages to which he has no right.

In short, Gerald's interpersonal difficulties will in all likelihood continue to present a significant vocational impediment to him and to plague those who work with him as well. Even more than his need for recognition and support, he needs clear guidelines about the limits of tolerance for his behavior and about the expectations of his work performance, and he may need them backed up by some higher authority, such as the threat of firing or lawsuit. Presenting such guidelines in a straightforward, detached, and respectful way, along with the consequences for noncompliance and accompanied by recognition for work well done, may improve his chances for tolerable relationships in the workplace.

Summary: Narcissistic Personality Disorder's Effect on Vocational Abilities

Level of Impairment

1. no impairment
2. mild—minimal impairment with little or no effect on ability to function
3. moderate—some impairment, which limits ability to function fully
4. serious—major impairment, which may at times preclude ability to function
5. severe—extreme impairment

Understanding and Memory

Remembers locations and basic work procedures

1____X____ 2_____ 3_____ 4_____ 5_____

Understands and remembers short, simple instructions

1____X____ 2_____ 3_____ 4_____ 5_____

Understands and remembers detailed instructions

1____X____ 2_____ 3_____ 4_____ 5_____

Concentration and Persistence

Carries out short, simple instructions

1____X____ 2_____ 3_____ 4_____ 5_____

Carries out detailed instructions

1____X____ 2_____ 3_____ 4_____ 5_____

Maintains attention and concentration for extended periods of time

1____X____ 2_____ 3_____ 4_____ 5_____

Can work within a schedule, maintain attendance, be punctual

1____X____ 2_____ 3_____ 4_____ 5_____

Sustains ordinary routine without special supervision

1_____ 2____X____ 3_____ 4_____ 5_____

Can work with or close to others without being distracted by them

1____X____ 2_____ 3_____ 4_____ 5_____

Makes simple work-related decisions

1____X____ 2_____ 3_____ 4_____ 5_____

Works quickly and efficiently, meets deadlines, even under stressful

conditions

1____X____ 2_____ 3_____ 4_____ 5_____

Completes normal workday and workweek without interruptions due to

symptoms

1____X____ 2_____ 3_____ 4_____ 5_____

Works at consistent pace without an unreasonable number or length of

breaks

1____X____ 2_____ 3_____ 4_____ 5_____

Social Interaction

Interacts appropriately with general public

1_____ 2_____ 3____X____ 4_____ 5_____

Asks simple questions or requests assistance when necessary

1____X____ 2_____ 3_____ 4_____ 5_____

Accepts instruction and responds appropriately to criticism from

supervisors

1_____ 2_____ 3_____ 4_____ 5____X____

Gets along with coworkers without distracting them

1_____ 2_____ 3_____ 4____X____ 5_____

Maintains socially appropriate behavior

1_____ 2____X____ 3_____ 4_____ 5_____

Maintains basic standards of cleanliness and grooming

1____X____ 2_____ 3_____ 4_____ 5_____

Adaptation

Responds appropriately to changes at work

1____X____ 2_____ 3_____ 4_____ 5_____

Is aware of normal work hazards and takes necessary precautions

1____X____ 2_____ 3_____ 4_____ 5_____

Can get around in unfamiliar places, can use public transportation

1____X____ 2_____ 3_____ 4_____ 5_____

Sets realistic goals, makes plans independently of others

1_____ 2_____ 3____X____ 4_____ 5_____

Summary: Vocational Strategies and Accommodations

To optimize the chances for vocational success, a person with narcissistic personality disorder needs:

- An unusually high level of praise for abilities and accomplishments, and of personal support and respect, because of hypersensitivity to criticism and rejection.
- The opportunity to work independently, not as part of a team, because of the tendency to manipulate or belittle others.
- Closely monitored interpersonal interactions, because of tendency to exploit others.
- Help from a mental health or rehabilitation professional in explaining sensitivities and the need for clear boundaries to supervisor.
- Clear guidelines with regard to the limits of tolerance for inappropriate behavior and with regard to expectations of work performance.

CHAPTER 6

The "Anxious" Cluster: Avoidant, Dependent, Obsessive-Compulsive, and Passive-Aggressive Personality Disorders

Reluctant and timid, meek and dutiful, perfectionistic and rule-obsessed, chronically late and forgetful: this is the "anxious" group of personality disorders. Those who manifest these disorders lead constricted, lonely lives, limited by their inability to form true connections with others, their relationships hampered by hidden animosities. A stew of resentment, alienation, and resistance simmers beneath their passive smiles and worried looks.

People with avoidant personality disorder tremble at the thought of rejection or humiliation, imagine its potential in every contact with others, and avoid or circumvent situations and responsibilities requiring social appearances. A guarded reticence characterizes their interactions. Hypersensitivity and misinterpretation haunt their relationships. They might yearn for emotional closeness but cannot bring themselves to open the door to it in the absence of unconditional guarantees of affection and acceptance.

Submissive, compliant, and deferential, people with dependent personality disorder rarely take a step on their own if they can help it. Docile and accommodating, obedient and polite, they are often willing to trade their own goals and desires for permanent refuge under someone else's umbrella. Independence and self-reliance are threatening words to them, and almost no price is too great to pay to ensure escape from the requirements of autonomy. Yet no amount of interpersonal security seems to be enough to ease their worries fully or to make up for the resentment they are likely to feel toward those on whom they depend.

People with obsessive-compulsive personality disorder are fearful of uncertainty, mistrustful of emotion, disapproving of pleasure, and preoccupied with the right way of doing things. They are often rigid

169

and uncompromising. Their decisions wallow unmade, bogged down in a sea of minor details. They fret and worry over possible mistakes. They find interpersonal relationships, messy and unpredictable as they are, profoundly threatening. They resent any incursion against their authority to maintain the control and orderliness they crave.

DSM-IV places passive-aggressive, or negativistic, personality disorder under a category called "Disorders in need of further study," rather than in the "anxious" cluster where it has appeared in previous editions of the DSM, because of inconsistency among clinicians in making the diagnosis. Nevertheless, its effect in the workplace is so pervasive and so destructive, and its occurrence is so frequent, that it requires a description.

Counting on people with passive-aggressive personality disorder is like counting on the weather—you can't, and they will get you if you try. They excel at passive resistance to reasonable demands for adequate performance. They procrastinate. They're late. They forget. They're slow. They dawdle. They're inefficient. They goof up and make mistakes. They may not overtly refuse requests or requirements or indicate their resentment in any direct way, but their opposition is unmistakable and their hostility thinly veiled. Their interpersonal relationships struggle for life in a poisonous atmosphere of negativity, pessimism, undue criticism, and discouraging, defeatist attitudes.

If interpersonal martyrdom were a virtue, the people in the "anxious" group of personality disorders would be saints. Their inability to relate adequately to others produces deep distress. They are perpetually tense, worried, and resentful. They become so absorbed in their own suffering that they are often unaware of others' needs and feelings. They find taking risks, making decisions, and expressing feelings largely beyond the scope of their ability. They put most of their energy into avoiding emotional pain and interpersonal responsibility.

Under the right circumstances, however, some members of the "anxious" group, especially those with dependent or obsessive-compulsive personality disorders, may make excellent employees. In a setting that nurtures their abilities without triggering worry or resentment, they can do very well.

AVOIDANT PERSONALITY DISORDER

Avoidant personality disorder is frequently diagnosed with mood and anxiety disorders, with dependent personality disorder, and with the "odd" cluster of personality disorders—paranoid, schizoid, or schizotypal. It seems to be equally common among men and women.

It appears in between 0.5% and 1% of the general population, and in about 10% of patients seen in outpatient mental health settings. Avoidant behavior may start early in childhood, with shyness or fear of strangers. While most shy children become less so as they get older, those who go on to develop avoidant personality disorder become more so. They tend to avoid social contacts and personal relationships during adolescence and early adulthood, when developing a social life and meeting new people are especially important. In adulthood, the disorder may diminish in intensity and become less evident with age (American Psychiatric Association, 1994).

Connie

The butterflies in Connie's stomach were nothing new, nor was the headache behind her eyes, nor the vague sense of impending doom clouding her consciousness. She suppressed a wave of resentment at her daughter, who had insisted she accept the invitation to this event, a wedding shower for her niece. Her daughter sat across the room from her now, chatting happily, oblivious to Connie's discomfort. Connie could not suppress her resentment at their hostess, who had just proposed a little get-acquainted activity as cheerfully and confidently as if everyone there would naturally be thrilled to participate.

Nervously twisting a napkin in her lap, Connie swallowed hard as the hostess called for the attention of the group. She looked down at the toes of her shoes—scuffed, she noticed, and out of fashion—as the introductions began. Each guest was expected to say her name and tell a little anecdote about her relationship to the guest of honor. Connie felt so flustered that she could remember nothing about her relationship with her niece over the last 25 years.

Moving around the circle, each guest sounded to Connie more witty and articulate than the last. Connie's daughter told a charming story about making cookies with her cousin in Connie's kitchen and ended with a warm gesture toward her mother. The guests responded with a little flutter of applause. Connie was overcome by embarrassment; she tried to hide from the harsh stares she felt by turning away until her face was nearly hidden in the couch pillows. She was appalled by her daughter's insensitivity.

Eventually, just two people were left before Connie's turn. Her hands were sweaty; the napkin in her lap was in shreds. Her shoulders, hunched over in a painful effort to diminish her presence, were tense. She could think of nothing to say. As unobtrusively as she could, she stood up and slipped out of the room. She went upstairs to the bathroom and stayed there for a good 15 minutes. She opened the door and heard the hostess' voice floating up the stairs: "What wonderful stories. We'll just have time for Connie's turn before our lunch is served." Connie pulled the bathroom door closed again.

What Avoidant Personality Disorder Is Like

- Pattern of social inhibition
- Feelings of inadequacy in groups, tendency to be quiet and "invisible"
- Hypersensitivity to anticipated or actual criticism
- Avoidance of work, school, or social situations

Pattern of social inhibition. Connie is shy, but shyness doesn't begin to describe what she experiences. Ordinary social situations are so difficult for her that she is nearly unable to sustain relationships outside of her immediate family. Many of the guests at her niece's shower were family members or lifelong acquaintances of either hers or her daughter's, yet Connie felt intimidated by them and overwhelmed by the situation. Her reluctance to communicate or to express herself takes the form of intense internal discomfort and confusion, to the point that even if she wanted to, she could not string together more than two or three words at a time.

At 53, Connie has lived with her condition for many years and has given up hope that it will change. When she was a teenager, her mother assured her that she would "grow out of it" and encouraged—forced—her to try to become an extrovert. Connie dutifully joined the high school debate team, the marching band, and a group that worked with children in a poor neighborhood after school. She felt that she had no choice but to appear, interact, or perform as required, but each instance was a new horror. It never got easier. She developed a repertoire of evasive measures, including a barely audible voice, a hairstyle that nearly hid her face, body posture that diminished her presence, and a habit of looking everywhere but directly at a person.

She married right out of high school; her husband was an engineering student who had lived next door for four years. They raised three children. When Connie's role as a homemaker began to diminish, she became restless and a little bored. At the same time, facing college expenses for their children, her husband suggested that she think about getting a job. She attended a college program especially designed for older women entering the work force. She obtained a bachelor's degree in social work, specializing in geriatrics. She felt comfortable in the program as long as she was diligent about meeting all of the academic expectations and could avoid speaking in class.

She got a job in a nursing home. She found that she liked the older people; they expected nothing of her but a willing ear, which she was happy to provide. Additional responsibilities, however, including calling family members and meeting with them, coordinating services with other professionals, and giving periodic talks to community members, severely taxed her ability to function. She managed to get out of doing the talks, but still she dreaded going to work every day, and after five grueling years, she quit. She felt like a complete failure.

Feelings of inadequacy in groups, tendency to be quiet and "invisible." Connie constantly compares herself to others and finds herself wanting on virtually every level. Others are more attractive, more intelligent, more interesting, and better informed than she. They do important things and hold valuable opinions. Their lives matter, and they have a right to take up space in the world. She, on the other hand, feels that she has nothing to offer, and that the less she says and the less she is noticed, the better for her and for everyone else.

Her children grew up to be decent, productive people, but she feels no sense of accomplishment in raising them. She is a skilled and creative cook, but she denigrates her ability, saying that anyone can learn to cook like she does. She has written poetry since high school; she keeps notebooks of her work and has on several occasions submitted poems to literary journals. Two were published, but Connie never told anyone except her husband, and she could barely bring herself to tell him. She thought the poets she met in a writing class she once took were doing important, significant work, but saw her own writing skill as useless and frivolous.

Self-esteem is a concept Connie doesn't understand. She has always felt inadequate compared with others. As she understands it, her responsibility in life is to trouble others with her presence as little as possible. She does her best not to exist. Her resentment at this state of affairs, however, sometimes wells up in her until she is afraid she will choke on it.

Hypersensitivity to anticipated or actual criticism. Connie would love to have friends. She imagines herself relaxed and at ease, familiar and affectionate, sharing ideas, expressing feelings, laughing. It is a compelling scenario to her, but not one she has encountered. The fear of being criticized keeps her from revealing anything of her inner life to others. She is fussy and exacting in everything she does, hoping that perfection will stave off criticism. Her home is spotless, her bills paid on time, her obligations met, and her responsibilities discharged, all with a sense of desperation and not joy or accomplishment on her part.

Her marriage is companionable in many ways, but Connie never disagrees with her husband, never states an opinion he might not share, and feels emotionally intimidated by him. He is exceedingly mild mannered and easy-going and would be amazed if he knew how hard she tries not to incur his disapproval. He is active in the political party he supports; after 35 years of marriage, he doesn't know that in every election Connie votes a straight ticket for the other party.

Connie's discomfort in social situations does not enhance her ability to experience empathy. In fact, it has the opposite effect; she is so worried about being criticized that she is oblivious to others' need for friendly or courteous responses. Rather than relating to them, she tends to be contemptuous of those who appear socially awkward. She attributes such a high level of social skill to others that she expects them to somehow divine and respond to her needs, and she is resentful when they don't.

Avoidance of work, school, or social situations. Connie successfully avoids most social situations and avoids interaction when she is forced to be with other people. She quit her job because of the interpersonal responsibilities it required. She tried her best to blend into the crowd in high school, and found the extracurricular activities she participated in deeply painful. She earned her college degree in a small program specifically geared to her needs, which provided a great deal of emotional support to its students and allowed her to succeed.

Avoidant Personality Disorder's Effect at Work

- Oversensitive to criticism
- Avoids taking risks
- Isolation may be ridiculed

Oversensitive to criticism. Feedback from supervisors about her work was so painful for Connie to hear that she asked to receive her performance reviews in writing only, a policy that the nursing home's parent corporation would not allow. Though much of the feedback was positive—she was extremely conscientious about paperwork and other responsibilities, and her listening skills provided a soothing presence for the residents—she heard only the negative parts, about her difficulty communicating and relating to staff and the public. Each review left her shaken and near tears.

She often heard criticism where none was intended. She interpreted innocuous or even friendly remarks in a negative light; she took everything from routine complaints about difficult residents to information about policy changes as criticism of her work. She became worried and preoccupied, confused and forgetful, she was prone to mistakes, and she was sometimes unable to carry out simple tasks.

Avoids taking risks. Connie kept her role at the nursing home as small as she could. She paid a great deal of attention to those aspects she found enjoyable and nonthreatening, like talking one-on-one to the residents and keeping meticulous written records. She avoided and procrastinated on the things she found difficult, like phone calls and meetings. She refused to take on additional duties that might have made the job more interesting, like offering educational groups for the residents or arranging for outside speakers and entertainment. She put forth no ideas at all about ways to make nursing home life more livable, even though creating and implementing such ideas had been part of her training in geriatrics.

Isolation may be ridiculed. Connie took little part in the social life of the nursing home, either among residents or staff. Her supervisors and coworkers were aware of her shyness and tried to be sensitive to it, but her ongoing resistance to most of their friendly overtures eventually wore them out. They began to see her as stuck-up rather than shy. They began to speculate about her life, wondering if she had something to hide. They stopped trying to be nice to her and began to mimic her hunched shoulders and monosyllabic conversation behind her back. While Connie was unaware of the ridicule, she knew she was not well liked. Her oversensitivity to disapproval and rejection heightened the problem and made her work life almost unbearable for her.

Before quitting her job, she went to see a psychotherapist, as a last ditch effort to salvage the situation somehow. She did not find the experience helpful, however, and wished she had saved herself the trouble. At first, the therapist seemed sensitive and understanding. After spending several sessions on history and assessment, she made a diagnosis of avoidant personality disorder and explained to Connie what that meant. While Connie found some relief in the idea that her problems were not of her own making, she also took the diagnosis to confirm her long-held belief that she was a hopelessly flawed human being, and that her flaws made her worthless and unacceptable; but she expressed none of that to the therapist.

The therapist took the tack of wanting to "support" Connie to "face her fears," to get out in the world, to experience new things and have some fun, to change her lifelong patterns of relating to others; she seemed unaware of the pain this caused Connie. She reminded Connie of her mother, whose endless plans for overcoming shyness and transforming her from an introvert into an extrovert made her childhood and adolescence so difficult. She wanted to be understood and accepted, though she found it difficult to articulate that need. She could not make a therapeutic connection, she resented the therapist's apparent desire to change her, and she was relieved when the 20 authorized sessions were used up.

Working with Avoidant Personality Disorder

A career in geriatric social work was one of the options available to participants in Connie's college program, and she made her choice without thinking it through. She imagined spending her time with lonely, nonthreatening senior citizens, who would appreciate her ability to listen quietly. She didn't imagine that the senior citizens would also have needs that required active intervention on her part, or family members who required ongoing interaction with her or information from her. She didn't imagine the need to attend staff meetings or to consult with other professionals. In short, she didn't think about the "social" part of social work.

As it was, she had virtually no chance of succeeding in a field that required her to confront her worst nightmares on a daily basis. She lacked both the necessary interpersonal skills and the desire to develop them. Her reticence and social anxiety, being fundamental aspects of her personality, are not amenable to treatment and are unlikely to improve significantly over time. Her ability to cope with her difficulties or to develop a degree of self-acceptance were likewise thwarted in a setting so antithetical to her nature.

The team atmosphere at the nursing home, which included medical, administrative, physical therapy, and support personnel, as well as many volunteers, was especially difficult for Connie to deal with. Her own role seemed vague and undefined in comparison with the other roles, especially since she tried so hard to keep her interpersonal contacts and public appearances to a minimum. She felt insignificant and superfluous, and she rarely voiced the ideas or opinions she had.

Difficult as her dealings with other staff members were, she found that contact with residents' families and members of the general public was harder. She communicated as much as she could in writing and relied heavily on voice mail and e-mail, but face-to-face meetings and live telephone conversations were inevitable. This aspect of her job never got easier, and in fact began to seem more and more threatening over time. She prepared as well as she could by using detailed notes about what she had to say, but still she was often tongue-tied and uptight, which made her appear unfriendly and led to questions about her competence.

Connie missed a great deal of work because of anxiety. She was too concerned about being criticized to ask for extra sick or vacation days, but she used the time off she was granted fully, and even pushed the limits a bit by leaving early when she was sure it would not be noticed. After quitting her job, she felt some relief from social pressure for a while. She went about her housework and gardening, cooked for her husband, sent packages of baked goods to her children away from home, wrote letters, read, and kept her poetry journal with a sense of freedom and release from pain, like a burden had been lifted.

But her period of peace and comfort was short-lived. Her chronic feelings of failure surfaced quickly and painfully. Her household activities seemed trivial and unsatisfying. Her husband never criticized her decision to quit work, and in fact expressed pleasure at coming home from his job every day to find her in the kitchen amid delicious cooking smells, but she didn't believe him. He assured her that they could pay the college expenses without an income from her, but she didn't believe him about that, either. She felt guilty and anxious, she felt that she had let him and their children down, she felt worthless and undeserving, and she believed she had to go back to work in order to feel better, which made her even more miserable and unhappy.

One day, after thinking about it for a long time, she worked up the courage to call the office of her college program. She thought she would speak to Mary, a guidance counselor there whom she had known and felt comfortable with. Mary no longer worked for the guidance and placement office at the college. She was doing career counseling and vocational rehabilitation work on her own. Connie took down the telephone number she was given.

Feeling unnerved and disappointed and telling herself she was foolish to take this as a personal rejection, she put the number aside, thinking she would call later. Several days went by, during which she worked herself up to a fever pitch of anxiety about making the call. Many times she picked up the note with the number on it and approached the phone. Before lifting the receiver, she would mentally rehearse what to say, and time after time she would walk away, sweaty and tense, unable to formulate a suitable opening to the conversation.

For one thing, she was sure Mary would not remember her, and she would have to explain herself. Next, she was sure that once Mary understood who she was and why she was calling, her voice would take on the disappointed and critical tone that Connie so feared and was so attuned to, because Connie had failed as a geriatric social worker. She agonized over exactly what to say and how to say it, actually writing herself a script at one point. She continued to put off making the call until she was so upset and overwrought that she could hardly stand herself. Finally she dialed the number, and got Mary's voice mail.

Having for some reason expected Mary herself, Connie was flustered and relieved at the same time. She left a message, completely inconsistent with her planned speech, barely remembering to include her name and phone number. After going over in her mind every word she had said in the message, and considering calling back to clarify it, she decided to let it go. She had done what she could for the time being, and now she had only to wait, which she didn't mind doing.

Mary called back later that afternoon. Her tone was businesslike but friendly as she asked what she could do for Connie. Overcoming a rush of shame, Connie explained that she wanted to rethink her career choice. Mary did remember her; she recalled her as being earnest and diligent in the program, though exceptionally quiet. They agreed to meet in Mary's office.

At first, as they talked, Mary had a hard time understanding exactly what had gone wrong with the nursing home job. From Connie's demeanor, she had the impression that something terrible had happened there. Through careful and patient questioning, however, she began to get an accurate picture of how inappropriate a career choice Connie had made, how painful some aspects of her job were for her, and how hard she had tried to succeed.

Encouraged by Mary's interest, soothed by her quiet tone, and guided by her insightful questions, Connie described her responsibilities at the nursing home and hinted at the extent of her interpersonal difficulties and the depth of her fear. Feeling overwhelmed by her shortcomings and inadequacies, she left a great deal for Mary to surmise. She felt accepted by Mary, but still found it difficult to express herself fully.

Mary asked for Connie's psychotherapy records, which Connie agreed to release. The information she found there, especially in the initial assessment, helped Mary fill in some of the gaps in Connie's story and gain a better understanding about how to relate to her in a way that would be helpful. At their next meeting, she directed the conversation toward those aspects of Connie's job that she had enjoyed and done well. Connie was at first unable to identify any, but as she began talking about her quiet, one-on-one talks with the nursing home residents, she relaxed and became almost animated.

Mary thought it would be a shame to waste Connie's college education. Connie agreed, but she didn't see how she could make use of it, either. The idea of putting herself in a situation similar to her nursing home job again was too frightening. Mary wondered if they might be able to find, or create, a situation for Connie that would allow her to do the part of her job she found easy and nonthreatening, without the level of responsibility and the kinds of interactions she found impossible.

That idea sounded a little too self-serving for Connie to consider. She believed she had to adapt herself to other people's needs. Identifying her own, and expecting that they be met, was not something she was used to doing. She seemed to shut down and back off from Mary. She almost seemed to prefer thinking of herself as devoid of job skills and therefore unemployable. But Mary persisted, in her calm, quiet, patient, and supportive style, to ask Connie to describe the kind of job setting in which she might feel comfortable.

Ideally, Connie thought she would like to work from her home. She expressed regret about her career choice, wishing she had instead learned computer skills, word processing, or something else that would allow her to set up a home-based business. Mary pointed out that while in that situation she might be able to spend most of her time alone, she would still have to drum up business and to interact with other people to some extent, and she would have no support or encouragement in doing so.

Mary thought that working alone but in a supportive environment would suit Connie better. She said that Connie's coworkers at the nursing home had backed off from her in response to what seemed to them to be Connie's negative attitude, leaving Connie no way to bridge the isolation around her. But if instead, Mary went on, her coworkers and supervisors could provide her with ongoing reassurance and support, it might make all the difference in the world. Connie thought that such a scenario was unlikely; how could she possibly ask for that kind of support, especially at work?

But Mary didn't give up; she was relentlessly supportive. She called Connie's fear of criticism an asset, saying it made her highly motivated to do well. Because she is so meticulous and conscientious, she would be well suited to solitary work with little supervision. Her persistence and her reliability would undoubtedly improve in a situation she found comfortable, one that involved little interaction with few people, without the distraction of the public or the expectation to work as part of a team.

Mary went on to talk about how valuable nursing home work was. She reminded Connie that she had felt comfortable with and appreciated by the residents she talked to. She acknowledged that she was unlikely to find a job exactly suited to her temperament, but she wondered about the possibility of working part-time, both to reduce Connie's sense of having too much responsibility and to ease her feelings of social pressure. She offered a few contacts at nursing homes for Connie to follow up with.

By the time of their next meeting, however, Connie had taken no action. She felt at ease enough with Mary to confide that she didn't feel ready to interview. Still patient and supportive, Mary took responsibility for the oversight—she should have known, she said—and spent some time working on interviewing skills, trying to build some confidence on Connie's part. Finally, Connie was able to arrange several interviews for part-time jobs in nursing home social service departments. She was eventually hired as a social service assistant, working not as part of a team but under one supervisor. Her primary job duties involved spending time with the residents, with the expectation that she keep written records, and that she report problems, difficulties, and special needs back to her supervisor.

At Connie's request, Mary spoke to her supervisor. She explained Connie's interpersonal sensitivity, her shyness, her difficulty expressing herself, her need for approval, and her discomfort in situations where she is the focus of attention. She said that Connie generally responds well to low-key efforts of others to show understanding and to put her at ease, when she believes that they accept her. The supervisor was glad to have the information, but she said that they didn't have a lot of time to go around "holding each other's hands" at the nursing home, since they were too busy with the patients' needs. But as long as Connie stuck to business, worked the hours she was supposed to work, met with the residents as needed, and "didn't get in anyone's way," she should do fine.

Concerned that the supervisor may have misunderstood, Mary emphasized that Connie did not need any hand holding, and in fact would likely do better with a minimum of supervision. What she did need was an extra measure of sensitivity with regard to supervisory functions such as routine feedback and constructive criticism; for these to be effective and produce the desired results, Connie needed them offered in a friendly, low-key, supportive way, with an understanding of her interpersonal difficulties. Mary went on to offer her services if needed; in the event of a supervisory problem in the future, she would be glad to serve as an intermediary since she already had positive rapport with Connie.

Connie can succeed in a job that doesn't push her past her self-imposed limits. Low rather than high responsibility, little interaction, little supervision, and relatively high autonomy in a supportive atmosphere will help her stay with a job and produce solid results.

Summary: Avoidant Personality Disorder's Effect on Vocational Abilities

Level of Impairment

1. no impairment
2. mild—minimal impairment with little or no effect on ability to function
3. moderate—some impairment, which limits ability to function fully
4. serious—major impairment, which may at times preclude ability to function
5. severe—extreme impairment

Understanding and Memory

Remembers locations and basic work procedures

1____X____2_____3_____4_____5_____

Understands and remembers short, simple instructions

1____X____2_____3_____4_____5_____

Understands and remembers detailed instructions

1____X____2_____3_____4_____5_____

Concentration and Persistence

Carries out short, simple instructions

1____X____2_____3_____4_____5_____

Carries out detailed instructions

1____X____2_____3_____4_____5_____

Maintains attention and concentration for extended periods of time

1_____2____X____3_____4_____5_____

Can work within a schedule, maintain attendance, be punctual

1_____ 2___X___ 3_____ 4_____ 5_____

Sustains ordinary routine without special supervision

1_____ 2___X___ 3_____ 4_____ 5_____

Can work with or close to others without being distracted by them

1_____ 2_____ 3_____ 4_____ 5___X___

Makes simple work-related decisions

1_____ 2___X___ 3_____ 4_____ 5_____

Works quickly and efficiently, meets deadlines, even under stressful conditions

1___X___ 2_____ 3_____ 4_____ 5_____

Completes normal workday and workweek without interruptions due to symptoms

1___X___ 2_____ 3_____ 4_____ 5_____

Works at consistent pace without an unreasonable number or length of breaks

1___X___ 2_____ 3_____ 4_____ 5_____

Social Interaction

Interacts appropriately with general public

1_____ 2_____ 3___X___ 4_____ 5_____

Asks simple questions or requests assistance when necessary

1_____ 2_____ 3_____ 4_____ 5___X___

Accepts instruction and responds appropriately to criticism from supervisors

1_____ 2_____ 3_____ 4_____ 5___X___

Gets along with coworkers without distracting them

1_____ 2_____ 3___X___ 4_____ 5_____

Maintains socially appropriate behavior

1_____ 2___X___ 3_____ 4_____ 5_____

Maintains basic standards of cleanliness and grooming

1___X___ 2_____ 3_____ 4_____ 5_____

Adaptation

Responds appropriately to changes at work

1_____ 2____X____ 3_____ 4_____ 5_____

Is aware of normal work hazards and takes necessary precautions

1____X____ 2_____ 3_____ 4_____ 5_____

Can get around in unfamiliar places, can use public transportation

1____X____ 2_____ 3_____ 4_____ 5_____

Sets realistic goals, makes plans independently of others

1____X____ 2_____ 3_____ 4_____ 5 _____

Summary: Vocational Strategies and Accommodations

To optimize the chances for vocational success, a person with avoidant personality disorder needs:

- An unusually high level of support and encouragement from coworkers to help counteract feelings of personal inadequacy.
- A relatively low level of responsibility, to help prevent feeling overwhelmed and the desire to avoid some aspects of the job.
- The opportunity to work alone, not as part of a team, with little interaction expected with coworkers, the public, or others, to help accommodate social anxiety.
- Supervision and feedback that emphasizes strengths and abilities rather than problems and difficulties, because of oversensitivity to criticism.
- Help from a mental health or rehabilitation professional in explaining shyness and interpersonal sensitivities to a supervisor, to help prevent misunderstanding and misinterpretation of behavior and to help engender a supportive environment.

DEPENDENT PERSONALITY DISORDER

Dependent personality disorder is one of the most frequently reported personality disorders in mental health clinics. In clinical settings, it seems to be diagnosed more frequently in women than in men, but other studies report similar prevalence rates for men and women. The diagnosis should not be made without reference to age, gender, and cultural issues. Dependent behavior, for example, is developmentally appropriate in children and adolescents. Some societies foster dependency in women, while discouraging it in men. In some cultures, traits such as passivity, politeness, and deferential treatment are the norm and should not be confused with characteristics of dependent personality disorder. Dependent behavior constitutes a disorder to the extent that it is outside the range of the person's cultural norms or reflects unrealistic expectations (American Psychiatric Association, 1994).

Bill

Bill felt the silence in his house like a presence. His footsteps thudded unnaturally loudly as he walked from room to room switching on lights, radio, TV. In the kitchen, he found a list of instructions about how to use the dishwasher and the microwave. He found three days' worth of prepared meals in neatly labeled plastic containers in the refrigerator. He found a single place set at the kitchen table—place mat, plate, silverware, cloth napkin, milk glass turned upside down so as not to collect dust, salt and pepper shakers near at hand.

In the living room, he found the TV guide folded open to today's date. He saw that his favorite weekend shows had been marked and the times circled with the purple marking pen his mother liked to use. The remote control lay on the arm of his chair, exactly at his fingertips. The troublesome window blind behind the TV had been drawn closed for him. Bill recognized all that his mother had done to take care of him in her absence, but he could not rid himself of the deep sense of abandonment he felt. In spite of everything, her annual trip to visit her sister still hurt his feelings.

What Dependent Personality Disorder Is Like

- Need to be taken care of
- Passive, submissive, unassertive, defers to others
- Low self-esteem, fearful of losing support
- Easily exploited

Need to be taken care of. Bill is 45 years old. He moved back to his mother's house 20 years ago after his brief marriage failed. Bill loved his wife, and he felt that he needed her. He wanted her with him all the time. He was reluctant to take on even routine tasks without her advice. He relied on her to make decisions not only about their life together, but also about how he should spend his leisure time, what clothes he should put on in the morning, and whether he should stop for gas on the way to or from the shopping mall. After just three months of marriage, they were in therapy to work on his dependency issues.

Bill tried hard to please both the therapist and his wife. He went out of his way to be accommodating. He rearranged his work schedule as needed, sometimes with great difficulty, so they could meet every week. When the therapist defined Bill's childhood as abusive, he supplied details supporting that view, though he did not think he had been abused, and some of the "memories" he produced in his effort to be agreeable stretched the truth considerably. He readily participated in relationship-building exercises; he was loving, supportive, open, communicative, and said he was willing to change. He balked only when the subject of his dependency on his wife arose. Then, he became tearful, begged his wife not to criticize him, and pleaded with the therapist to help him. His wife filed for divorce within a year.

Devastated, Bill saw no recourse but to return to his mother's house. He was terrified of being abandoned again, and he resigned himself to his mother's sharp tongue and relentless faultfinding in exchange for the security of his childhood home. Despite painful memories—his father's death in a car crash when Bill was 11, his older brother's bitterness and eventual dissipation into drugs, his mother's unresolved grief and taut emotional distance—home felt safe.

His mother had not favored his marriage, had predicted its failure, had ridiculed his attempt to leave her protection, and had gloated upon his return home. But she was willing to take care of him. In return, he took her to the doctor, helped her with housework, put up with her constant criticism, jollied her out of her crabby moods, and gave up his own social life to be with her. He didn't think it was a fair trade-off, and he felt resentful, but he saw no alternative.

Bill continued in individual psychotherapy after his marriage broke up. First he saw the same therapist he and his wife had seen, but she declared him cured after a year and a half and cheerily sent him on his way. Bewildered and hurt and feeling far from cured, Bill found another therapist. She saw him for two years; then she left the field for a new career. Bill found still another therapist. He participated in group therapy, assertiveness training, self-esteem building, ongoing support groups, and programs designed to help him take charge of his life. He tried different psychotherapeutic approaches: Jungian analysis, Gestalt therapy, cognitive-behavioral therapy. After 20 years, however, he is still in therapy, and still feels that he needs it.

Passive, submissive, unassertive, defers to others. Bill does not make decisions on his own. He turns to his mother, his therapist, his boss, or his support group members for guidance and direction. He assumes that they know more than he does, and he listens attentively, sometimes taking notes, as one or another of them tells him how he feels, what he thinks, what he needs, and what he should do. He abides by their advice, or tries to, unless it involves taking some independent action, in which case he becomes prickly and resentful.

He defers to his mother's taste in music, TV shows, sporting events, and politics. He holds few opinions of his own and rarely expresses them. He submits to her household rules unquestioningly: he comes directly home from work, he doesn't bring home unexpected guests, he keeps his room neat and tidy, he takes his shoes off at the door, he leaves the toilet seat down, and he doesn't answer the phone after 10:00 at night. He does not react to her criticism, and he attempts to comply with her sometimes unreasonable demands. He stopped seeing a woman he met in his support group after two dates, though he liked her quite a lot and the feeling seemed to be mutual, because his mother complained about being left alone in the evenings.

Bill works as an assistant chef in an elegant restaurant in a large hotel. He started as a dishwasher when he was 16 and has been a steady and reliable employee ever since. Recently, the hotel was bought out by a large corporation, which plans to change the character of the restaurant, automate the kitchen, and eliminate Bill's job.

Considering Bill's nearly 30 years of service to the hotel, his boss thought he deserved better than to be simply let go. He offered to help Bill arrange a meeting with the new vice-president. Bill's mother thought they should hire a lawyer and sue. His therapist encouraged Bill to empower himself by confronting the new management. Bill preferred the advice of his support group; the members sympathized with him, shook their heads, and said that life's unfair and there's not much you can do about it.

Low self-esteem, fearful of losing support. Bill is convinced that he cannot function adequately on his own. He places pleasing others above all else in importance, fearful that otherwise he will lose the support he requires. He feels incompetent without someone standing next to him telling him he is doing OK. He is willing to give virtually anyone authority in his life; he attributes expertise in diagnostic medicine to the check-out clerk at the drug store and superior interpersonal insight to his barber. He constantly asks their advice and that of many other people he encounters. He does his best to express his appreciation and to cultivate and maintain pleasant relationships, in order to get what he needs from others.

Important as the advice and support of casual acquaintances is to Bill, he is most concerned about the relationships he relies on: his current therapist, his boss, and his mother. Displeasing any of them in any way is a frightening prospect for Bill, although one he is not always able to avoid. His situation at work is especially stressful because his inability to stand up for himself has disappointed all of them. His solution is to fall back on his claims of incompetence and beg others to take care of him because he is too overwhelmed to cope with anything.

Easily exploited. Bill's dependency needs make him vulnerable to exploitation by others. Sometimes, he is a willing if resentful participant, as in his relationship with his mother. Other times, he may be simply duped. Neighbors, coworkers, support group members, or anyone he has come to know, feel free to borrow money, tools, equipment, even clothes, from him. He is willing to lend and unwilling to ask for the return of his things; he may or may not get them back. People ask him to help them move, to baby-sit their kids or care for their dogs, to mow their lawns when they are out of town, to pick them up when they've had a little too much to drink, and on and on. They rarely offer to reciprocate, and Bill rarely asks them to.

He does all these things and more, in the belief that he is thereby earning the support he needs from the people in his life. He might come to realize that he has made a poor trade and to feel badly let down and deeply resentful. But rather than change his behavior, ask for what he wants from others, or end a relationship, he is more likely to redouble his efforts to please. He rarely turns down panhandlers or door-to-door salespeople, and he has difficulty refusing telephone solicitors; he does so only with a flurry of polite apologies. He is vulnerable to scams and frauds, and he once contributed a sizable amount of money over several months to a phony charity because he didn't want to offend the person who came to his door.

Dependent Personality Disorder's Effect at Work

- Excellent employee when feeling adequately supported
- Seeks reassurance
- Self-presentation as incompetent may be annoying to others
- Unassertive with coworkers and supervisors

Excellent employee when feeling adequately supported. Bill has no formal training as a chef, but he worked hard to learn his trade, and he does a good job. What he lacks in creativity and flair he makes up in solid, reliable service. He has won awards for attendance and punctuality, for longevity, for best attitude, and for service to the organization. He has a genuine desire to please the diners in the restaurant as well as the management of the hotel and his boss, the head chef.

He has a special talent, the ability to mollify even the most unreasonable customers. Listening to complaints from diners and offering pleasing solutions was a task the entire restaurant staff was happy to hand over to him. He was happy to do it, along with other unusual tasks and special assignments that came up from time to time. Bill rarely refused any request. He was never late, he seldom missed a day, he always had a smile and a greeting, and he didn't complain.

Bill thought his job rested on a kind of bargain: the hotel would continue to take care of him as long as he continued to please everyone. He worried about keeping up his end of the deal and tried his best to do so; the sense of betrayal he felt on being abandoned anyway was profound. Losing his job confirmed his deepest sense of himself: that he is incompetent, that he needs others to take care of him, and that his ability to acquire the necessary level of care is precarious, a fact he deeply resents.

After learning that his job would be eliminated, Bill's attitude at work changed. He became depressed and frequently irritable. He often called in sick. He felt anxious, unable to concentrate. He made mistakes and balked at correcting them or dealing with their effects. He felt that nothing he did was adequate or acceptable, and that no effort he made would solve his problems. He felt helpless and hopeless, resentful, angry, and bitter. Even with his boss's help, he couldn't imagine standing up for himself with the new management. He felt incapable of any effort on his own behalf and also couldn't imagine finding another job.

Seeks reassurance. Bill's position in the restaurant was never stressfree. From the beginning, he felt he was on thin ice, undeserving of the position he had, and he sought reassurance at every turn. His boss, who had been at the restaurant even longer than Bill had, took an interest in him early on. He elevated Bill from dishwasher to kitchen helper, taught him and coached him, and eventually promoted him to assistant chef. He was sometimes testy in response to Bill's constant needs and questions, especially after nearly 30 years of working together, but he enjoyed his role as mentor and was generally willing to allow Bill to depend on him.

Self-presentation as incompetent may be annoying to others. Problems arose, however, if his boss was gone, busy, or unavailable. Then, Bill's fears would often take over, and he might become flustered and nearly paralyzed unless other members of the kitchen staff stood by to help him out. They were for the most part far less indulgent than their boss. As assistant chef, Bill was their supervisor on the shift, and they resented his indecisiveness and his refusal to take charge, especially when the restaurant was busy and orders had to be filled fast. They saw him fulfill all the expectations of his job smoothly and well when his boss was at his side, and his sudden floundering when on his own seemed like a manipulative ploy.

Unassertive with coworkers and supervisors. Bill was unlikely to make requests of the people he worked with. If he needed help on a task, he would usually attempt to do it alone, hoping someone would notice and come to his assistance. More than once, he spilled or broke things, causing extra work for himself and others, when a simple request for help could have prevented it. If he wanted a particular day off, he would hint around, hoping his boss would catch on. Each year he took a short vacation in the fall to work on his house and yard; he never once asked for it directly, but instead began to talk about cleaning his gutters, painting his fence, washing his windows, fertilizing his lawn, and so on, until his boss asked if he wanted a few days off.

He rarely expressed interpersonal needs or negative feelings. If he felt angry, resentful, or let down in some way, he would retreat into a cold silence and deny the feelings if asked directly. If he sensed a coworker's annoyance, he would avoid that person rather than ask what the problem was and how it could be solved. He knew that his coworkers let him take on the tasks that no one else wanted, and for the most part he didn't mind. He would work extra shifts, fill in for people on a moment's notice, even cover for someone who was late from a break or who wanted to leave early. He thought that these things were expected, even required, of him, but sometimes he felt overworked and underappreciated. Still, he would not assert himself, either to refuse a task or to ask for thanks for it.

Working with Dependent Personality Disorder

To the extent that he is expected to function as an autonomous and independent adult, Bill has problems. But the trade-off he is willing to make—compliant attitude and desire to please in exchange for ongoing care and support—can create an excellent situation for both him and an employer, and in fact worked quite well for nearly 30 years. He is a loyal employee, hardworking, dependable, agreeable, willing to take direction, and easy to supervise, unless the level of support he requires is withdrawn.

Concerned over what would happen to Bill and convinced that he was unlikely to take action for himself, Bill's boss approached the new hotel management on his behalf. He showed them Bill's work history, performance reviews, and the employee awards he had received over the years. He praised Bill's social skills and his ability to work well with the public. He asked if a place couldn't be found for Bill in the new organization. The new manager expressed regret. He said that with the new restaurant format, he did not have enough staff positions available to allow him to keep Bill on. He offered severance pay and out-placement services.

Bill was grateful to his boss. He didn't want to change jobs, and he was extremely nervous about his ability to do adequate work for anyone else, but he found the idea of out-placement services comforting; at least he would have some help and support through a difficult transition. He scheduled an appointment with Rick, the out-placement counselor, as soon as he could.

Bill felt comfortable and at ease in the recipient role of a helping relationship. He approached the meeting with his characteristic obsequious, pleasant manner. His one concern had to do with how much would be expected of him and to what extent he would be asked to function independently. It was a concern he felt each time he started a new psychotherapy relationship, and he made small distinction between out-placement services and psychotherapy. He therefore set out to show Rick how inadequate and limited his abilities were and how much help he would need.

Lack of self-confidence is fundamental to Bill's personality. Still, he does better than he thinks he can and quite a bit better than he says he can. His performance on specific tasks is at least adequate and often exemplary. Looking at his work history, his awards, and his performance reviews, Rick was mystified by his presentation as helpless and incompetent. Used to working with ambitious people who, if anything, inflated their abilities, Rick didn't know what to make of Bill, who seemed to be deliberately trying to look less able than he was.

Bill disclosed that he was in therapy, and suggested that it might be useful for Rick to talk to his therapist. Rick followed up but found the conversation not as informative as he had hoped. The therapist said that Bill was recovering from a bad childhood. He had problems in his relationship with his mother. He needed to expand his social life. The therapist knew little of Bill's work life. She mentioned that he had dependency issues but did not regard them as central. She was treating him for chronic mild depression and had been for the past three years.

This information did not provide Rick with a satisfactory explanation of the divergence between Bill's low self-concept and his relative success as an employee. He still felt unclear about what kinds of vocational help Bill could best make use of and what method of working with him would be most effective. His initial approach had been to encourage Bill to use this opportunity to advance his career, to move forward, perhaps into a head chef position. Rick had even been excited about Bill's prospects, thinking that with an employment record like his, a good placement, beneficial to everyone, would be easy to find. But Bill continued to present himself as incapable of advancing his career, or even of preparing a résumé and conducting job interviews without significant help from Rick. He responded with resentful denials to Rick's efforts to encourage him and bolster his self-confidence.

Rick consulted a psychologist he sometimes worked with. He thought that a psychological evaluation might help him in working with Bill. The psychologist agreed, but asked if, given all his years of psychotherapy, such an evaluation did not already exist in Bill's records. When Rick asked him, Bill said that it did not. He had once taken a personality test, and the results had been passed on to subsequent therapists, but he had never had a formal evaluation. He readily agreed to do so.

After reading the psychological report, which included a diagnosis of dependent personality disorder and a description of its effects, Rick changed his approach to Bill and Bill's situation. He still believed that Bill could find a good job, commensurate with his years of experience and his worth as an employee, but he saw that getting Bill to seek and then accept such a position would be harder than he had at first anticipated. He stopped talking about advancing Bill's career and talked instead about finding a job Bill could do. He switched from a "you can do it," empowering approach to a hands-on, supportive, sympathetic, gently reassuring approach. Their relationship improved immediately, and Rick found Bill much more willing to take part in the process.

They worked on a résumé. As they discussed its format and content, Bill took notes, so he could be sure to use the exact words and phrases that Rick mentioned. They worked on interviewing skills, doing role play after role play until Bill felt he had memorized and could reliably repeat the appropriate attitude, facial expression, and wording of questions and responses. He asked if Rick would accompany him on job interviews, at least the first few. Rick refused, explaining that his presence would do nothing to help Bill get hired. Bill was hurt, however, and his abandonment fears were triggered. Their relationship suffered a temporary set-back until Rick offered to be available by phone on the days Bill had interviews scheduled.

They had also been researching job possibilities. Bill liked his old job and wanted to do something similar. Rick agreed that a service-oriented field such as restaurant work was a good match. Bill's desire to please others, which for him was almost a survival skill, helped him perform well. Rick saw that such a setting could easily backfire, however, if Bill should feel that he was not getting adequate support, reassurance, recognition, and direction from supervisors and coworkers. He would resent doing for others if he felt that he was not getting what he needed for himself.

Likewise, he could be a good team member, very concerned about doing his part, keeping things running smoothly, and keeping relationships strong. But since his primary motivation has to do with meeting his dependency needs, his anxiety and resentment would sabotage his efforts to do well if the expected payoff were not forthcoming.

As he began interviewing, Bill's primary concern was whether or not the place was "nice," by which he meant not the quality of the restaurant but the nature of the staff. He had many opportunities, but often the job didn't fit well with his personality and his emotional needs. He turned down a job that would require him to take on the duties of head chef from time to time. He refused even to interview for a job as assistant chef at a famous French restaurant, because he had heard that the head chef was a tyrant who drove his staff hard.

Eventually, he accepted a job as an assistant chef at a country club. The club was large, with two restaurants and a snack bar. Many staff members had worked there for 20 years or longer, and it had a family-like feel that Bill found comforting. The restaurant staff was organized into teams, each with specified responsibilities and a designated team leader. As assistant chef, his job included interaction with wait staff and with club members as needed, as well as kitchen duties. His team leader was the head chef.

Bill easily took to the setting. He wanted his teammates to like him, so he worked hard, and he was pleasant and accommodating. He wanted the club membership to like him, so he was friendly and helpful, he made it a point to learn names and menu preferences, and he provided extra services whenever he could. After several weeks on the job, he called Rick and asked to meet with him again to talk about how he was doing.

He was doing quite well. He liked the club, and he liked his job. For the most part he liked the management and his coworkers. He was concerned, however, about receiving the kind of ongoing support he felt he needed. He said that everyone had been very helpful to him in the beginning, but now they seemed to feel he should know his way around, and they didn't seem as caring and understanding anymore. Rick assured him that was nothing personal; it was the normal way things were in a work setting. He reassured Bill that he could function just fine, and that soon he would feel just as comfortable as he had in his old job. Seeing that Bill was unconvinced, he also offered to call Bill's team leader to provide suggestions for helping Bill contribute his full potential.

Rick explained that while Bill obviously has great value as an employee, he lacks self-confidence, and he needs an unusually high level of emotional support and reassurance. In the absence of such support, he could still do acceptable work, but his feelings of abandonment and betrayal might cause significant interpersonal problems in the workplace.

If his team members could understand and accept him, while simultaneously helping him to increase his independence, Bill would be a loyal and dedicated employee. Ongoing reassurance that he is doing a good job, frequent recognition of his achievements, companionship and teamwork in accomplishing tasks, straightforward help in making decisions, instruction, direction, and guidance—these kinds of supervisory techniques will help him do his best. Frequent supervisory meetings, with the goal of encouraging Bill to be more assertive and keeping him informed about how he is doing and what he needs to do to do his job well, would also be useful. The expectation of full independence and autonomy, on the other hand, would place an unmanageable burden on him and lead to dissatisfaction and possibly failure.

Summary: Dependent Personality Disorder's Effect on Vocational Abilities

Level of Impairment

1. no impairment
2. mild—minimal impairment with little or no effect on ability to function
3. moderate—some impairment, which limits ability to function fully
4. serious—major impairment, which may at times preclude ability to function
5. severe—extreme impairment

Understanding and Memory

Remembers locations and basic work procedures

1_____X_____ 2_____ 3_____ 4_____ 5_____

Understands and remembers short, simple instructions

1_____X_____ 2_____ 3_____ 4_____ 5_____

Understands and remembers detailed instructions

1_____X_____ 2_____ 3_____ 4_____ 5_____

Concentration and Persistence

Carries out short, simple instructions

1_____X_____ 2_____ 3_____ 4_____ 5_____

Carries out detailed instructions

1_____X_____ 2_____ 3_____ 4_____ 5_____

Maintains attention and concentration for extended periods of time

1_____X_____ 2_____ 3_____ 4_____ 5_____

Can work within a schedule, maintain attendance, be punctual

1_____X_____ 2_____ 3_____ 4_____ 5_____

Sustains ordinary routine without special supervision

1_____ 2_____ 3_____X_____ 4_____ 5_____

Can work with or close to others without being distracted by them

1_____X_____ 2_____ 3_____ 4_____ 5_____

Makes simple work-related decisions

1_____ 2_____ 3_____X_____ 4_____ 5_____

Works quickly and efficiently, meets deadlines, even under stressful conditions

1_____ 2_____ 3_____X_____ 4_____ 5_____

Completes normal workday and workweek without interruptions due to symptoms

1_____X_____ 2_____ 3_____ 4_____ 5_____

Works at consistent pace without an unreasonable number or length of breaks

1_____X_____2_____3_____4_____5_____

Social Interaction

Interacts appropriately with general public

1_____X_____2_____3_____4_____5_____

Asks simple questions or requests assistance when necessary

1_____2_____X_____3_____4_____5_____

Accepts instruction and responds appropriately to criticism from supervisors

1_____2_____X_____3_____4_____5_____

Gets along with coworkers without distracting them

1_____2_____X_____3_____4_____5_____

Maintains socially appropriate behavior

1_____2_____X_____3_____4_____5_____

Maintains basic standards of cleanliness and grooming

1_____X_____2_____3_____4_____5_____

Adaptation

Responds appropriately to changes at work

1_____2_____3_____X_____4_____5_____

Is aware of normal work hazards and takes necessary precautions

1_____X_____2_____3_____4_____5_____

Can get around in unfamiliar places, can use public transportation

1_____X_____2_____3_____4_____5_____

Sets realistic goals, makes plans independently of others

1_____2_____3_____4_____5_____X_____

Summary: Vocational Strategies and Accommodations

To optimize the chances for vocational success, a person with dependent personality disorder needs:

- An unusual level of emotional support, reassurance, and recognition of work well done, to offset feelings of low self-confidence.
- The opportunity to work as part of a team, not alone, to help offset fears of abandonment and feelings of inadequacy.
- Little expectation of functioning independently or autonomously, to avoid triggering feelings of abandonment or resentment.
- Encouragement to be as assertive as possible in requesting appropriate help in accomplishing work-related tasks.
- Help from a mental health or vocational rehabilitation professional in explaining interpersonal needs to supervisors and coworkers, in order to avoid misunderstanding and misinterpretation of behavior and to ensure optimal vocational performance.

OBSESSIVE-COMPULSIVE PERSONALITY DISORDER

Many characteristics of obsessive-compulsive personality disorder—time urgency, competitiveness, or hostility, for example—are the same as those that define "type A" personality, and are also present in people at risk for heart attacks. People with obsessive-compulsive personality disorder may also have mood or anxiety disorders. While some studies have shown an association with obsessive-compulsive disorder, listed as an anxiety disorder, most people who have obsessive-compulsive disorder do not show a behavior pattern consistent with obsessive-compulsive personality disorder. The disorder is diagnosed about twice as often in men as in women. It should not necessarily be diagnosed in members of cultures that place a great deal of emphasis on work and productivity, even if some behaviors seem to warrant it. Prevalence of obsessive-compulsive personality disorder is about 1% in community samples and about 3%–10% in people who go to mental health clinics (American Psychiatric Association, 1994).

Judy

Judy tapped the sharp point of her pencil on the page of neatly written notes in front of her, reading them over carefully for the third or fourth time to be sure of their contents. Twin creases of worry and annoyance furrowed her brow. Her mouth was drawn into a tight little frown. She glanced nervously around the table at a group consisting of five of her neighbors and their representative on a city planning committee. They were meeting informally to generate ideas regarding a parking problem in their neighborhood.

Judy's notes on the subject were arranged in perfect outline form. No one else had notes. The city planning person arrived late. The hostess served coffee and donuts first thing, so crumbs and napkins littered the table. Twenty minutes into the scheduled time, no one had addressed the issue at hand. Finally the meeting began, in what seemed to Judy a disorganized and overly casual manner.

She continued to tap her pencil. She cleared her throat. The lack of proper procedure made her nervous. The level of informality irritated her. She regretted that she hadn't made copies of her outline for everyone, but she decided to plunge ahead anyway. She interrupted the freewheeling, laughter-filled discussion to elucidate her first point. She was about to cover the supporting points, when someone raised a concern about lighting in the alleys, a topic that seemed to Judy to be completely unrelated and off the subject. Still, it led to a lively conversation, which somehow produced several viable solutions to the parking problem. The city planning representative was especially excited, saying that these were the kinds of ideas that would help his committee do a good job.

Feeling as she did that some sort of order must prevail, Judy felt forced to intervene again. She asked if she may have the floor, then proceeded to read every point on her outline. She went on to suggest a task-force to study how other neighborhoods and other cities dealt with similar problems. She offered to prepare a historical overview of the parking situation and asked if someone could procure a detailed map of the community. She said that once the data were in, they could begin to consider solutions. Looking around at the now silent group, she declared the meeting adjourned with a final tap of her pencil.

What Obsessive-Compulsive Personality Disorder Is Like

- Perfectionistic and inflexible
- Preoccupied with order and control
- Detail oriented, excessive checking for mistakes
- Indecisive

Perfectionistic and inflexible. Judy has definite ideas about how a meeting should be conducted, as she has about everything in life. An informal discussion at a table littered with donut crumbs does not fit her definition of a meeting, nor can she give credence to the outcome of any such discussion. The fact that her neighbors had generated an impressive list of possible solutions to a prickly problem without benefit of parliamentary procedure was beyond her ability to grasp; to her, the process must adhere to a prescribed format and cover every possible eventuality.

Judy lives according to the belief passed on to her by her father that perfection is not only achievable in all things, it is required. She is aware that others for the most part do not share this belief, which makes her very anxious. Her need to control her environment supersedes any other needs she may have. Deviating from tried and true methods, leaving stones unturned, cutting corners, "going with the flow," having fun, "getting loose," trusting creativity over logic: all of these seem to her to be dangerous practices. She believes in one right way of doing things, and she does not deviate from it nor, to the extent possible, does she allow others to deviate from it.

Preoccupied with order and control. Judy is likely to try to take charge of any situation she is in because she does not trust others to do things right. She dislikes uncertainty, and placing herself in control helps reduce it. She likes to know what the rules are, she expects to follow them, and she expects everyone else to follow them too. She suppresses emotional needs and even bodily needs in favor of following a schedule and sticking to a routine.

The clothes in her closet are organized by season, color, style, and function. Her kitchen drawers and cupboards are labeled with small, neat signs listing their contents in the order most often used. She brings her car in for servicing on the second Tuesday of February, May, August, and November. She gets up at the same time every morning, works out for exactly 20 minutes on her exercise bicycle, showers, reads the paper, eats a bowl of cereal and an orange, and gets dressed. Changes in her routine—if, for example, her paper is late—make her anxious and angry and can ruin her day.

Judy is 32 years old. She has never married, and she has had few close relationships. She lives alone in a small, neat house she bought with her father's help. She has a degree in business administration. She worked for seven years in a middle-management position in the marketing division of a large food manufacturing corporation. She was recently laid off in what the company called a "temporary downsizing," but her supervisor made it clear in her exit interview that she would not be hired back.

In many ways she performed well at work. However, her insistence on doing things her own way and her rigid noncompliance with changes in management style the company wanted to initiate made her hard to work with. Furthermore, she worked in a division that required quick responses to unpredictable market forces, and her slow, methodical, conventional, noncreative approach was a liability.

Judy was stunned and deeply distressed by the layoff, and as a result felt even more urgently the need to control her life and her environment. She took advantage of an offer of individual psychotherapy her company made as part of her transition out, but she did not find it useful. She felt that the therapist's credentials were insufficient. She didn't think he took enough time to understand fully the details related to her employment and her layoff. He wanted her to talk about her anger and sadness, and he seemed uninterested in her thorough explanation of the facts. When he asked her to come to their sessions without pages of notes about material she wanted to cover, she quit going.

Detail oriented, excessive checking for mistakes. Judy's concern with minutiae prevents her from fully participating in life; she would rather keep her kitchen cupboards orderly, for example, than use their contents to cook a good meal. She is likely to lose sight of a goal as she gets bogged down in the steps toward it. She focuses on dotted i's and crossed t's to the exclusion of sentences and paragraphs. Small details are manageable, as Judy sees it, while the large picture is not. Nevertheless, the small details sometimes overwhelm her.

The possibility of making a mistake, even a minor and inconsequential mistake, worries Judy to a considerable extent. On the rare occasions when her bank statement does not agree exactly with her check register, she won't make an adjustment even for an amount of a few cents but searches until she finds the discrepancy and corrects it. At work, every project she ever took part in was subject to incessant checking at every level for the elusive hidden error; her initial effort was so thorough and laborious that she rarely found any mistakes, but she never gave up the search.

Indecisive. Judy has great difficulty making decisions, because she can see endless alternatives and a great swarm of potential problems around each. Should she go to a movie on Saturday afternoon, or would that be a waste of time? She might decide to go, then wonder if she made the right decision. Should she spend her money on one movie when another might be superior? How will she know if the critics were right if she doesn't see the movie? Did she read the right reviews? Who decides which movies are worth seeing, anyway? Movie critics? Or should it be her, the audience, since she knows what she likes? Or does she? If she stays home, she might miss her chance to see the movie. Would that be a good thing, or would she regret it? What would she do instead? Should she begin her spring yard work, or is it too early in the season? Does raking early damage the grass? Does raking late? Which is better? How can she know for sure? And so on. Judy faces some version of this internal dialogue virtually every time she makes a decision.

Obsessive-Compulsive Personality Disorder's Effect at Work

- Hard worker, good employee
- Slow pace
- Formal, strained relationships
- Rigid, inflexible, rule-bound

Hard worker, good employee. Despite her interpersonal flaws, Judy has the capability of being an excellent employee. She is reliable, dependable, and conscientious in the extreme. She is devoted to her work to the exclusion of all diversions. She is tireless in her pursuit of excellence, and she strives for perfection in the belief that she can and should achieve it. All through high school and college, she pushed herself beyond ordinary limits of endurance to earn an A average, though her scores on standardized tests showed her to be less intellectually gifted than many of her peers.

At her job, she made it her business to attend to every detail of every project her department was assigned. She developed a management style designed to get the results she wanted from her supervisees. She would not accept shoddy work or halfhearted effort. She came in early and left late. She rarely took a lunch break. She never missed a day. She took her vacation time only when she had accumulated so much that she was in danger of losing it.

Slow pace. There were drawbacks, however. Her perfectionism and her dread of mistakes required her to work at a pace much slower than upper management needed from her department. Despite her long hours on the job, she frequently missed deadlines. The exemplary quality of her work did not make up for her delay in completing it, and her supervisor was constantly under pressure to get her to work faster. She was unable to do so. Even when the needs of the company were clearly spelled out to her—in many cases, speed was considered more valuable than high-quality efforts—she could not let go of her perfectionist approach. Further, she became angry and resentful at what she experienced as intrusion and interference.

Formal, strained relationships. Judy doesn't relax with other people, even in social situations. She doesn't laugh, chat, or engage in small talk. Her work is her only real interest, and she defines her work in narrow, constricted terms. Her need to control her environment extends to her interactions with other people; she prefers a stiff, formal, predictable exchange to the usual give-and-take of conversation. Her ambivalence and her indecisiveness constantly call into question other people's sincerity, trustworthiness, integrity, and capability. She is never sure if interacting with them at all is worth her time. For coworkers, supervisors, and supervisees, talking with Judy was an unpleasant fact of working life.

Rigid, inflexible, rule-bound. At the time of her layoff, Judy's company was in the midst of restructuring and redesigning the way work was assigned and accomplished. The traditional management hierarchy no longer fit the company's needs nor its image of itself. It strove instead for a more horizontal structure, based on a collaborative model, in which employees were encouraged to express and implement their ideas, to discover and focus on their range of expertise, and to use techniques such as brainstorming and imaging for the free exchange of thoughts.

Judy's department received new office furniture, arranged in such a way that the work teams could easily interact with each other. Judy's work station was moved from what she considered its place of respectable distance from those who worked under her, to the middle of everything. She found the hubbub of teamwork in progress distracting. She felt out of control and anxious, and she took what measures she could to limit the extent and nature of the interactions that took place around her.

Despite revised management guidelines and a series of training sessions to help accomplish them, she insisted on using the standard supervisory techniques she learned in college. She continued to require that all communication be submitted in memo form to her, and she continued to parcel out tasks without regard to employees' newly identified skills and abilities. Judy's inflexibility, her unwillingness to consider new methods, her rigid adherence to old rules, and her flouting of authority in favor of doing things her way were the major causes of her dismissal.

Working with Obsessive-Compulsive Personality Disorder

For Judy, the balance of perfection and necessity is so delicate as to be nearly unattainable; she might tweak here and nip there forever, never completing anything, because nothing is ever quite good enough. She can't reconcile herself to the flaws or uncertainty of real life. She can't fully understand situations or circumstances because she is entangled in their details. She can't resolve arguments or concede points because of the possibility that she might have overlooked some angle or nuance. She is a prisoner of her own need for order and control. She could not adapt to the kinds of changes required in her job.

She had quite a bit of money saved and had made some prudent investments, and, with her severance pay, she thought she could manage financially for several months while she considered her options. Her transition package included out-placement services, but Judy had lost trust in the company, and she declined to use them. She doubted the value of any such services, but she also didn't want to leave herself at a disadvantage. Accordingly, she called all the career consultants and vocational counselors she found listed in the Yellow Pages. She asked each a prepared set of questions about his or her training and experience, areas of specialization, methods of working, interpersonal preferences, and convenience of office location. In this way she gathered a great deal of information about career counseling, but she was unsure how to organize it or make use of it for herself. She labeled her notes and filed them for future reference.

Judy considered herself an exemplary employee who had been misunderstood and mistreated by her employer. She recognized, however, that many aspects of her former job presented unusual challenges to someone with her high performance standards and her personality style. That values such as creativity and speed took precedence over high-quality, error-free results had always annoyed her, as had her department's lack of interest in her opinion on the matter and its constant pressure on her to provide what she considered careless work quickly. The high level of interpersonal interaction, both social and work-related, had been difficult and distracting for her, and she knew she had not always responded appropriately to coworkers or supervisors.

Her father had steered her toward a business degree and in fact had made her decision for her when she expressed ambivalence. Once committed, she never questioned her choice. She had always been drawn, however, to the scientific and the technical fields where she believed an ability to focus on details would be more highly valued and understood. Her father, who was still very much involved in her life, agreed that she had been treated poorly by her former employer, but he saw no reason for her to change career paths. The business world is a cutthroat environment, he counseled her. Only the strong survive and she was one of the strong. She should cut her losses, forge ahead, seize the opportunity, and make the situation work for her.

Judy listened to her father's advice, but she also wanted to explore vocational possibilities outside of the business world, in the hopes of finding a setting more suited to her capabilities. She was concerned about provoking her father's disapproval, and she was also hampered by her fear of uncertainty and by her habitual indecisiveness. In an effort to gain a sense of control, she wrote down, in outline form, as clearly as she could, the issues she was faced with and some ideas for dealing with them. She needed to convince her father that a career change might be a good thing, she needed to understand the job market in the fields that interested her, and she probably needed retraining.

She then listed all of the colleges, universities, and technical schools in her area. She requested course catalogues, studied these for appropriate programs, noted those she found, and made appointments to meet with the program heads. In each interview, she asked her prepared questions and took careful notes, which she then labeled and filed. Again, she gathered a great deal of information but didn't know what to do with it. Her anxiety increased as she completed the interviews on her list; soon her information-gathering phase would be complete, and she would have to begin a decision-making phase. She felt very far from being able to make a decision.

One of her last meetings was with the head of a Bachelor of Science program in aeronautics safety. The field didn't especially interest her, but she found herself feeling at ease with Derrick, the program head. Judy rarely felt at ease with anyone. With uncharacteristic spontaneity, fueled to some extent by anxiety, she told him about her business background, her frustrations with her old job, her conflict with regard to the direction her career should take, her uncertainty, her difficulty making decisions. She even mentioned her father's opinion that she should stay in a business career and her desire to avoid antagonizing him.

Derrick listened thoughtfully and sympathetically. Based on his conversation with her, and on his observation of her habits and behavior, he believed that Judy was a natural for his program. He thought she was likely to be a conscientious student who would move on to a technical position in an aeronautics firm, an independent consulting or inspection company, or the government, and be a credit to him and his program. But he understood her need to consider all possibilities, and he didn't want to rush her into a decision.

He also wanted to know more about her interests and abilities and her educational and employment history. He therefore suggested that her next step might be to seek vocational counseling. He recommended a counselor who worked through the technical college and offered to arrange an appointment.

Judy thought she should arrange her own appointment. She went home and checked her notes on vocational counselors. She found the name Derrick had given her and saw that her notes indicated her telephone interaction had been favorable. She scheduled an appointment for interest and aptitude testing. The results were quite clear in some ways. First, Judy should not be in a field that requires speedy decisions, quick action, or hastily scraped together projects. One that relies instead on careful consideration of all factors, methodical sifting of all information, and vigilant attention to all possible permutations would make use of her strengths and not tax her weaknesses.

Further, her interpersonal style does not lend itself to dealing with the public. She tends to approach others with a formal, distant style that can appear standoffish and unfriendly, and she does not value or enjoy interpersonal interactions no matter what their purpose. Collaboration and cooperation do not come naturally to her, but she can work adequately on a team in a role that suits her. She has no desire to sabotage relationships or undermine the work at hand, only to reduce uncertainty and to cover all the bases. If a team can allow her enough individual control so she isn't anxious or angry, she can be a positive, contributing member of it.

She feels driven to work hard and to produce excellent results. She was an above-average student, not because of innate ability, but because she pushed herself to capacity. But meeting deadlines was always a problem; in school, she agonized over turning in less-than-perfect assignments on time or turning in more perfect versions late, knowing her grade would be reduced accordingly. At work, she faced the same dilemma, but the stakes were higher. With some guidance in coping with her perfectionism and directing it properly, it could be an asset and not a liability.

Likewise, she is amenable to supervision if it is offered in a way that triggers her strengths and not her anxiety. She likes to "improve" upon assignments she is given; if a supervisor values her attention to detail, her low error rate, and her desire for order and predictability, and puts her in a role that highlights those skills, she can be an excellent employee.

After meeting with Judy to discuss these and other testing results, the vocational counselor offered to pass them on to Derrick. Judy agreed. Though initially not drawn to the field of aeronautic safety, she had in the meantime studied the vocational possibilities there and felt that it might be a good fit for her. Once she had done enough research to feel reasonably confident of her ability to discuss it, she expressed her interest to her father. She needed not only his emotional support to make a career change, but also his financial support to complete the training program. Her father surprised her by being amenable to the idea. He pointed out that she could still make use of her business background and that her management and marketing experience could be an asset in the new field.

Accordingly, after completing an application process and meeting several more times with Derrick to discuss various aspects of the program and what she would gain from it, Judy enrolled. She found the work difficult, especially at first. But, unlike her experience while working toward her business degree, she felt that she fit in. She did well, and after completing the program she was hired as an analyst for a company that offered safety inspection and crash analysis to small airlines.

Summary: Obsessive-Compulsive Personality Disorder's Effect on Vocational Abilities

Level of Impairment

1. no impairment
2. mild—minimal impairment with little or no effect on ability to function
3. moderate—some impairment, which limits ability to function fully
4. serious—major impairment, which may at times preclude ability to function
5. severe—extreme impairment

Understanding and Memory

Remembers locations and basic work procedures

1___X___ 2_____ 3_____ 4_____ 5_____

Understands and remembers short, simple instructions

1___X___ 2_____ 3_____ 4_____ 5_____

Understands and remembers detailed instructions

1___X___ 2_____ 3_____ 4_____ 5_____

Concentration and Persistence

Carries out short, simple instructions

1____X____ 2_____ 3_____ 4_____ 5_____

Carries out detailed instructions

1____X____ 2_____ 3_____ 4_____ 5_____

Maintains attention and concentration for extended periods of time

1____X____ 2_____ 3_____ 4_____ 5_____

Can work within a schedule, maintain attendance, be punctual

1____X____ 2_____ 3_____ 4_____ 5_____

Sustains ordinary routine without special supervision

1____X____ 2_____ 3_____ 4_____ 5_____

Can work with or close to others without being distracted by them

1_____ 2____X____ 3_____ 4_____ 5_____

Makes simple work-related decisions

1_____ 2____X____ 3_____ 4_____ 5_____

Works quickly and efficiently, meets deadlines, even under stressful conditions

1_____ 2_____ 3_____ 4____X____ 5_____

Completes normal workday and workweek without interruptions due to symptoms

1____X____ 2_____ 3_____ 4_____ 5_____

Works at consistent pace without an unreasonable number or length of breaks

1____X____ 2_____ 3_____ 4_____ 5_____

Social Interaction

Interacts appropriately with general public

1_____ 2____X____ 3_____ 4_____ 5_____

Asks simple questions or requests assistance when necessary

1_____ 2____X____ 3_____ 4_____ 5_____

Accepts instruction and responds appropriately to criticism from
supervisors

1_____ 2___X___ 3_____ 4_____ 5_____

Gets along with coworkers without distracting them

1_____ 2___X___ 3_____ 4_____ 5_____

Maintains socially appropriate behavior

1_____ 2___X___ 3_____ 4_____ 5_____

Maintains basic standards of cleanliness and grooming

1___X___ 2_____ 3_____ 4_____ 5_____

Adaptation

Responds appropriately to changes at work

1_____ 2_____ 3_____ 4___X___ 5_____

Is aware of normal work hazards and takes necessary precautions

1___X___ 2_____ 3_____ 4_____ 5_____

Can get around in unfamiliar places, can use public transportation

1___X___ 2_____ 3_____ 4_____ 5_____

Sets realistic goals, makes plans independently of others

1___X___ 2_____ 3_____ 4_____ 5_____

Summary: Vocational Strategies and Accommodations

To optimize the chances for vocational success, a person with obsessive-compulsive personality disorder needs:

- An opportunity to use and be valued for ability to focus on details, consider all aspects, investigate all possibilities, and produce results with few errors.
- Freedom, to the extent possible, from time pressures and constraints, in order to accommodate need to be exact and desire to be perfect.
- Guidance in organizing information into usable form, in order to aid decision making and problem solving.
- Supervision that recognizes and rewards efforts to produce high-quality work, while limiting tendency to put off completion of a project until perfection is achieved.

- Little interaction with the public or coworkers because of stiff and formal interpersonal style and discomfort in interpersonal situations.
- Enough autonomy on the job to feel some control over the work process and results.

PASSIVE-AGGRESSIVE PERSONALITY DISORDER

Though it has been listed in previous editions of DSM, passive-aggressive, or negativistic, personality disorder now requires further study before it will be fully included in future editions. Its characteristic behavior patterns and traits are ambivalence, indecisiveness, interpersonal conflicts and disappointments, desire for self-assertion, co-existing uneasily with dependence on others, poor self-confidence, superficial bravado, defeatist attitude, frequent complaints, and tendency to evoke hostile and negative responses from others. These behavior patterns also occur in borderline, histrionic, paranoid, dependent, antisocial, and avoidant personality disorders. Further, passive-aggressive behaviors occur often in everyday life, especially in authoritarian situations such as the workplace or the military. When such behaviors are inflexible, maladaptive, and cause significant functional impairment or subjective distress, they may constitute a disorder. DSM-IV has established research criteria to determine if such a disorder exists separate from other personality disorders. People who meet the current research criteria would be diagnosed with personality disorder, not otherwise specified (American Psychiatric Association, 1994).

Ray

Ray knew he had overslept; he could tell by the way the sun slanted in past his window shade. He must have forgotten to set his alarm clock again. He was due at his ex-wife's apartment to pick up their son in 20 minutes. He could just make it if he hurried, but instead he made coffee, took a shower, and read the morning paper before setting out. He was annoyed with his ex-wife. She had changed her work hours, and now expected him to pick up their son and bring him to preschool by 8:00 in the morning on his days off.

The sight of her, pacing and checking her watch in front of the apartment building, increased his annoyance. He responded with a sullen glare to her complaints that she couldn't count on him. He turned his back when she tried to hand him their son's lunch box and back-pack. He moved in slow motion, clearing a place on his cluttered car seat, carefully stowing each item, then rearranging them. "Will you please hurry?" his ex-wife said. "If I'm late again, Ray. . . ." "Sorry," Ray said; his sarcasm mangled the word almost beyond recognition. "I forgot what an important person you are to your bigshot employer."

What Passive-Aggressive Personality Disorder Is Like

- Negativistic attitudes
- Passive resistance to reasonable demands by others
- Excessive complaining about and criticism of authority figures

Negativistic attitudes. Ray responds to most situations he encounters with disdain. To him, few things are worthwhile, few people deserve respect, and few requirements are worth honoring. He's a negativistic cliché—a spoiler, a wet blanket, a nay-sayer with a chip on his shoulder. He is Eeyore with an attitude. He sees the world as a bleak and thankless place, and he resents expectations that he perform adequately in it. He is discouraging, defeatist, pessimistic, gloomy, and prepared to fail.

Generalized hostility characterizes his approach to life, but he doesn't express it directly. He transforms anger and anxiety into cynicism and stubbornness. He relates to others by means of sarcasm and derision. He filters experiences, decisions, and judgments through a thick screen of bitterness and contempt.

Ray is 35 years old. He was a 10-year veteran of the police force in a mid-sized city. He was assigned to a desk job, a position known to those on the force as the "rubber gun squad." He was taken off the street three years ago because of a series of complaints from citizens, problems getting along with coworkers, and ongoing difficulty dealing with authority. The city tried to get him fired because of his failure to complete routine paperwork and other aspects of his job adequately or on time.

Through his union, he appealed twice. He lost the first appeal. The second appeal, after a lengthy process of complex negotiations, resulted in his losing his job on the police force but remaining a city employee. He was married for five years and has been divorced for two. His ex-wife has custody of their four-year-old son.

Ray says that his son is a sissy who'll never amount to anything. He says that his marriage was doomed from the start because of his wife's demands on him. He describes his fellow police officers and their work as "a bunch of morons trying to outsmart a bunch of jerks." Of his own generally shoddy performance, he says, "Good enough for government work."

Passive resistance to reasonable demands by others. Ray resents any requirement, demand, deadline, or expectation imposed on him by others, but he believes that open resistance to such expectations is dangerous. Passivity is thus the only means available to him. He has developed oppositional techniques that are highly effective both in reducing his obligations and antagonizing those around him.

If he doesn't want to do something, he forgets about it, or he forgets a crucial part of it, or he forgets the deadline for it. If he doesn't want responsibility for a certain task, he performs it poorly; he makes mistakes, he's sloppy, slow, and inefficient. If he doesn't like an assignment or a request or if he is anxious about it, he procrastinates; he puts it off until it's too late to follow through. If anyone complains about any of this, he becomes stubborn and recalcitrant. These behaviors are built into the structure of Ray's personality, and, while he is fully capable of planning his passive get-backs, they are often not the product of conscious decision making.

Excessive complaining about and criticism of authority figures. As a teenager, Ray was popular among his peer group because of his disregard for authority and his ingenious plans for getting back at those in charge. Getting out of household chores, cutting class, letting air out of teachers' tires, "accidentally" leaving a large, wet sponge on the driver's seat of his father's newly washed car, and similar activities earned him the respect of other boys his age.

As an adult, most people seem like authority figures to Ray, because of the passive stance he takes in life. He refused to take on much responsibility for his home and marriage, forcing his wife to do so and then complaining about her bossiness. He couldn't relate to other officers of his rank as colleagues because he wouldn't accept the level of responsibility that went with the job. He forced them to tell him what to do and to pick up the slack, leading to animosity on both sides.

His biggest problems with authority, however, came as a result of the hierarchical nature of the police department. Accepting its authoritarian structure is a prerequisite for the job, and Ray couldn't do it. He complained about superior officers behind their backs, he scorned their right to give orders, he mocked rules and regulations, he fomented dissatisfaction with his constant faultfinding, he muttered nasty comebacks under his breath. In response to the complaints made against him by citizens and by fellow officers, he ridiculed their right to do so and was uncharacteristically bold and direct in his criticism of the department for taking them seriously.

A police psychologist who evaluated him for fitness for duty recommended that he receive six months of individual psychotherapy and then be retested to see if he could go back on the street. Ray approached the therapy process with defiance and hostility, daring the therapist to get him to talk and mocking her ability to help him. He came late to the sessions, he missed appointments without calling, and he sat mostly silent on the occasions he did show up. He completed the six months only because he understood that keeping his job depended on it. On re-evaluation, the police psychologist not only recommended that he not be returned to the street, but declared him unfit for duty on the police force, thus beginning the lengthy process of firing him.

Passive-Aggressive Personality Disorder's Effect at Work

- Obstructs efforts of others, impedes work completion
- Argumentative with supervisors
- Chronic complaining

Obstructs efforts of others, impedes work completion. Simply put, Ray just doesn't do his share of the work, no matter what job situation he is in. He makes it hard for others to do their work, because they can't count on him. His reason for wanting to be a police officer in the first place had to do primarily with his desire to drive fast, to park wherever he wanted, and to get some respect. Once he understood that the job required serving the public and following orders, and that he was not exempt from these requirements, his pattern of angry, passive resistance took over.

On the street, he routinely delayed responding to calls in his area, he invariably let his partner take the initiative, he occasionally turned off his radio "accidentally," and he once fell asleep while on patrol. He sometimes refused assignments altogether. No other officer wanted to work with him. At his desk job, he was notoriously slow in meeting deadlines, he made mistakes, he "forgot" to do things, he procrastinated in completing assignments, he "lost" things, he failed to comply with established protocols. His work area was a mess. Any paperwork that had to pass through him might be delayed indefinitely.

Argumentative with supervisors. Ray is always quick with an argument. He can come up with a long list of reasons why he shouldn't have to do something, why it should be done some other way, why it shouldn't be done at all. "That's not my area, that's not in my job description, that's not what the training manual says, I don't have time for that, I'm not trained to do that, I don't do it that way, that's not my responsibility, it's not my fault," and similar phrases roll easily and automatically off his tongue. Rarely does he simply do what he is told.

If he can't refuse an assignment, he complies begrudgingly. He slams doors and drawers, he flings files down, he throws or breaks pencils, he mutters curses under his breath, and he procrastinates as long as possible before proceeding with the task in his characteristic sloppy manner.

Chronic complaining. Like arguing, complaining comes as naturally as breathing to Ray. He whines and he blames: other people cause his problems and fail to support him; other people don't do their share; other people don't do things right; other people make him look bad; other people interfere in his life and expect too much. Other people, in Ray's view, are incompetent jerks, and he feels free to expound on the details to anyone who will listen.

Whether it's his supervisors on the police force, his ex-wife, or the check-out clerk at the grocery store, Ray finds them all blameworthy and himself exempt from responsibility. If he can't pinpoint an actual person to complain about, he turns to larger forces—life dealt him a bad hand, life isn't fair. Anything from elected officials to the weather can provide a reason that Ray doesn't perform adequately.

Ray thinks of himself as an affable sort of fellow, easygoing and pleasant when people treat him right and let him go about his business. The fact that he is frequently irritable and nasty is, naturally, not his fault. Likewise, he doesn't think he makes mistakes; anything that goes wrong is someone else's fault or beyond his control, and in any case he won't take responsibility for it.

Working with Passive-Aggressive Personality Disorder

Police work is not a good field for Ray, a fact that even he acknowledged after his second appeal failed. He has trouble with hierarchy and authority, and he resents the idea of being helpful and providing a service. He doesn't work well on a team or in a partnership, he doesn't do his fair share of the work, and he blames others for failures. The more he is pushed to perform, the more he resists; the more he is left to his own devices, the less he does.

While the city was free to fire him from the police force, it was obligated, under the agreement made with union lawyers, to find him another city job and to retrain him if necessary. Keeping him on his desk job in the police department would have been easier and cheaper for the city, but the chief had enough influence and authority to ensure that would not be the case.

Accordingly, Ray was referred to the city human services department, where he was assigned to work with Steve. Ray's circumstances and his reputation were well known throughout the city offices. Steve, who was semi-retired and looking forward to complete retirement soon, didn't exactly relish the assignment. But he was highly experienced and had always provided thorough and effective services. He, if anyone, could help Ray find a situation in which he might succeed.

Steve had at his disposal all of Ray's employment records from the police department, as well as records relating to the city's efforts to fire him. Still, his first step was to ask Ray to undergo another psychological evaluation. He wanted both documentation and back-up support for any decisions he might make involving Ray's employment abilities, and he wanted specific information about Ray's current psychological state and his intelligence level.

The psychologist specialized in evaluations related to vocational issues. Her report indicated that Ray had approached the evaluation in a hostile and very defensive manner, making the results unclear and difficult to interpret. She nevertheless was able to confirm the diagnosis that the police psychologist had made of passive-aggressive personality disorder. Ray clearly harbored a great deal of underlying anger but did not show symptoms of depression or anxiety and did not seem to be experiencing an especially high level of stress. Intelligence testing, which had not been done before, placed Ray in the high-average range. The report also included information about employment conditions that could increase Ray's chances of succeeding in a job.

Steve's next step was interest and ability testing for Ray. He thought that the more objective, concrete information he could hold in his hand, the better, and the less effective Ray's inevitable arguments and objections would be. He believed that involving Ray in the process of identifying options and choosing among them might increase his chances of success. He also wanted to limit to the extent possible the amount of time he spent in face-to-face interaction with Ray, thinking that he was likely to get more and better information in other ways.

Ray's cynical approach to the testing might adversely affect the accuracy and usefulness of the results, but Steve still thought it worthwhile. As it was, the results were mixed. Ray showed surprising aptitude in a variety of fields. He demonstrated an ability to work with numbers, for instance, as well as an ability to attend to details and an excellent memory. Unfortunately, he seemed to have no vocational interests at all.

Having gathered as much information as he could about Ray, Steve scheduled their first interview. Ray called about an hour before the appointed time to reschedule for the following day, then arrived 15 minutes late for that appointment. He appeared unprepared for a meeting, especially one that had to do with his employment possibilities. His clothes were casual and rumpled, his hair was uncombed, and he seemed not to have showered or shaved for several days. He sat down without accepting Steve's handshake or returning his greeting.

Steve showed Ray the pile of information he had: employment records, psychological reports, vocational testing results, packets describing city departments and their hiring needs. He commented that they had a lot to work with, and asked Ray where he would like to begin. Ray, sitting slumped in his chair, said that he didn't care. Steve expressed surprise and disappointment at this response. He said that was unfortunate, because he was very busy and didn't have time to work with Ray until Ray was ready to participate fully. He then stood up, indicated the door, and said that Ray should come back when he had some idea of how they might work together to find a suitable job for him.

Steve later learned that Ray had subsequently asked to be reassigned to a different human resources professional, and that this request had been refused. Eventually, after several weeks, Ray returned to meet with Steve. His appearance and his social skills had not changed, but he did show slightly more enthusiasm for the interview and more willingness to engage in the process. He asked about current city job openings, which Steve considered a positive sign for their relationship.

Steve responded by showing Ray his comprehensive list of city hiring needs. He went on to offer a brief description of each department, then asked Ray where he wanted to work. Ray laughed and said that he didn't want to work at all. Steve laughed, too, and said he was looking forward to retirement himself. He repeated his question, however, and was prepared to end the interview prematurely if Ray was unwilling to take responsibility for his part in it.

Ray looked at the pile of file folders on Steve's desk. Settling back in his chair, he asked what the so-called experts had concluded about him. Steve responded to this opening and described what he saw as Ray's vocational strengths and weaknesses. He talked about Ray's intelligence level and about the range of vocational abilities that had shown up on the testing. He went on to discuss Ray's chronic problems with authority and supervision. He said it was too bad that Ray had never worked up to his ability and that he seemed to be his own worst enemy.

Ray sat silently for a few minutes, then asked what Steve wanted him to do. Steve said he didn't care what Ray did, but he was there to help him find another city job if he wanted one. He hoped that Ray would declare a vocational preference or indicate a choice of some kind, so that he would be more interested in the outcome of a job search and less likely to be oppositional. Ray, however, was expert at remaining passive; taking responsibility now would reduce his power of refusal later on. He seemed to want to be told what to do so he could resist and oppose.

Steve was aware of a job opening for an inspector in the city housing inspections office. He knew something about that department, and thought that the job met most of the conditions that might allow Ray to succeed. Flexible scheduling, which the inspectors arranged themselves, would render Ray's chronic lateness irrelevant. The inspectors worked mostly alone, so Ray would have no one to directly oppose and no one to antagonize by his failure to take on his share of the work. The inspectors' compensation was tied to their performance, since they were paid for projects completed, a practice that might help Ray improve his work habits.

The director of housing inspections was a firm and unequivocal supervisor. He set high standards for thorough, accurate, and timely inspection reports, and had been known to delay payment until he was satisfied with the quality of the work, or deny payment altogether if he was unsatisfied. While this set of conditions might set Ray up to resist and oppose, it gave him little leeway to do so and made him the only one to suffer if he did. Ray had no experience in the field, but his aptitude testing indicated that he could do the work. The inspectors followed a detailed protocol, and, after a short course in city building codes, they received on-the-job training concurrent with a probationary period.

Steve was quite excited about the possibilities for Ray as a housing inspector; he saw it as a very good fit. He was aware of Ray's oppositional nature, however, and he figured that anything he was excited about or seemed to push on him, Ray would resist. If Steve arranged an interview with the director of housing inspections, and Ray either didn't want the job or wanted to thwart Steve, he would simply sabotage the interview.

At their next meeting, Steve told Ray about the housing inspection job, along with three other openings that he was aware of in other departments. He made sure to mention potential problems with the housing inspection job—he said, for example, that the director of the department was exacting and uncompromising—but otherwise expressed no opinions and urged Ray to apply for all four. Unaware that he had been out-manipulated, Ray insisted that the housing inspector job was the only one he would consider. Steve offered to work with him on interviewing skills, but Ray declined, saying he knew how to get himself hired.

Steve arranged the interview. On his own, Ray had apparently read up on housing inspection in general and had also become familiar with the practices of the housing inspection department in his city. He showered and shaved and wore a suit to the interview, conducted himself appropriately, and was hired. Steve followed up by calling the director to make sure he knew about Ray's difficulties with supervision and to offer some suggestions for working with him.

Ray needs the chain of command and grievance procedures spelled out clearly from the start. He needs unequivocal standards for work quality and performance. He needs a supervisor who will set and maintain unambiguous limits and consequences for nonperformance. Unfortunately, even in a setting suited to his abilities and interests and equipped to deal with his personality problems, Ray's tendency to avoid responsibility and to argue and complain, his passive resistance to reasonable demands, his negativity and his obstructionism, mean that he will likely remain a difficult employee. But, in the right setting, he can be productive and meet minimum expectations.

Summary: Passive-Aggressive Personality Disorder's Effect on Vocational Abilities

Level of Impairment

1. no impairment
2. mild—minimal impairment with little or no effect on ability to function
3. moderate—some impairment, which limits ability to function fully
4. serious—major impairment, which may at times preclude ability to function
5. severe—extreme impairment

Understanding and Memory

Remembers locations and basic work procedures

1_____ 2___X___ 3_____ 4_____ 5_____

Understands and remembers short, simple instructions

1_____ 2_____ 3____X____ 4_____ 5_____

Understands and remembers detailed instructions

1_____ 2_____ 3_____ 4____X____ 5_____

Concentration and Persistence

Carries out short, simple instructions

1_____ 2____X____ 3_____ 4_____ 5_____

Carries out detailed instructions

1_____ 2_____ 3____X____ 4_____ 5_____

Maintains attention and concentration for extended periods of time

1_____ 2____X____ 3_____ 4_____ 5_____

Can work within a schedule, maintain attendance, be punctual

1_____ 2_____ 3____X____ 4_____ 5_____

Sustains ordinary routine without special supervision

1_____ 2_____ 3_____ 4____X____ 5_____

Can work with or close to others without being distracted by them

1_____ 2____X____ 3_____ 4_____ 5_____

Makes simple work-related decisions

1_____ 2_____ 3_____ 4____X____ 5_____

Works quickly and efficiently, meets deadlines, even under stressful conditions

1_____ 2_____ 3_____ 4_____ 5____X____

Completes normal workday and workweek without interruptions due to symptoms

1____X____ 2_____ 3_____ 4_____ 5_____

Works at consistent pace without an unreasonable number or length of breaks

1_____ 2_____ 3_____ 4____X____ 5_____

Social Interaction

Interacts appropriately with general public

1_____ 2_____ 3_____ 4____ X ____ 5_____

Asks simple questions or requests assistance when necessary

1_____ 2_____ 3____ X ____ 4_____ 5_____

Accepts instruction and responds appropriately to criticism from supervisors

1_____ 2_____ 3_____ 4_____ 5____ X ____

Gets along with coworkers without distracting them

1_____ 2_____ 3_____ 4____ X ____ 5_____

Maintains socially appropriate behavior

1_____ 2_____ 3____ X ____ 4_____ 5_____

Maintains basic standards of cleanliness and grooming

1_____ 2_____ 3____ X ____ 4_____ 5_____

Adaptation

Responds appropriately to changes at work

1_____ 2_____ 3____ X ____ 4_____ 5_____

Is aware of normal work hazards and takes necessary precautions

1____ X ____ 2_____ 3_____ 4_____ 5_____

Can get around in unfamiliar places, can use public transportation

1____ X ____ 2_____ 3_____ 4_____ 5_____

Sets realistic goals, makes plans independently of others

1_____ 2_____ 3____ X ____ 4_____ 5_____

Summary: Vocational Strategies and Accommodations

To optimize the chances for vocational success, a person with passive-aggressive personality disorder needs:

- Flexible scheduling, to accommodate the tendency to be late.
- The opportunity to work mostly alone, because of interpersonal difficulties and the tendency to oppose and antagonize coworkers.

- Compensation tied to work performance, as in payment for piece work or completed projects, because of tendency to avoid performing adequate work.
- Supervision that is clear and unequivocal and that provides for immediate and consistent consequences for noncompliance or poor performance, because of tendency to blame others, shift responsibility, and evade expectations for adequate performance.

PART III

Problems with Reality

Most of us know most of the time that the things we see, hear, experience, and believe to be true exist in a context that we share with other people. Our expression of these things might meet with agreement or derision, but generally not with complete lack of recognition or understanding. People with psychotic disorders have no shared context. Their world is erratic and unpredictable. The things they see, hear, experience, and believe to be true may have no existence at all outside of their own minds. Their expression of these things is likely to meet with a blank stare or a cautious backing away on the part of the listener.

Delusions (believing, for instance, that one is the Virgin Mary or the object of a CIA plot when one is not) and hallucinations (seeing or hearing things that are not present) are the most obvious features of schizophrenia, but perhaps not the most debilitating. Intense and overwhelming anxiety, constant confusion, disorganized speech and behavior, inability to form relationships, inability to manage the normal activities of daily living or to withstand even mildly stressful situations—all of these make life painful and uncertain for those who must live with schizophrenia. It is a chronic disorder, with active and residual phases. Medication is extremely helpful, but not a panacea, not as effective for some as for others, and fraught with its own problems and side effects.

Schizoaffective disorder includes a major depressive episode or a manic episode concurrent with schizophrenia. Brief psychotic disorder and schizophreniform disorder involve symptoms of schizophrenia in relatively shorter time frames and are not chronic disorders. Delusional disorder involves a fixed set of delusions with a theme, such as being loved from afar, being treated malevolently, being deceived, or having a special relationship to a deity or celebrity. All of these disorders can cause serious workplace problems for everyone involved.

CHAPTER 7

Schizophrenia and Other Psychotic Disorders

SCHIZOPHRENIA

The onset of schizophrenia usually occurs between the late teens and the mid-thirties. Women are likely to have a later onset and a better prognosis. Hospital-based studies suggest a higher rate of schizophrenia for men than for women, but community-based surveys suggest an equal ratio of men and women. Taking a variety of sources of information into account, the lifetime prevalence of schizophrenia is estimated to be between 0.5% and 1%. Schizophrenia is a chronic illness; while some people may experience exacerbations and remissions, a complete return to premorbid functioning is rare. Onset may be abrupt or insidious, but most people show some kind of prodromal phase, including social withdrawal, loss of interest in school or work, deterioration in personal hygiene, and unusual behavior or angry outbursts. First degree biological relatives of people who have schizophrenia are 10 times more likely than the general population to develop it (American Psychiatric Association, 1994).

Kelly

Kelly sat at her kitchen table looking at her grocery list. She kept the list just the way her independent living aide had taught her, writing down each item when she used it up, so the task would not be overwhelming on shopping day. Still, the slip of paper shook in her hands. Just thinking about the steps involved in grocery shopping made her nervous. She had to walk to the store, hold on to her list, search the aisles for the things she needed, and keep track of her money so she would have enough left for cigarettes, all the while dealing with her uncertainty and fear of the other people she saw there.

She began to hear bells clang from a corner of her apartment. She recognized the sound as a hallucination, one she heard often. She lit a cigarette, then began to gather her things to go to the store. From outside her apartment door, she heard her mother's voice. "She's no good," the voice said. "She should die." Kelly hesitated. This, too, was a frequent hallucination. The voice was continuous, repeating the same sentences over and over. A nurse at the hospital had taught Kelly to recognize hallucinations, and to ignore them. Still, she went to the door, unlocked it, and looked out. She had once been hospitalized because she heard her mother's voice, and she screamed back until someone called 911. This time, she closed the door and stood leaning against it, shaking and breathing hard.

She lit another cigarette. Pacing around her tiny apartment, she noticed her coin purse and her grocery list on the kitchen table, and remembered that she had to go shopping. She sat down again. She sometimes thought that the checker at her corner grocery received messages about her from outer space. She knew that the other shoppers in the store looked at her strangely and talked to each other about her. She felt too weak to walk the block and a half to the store.

Still, she was out of milk, bread, toilet paper, and cigarettes. Her independent living aide would arrive in the afternoon; Kelly had to show that she could take care of herself, or she would be sent back to live in a group home. She smoked another cigarette and wondered which was worse, going to the grocery store now or living in a group home maybe forever.

What Schizophrenia Is Like

- Poor reality operations—unusual beliefs, illogical thinking, hallucinations, delusions
- Flat affect, disinterested, amotivational, socially withdrawn
- Sleeping problems, low energy, fatigue; poor concentration, memory, and decision-making abilities
- Poor communication skills, unusual language, unusual appearance, disorganized speech and behavior
- Suspicious and argumentative; lacking insight

Poor reality operations—unusual beliefs, illogical thinking, hallucinations, delusions. Kelly was always considered odd. All through high school, she kept pretty much to herself and rarely spoke. Her mother warned her that unless she got out more, she would end up like her grandfather and her Aunt June, both of whom spent large parts of their lives in mental institutions. Her school notebooks contained pages and pages of intricate geometric designs or single sentences written over and over again. Still, she managed to make nearly average grades and to escape notice until the middle of her senior year.

She came to believe that her history teacher communicated with her telepathically. She spent more and more time alone in her room, attempting to receive his messages. Gradually, she began to believe that he was evil and intended her harm. Many times she heard him instruct her to go back in time—by which she thought he meant her death. She saw him standing in the corner of her room dressed like a Roman warrior threatening her with a battle ax. She stopped going to history class but would stand just outside the classroom door throughout the class period.

Her classmates began to make fun of her. She quit going to school altogether, finding her experiences and her anxiety overwhelming. She spent her days wandering in the woods near her home. One day she saw her mother and her history teacher standing together on a bridge, both of them shouting that she was no good and should die. She jumped off the bridge into the river.

She was subsequently hospitalized, diagnosed with schizophrenia, and started on medication. She went home to live with her mother, but she began to wander the woods again and to sit and stare at her mother saying nothing for hours at a time. She was hospitalized twice more before her mother decided she could no longer live at home.

With help from the hospital social worker, Kelly's mother found a group home for her. As a requirement for living there, her time had to be structured and her days filled. She was referred to a day treatment program for individual and group psychotherapy, social skills training, and daily life skills training. She did well there, and within a few months began a vocational training program that specialized in helping people with mental illnesses.

Kelly practiced such skills as arriving on time, staying all day, staying on task, responding when spoken to, and making eye contact, and was eventually placed in a small assembly plant. Once placed in a job, she was allowed to leave the group home to live in her own apartment, in a supported living arrangement, visited several times a week by an independent living aide. Kelly had never lived on her own before. Her experiences in the hospital and in group homes had been painful and difficult. She found the solitude and freedom of her own apartment to be soothing and pleasant, usually well worth the stress of taking care of herself and her personal needs.

Flat affect, disinterested, amotivational, socially withdrawn. She was no longer having significant delusions or hallucinations, but she found the assembly work extremely stressful. She responded by withdrawing so completely from the work and from the other people in her unit that her coworkers complained that she was "spooky," that she refused to keep up the necessary pace, and that nothing they said or did made any difference to her.

Sleeping problems, low energy, fatigue; poor concentration, memory, and decision-making abilities. For Kelly, just showing up every morning at 7:00 a.m. took an enormous amount of energy. Her sleep had always been troubled and erratic, and her medication contributed to a feeling of constant fatigue. Once at work, she had a hard time concentrating on what she was supposed to be doing; she was distracted by sights and sounds around her, by her coworkers' talking and laughing as they worked, and by her own thoughts and perceptions. She couldn't remember the order in which certain tasks had to be done and required constant reminding. Each day she had a choice of when to take her lunch break—11:30 or 12:00 noon—and each day she agonized over the decision for most of the morning, often audibly muttering to herself about it.

Poor communication skills, unusual language, unusual appearance, disorganized speech and behavior. Kelly spoke very little, and when she did she kept her eyes fixed on a point just beyond her left shoulder. She spoke rapidly and tended to repeat words or phrases over and over. She spoke in half sentences, rarely completing a thought. Her voice was a flat monotone, expressing no emotion. She rarely responded directly to what others said to her. When she worked at it and tried very hard, she could carry on a short conversation and make eye contact, but the effort was exhausting.

Her appearance was odd, but in a way difficult to pinpoint or describe. An air of strangeness seemed to surround her. When she walked, her gait was just a bit off. Her movements seemed a little awkward. Her glasses sat slightly crooked on her face and were usually smudged. Her facial expression was often inappropriate to the situation. Her clothes seemed to fit her oddly. She herself believed that her illness was obvious in her appearance, that others could look at her and see that she was "different," and that they targeted her for ridicule, contempt, or abuse as a result.

Suspicious and argumentative; lacking insight. After three months at the assembly plant, Kelly was sent back to the vocational training program. Her supervisor indicated that her presence was disruptive to the other employees in her unit. They complained that she watched them. She argued with instructions and directions, and even with efforts to offer encouragement or support. When her supervisor assigned her a regular lunch time, seeing how difficult the daily lunch time decision was for her, Kelly took it as evidence that she was being singled out and ridiculed.

Kelly understands that she has a mental illness, and she understands quite a bit about its effects. She can recognize hallucinations, for example, and generally cope with them. She knows that most people don't see things the way she does, and that her perceptions are often erroneous. Unfortunately, she has very limited understanding of how her behavior affects others. She has great difficulty regarding others' actions toward her with anything but suspicion, but cannot see how her responses contribute to the problem.

Schizophrenia's Effect at Work

- Profound impact on relationships with coworkers and supervisors
- Disinterested in achievement or promotions; passive or avoidant in response to performance demands
- High error rate, frequent miscommunication
- Poor stress tolerance

Profound impact on relationships with coworkers and supervisors. Part of Kelly's problem at the assembly plant was that she could not form relationships with the other people there. She ate her lunch and took her breaks alone. She didn't participate in the casual trading of cigarettes, snacks, recipes, craft patterns, and idle conversation that the rest of the group enjoyed. She didn't attend the social functions they occasionally organized.

She did her part of the assembly work as best she could, but had no sense of herself as part of a team and made no attempt to pace herself in accord with the others, diminishing the efficiency of the whole group. Feedback from coworkers and from her supervisor about these things had limited and short-lived impact on her behavior. She tended to view any criticism as an attack and to become defensive in return. The more withdrawn Kelly became, the more her coworkers distanced themselves from her. They quickly began to dislike her, then became overtly hostile, thus justifying her suspicion of them and helping to perpetuate a vicious cycle.

Disinterested in achievement or promotions; passive or avoidant in response to performance demands. Kelly's work group had a quota to meet each day. If they exceeded the quota, they were eligible for rewards ranging from a notice of praise on the bulletin board to financial bonuses. Meeting the quota was no problem, but no amount of encouragement or pressure or coercion could get Kelly to work more effectively within the group so they could exceed the quota. She responded to all efforts at persuasion with complete passivity. Even threats to dock her pay were ineffective. The incentives meant nothing to her, nor did the anger and frustration of her coworkers.

The only things that did seem to matter to her were breaks and cigarettes. She focused on the clock, literally counting the minutes until she could go have a cigarette. Still, her supervisor's attempt to tie break times to improved performance—first in the form of incentives and later with threats to curtail her breaks—was met with the same passivity and withdrawal that Kelly habitually showed.

High error rate, frequent miscommunication. Kelly made lots of mistakes because of her problems with memory and concentration. She couldn't remember which step came first or what to do with pieces she completed. She was easily distracted from the task at hand. She processed information in unusual ways, leading to confusion and misunderstanding. She might spend hours trying to "decode" a simple remark from a coworker, and then respond with a remark of her own that made no sense at all to anyone else. She might misinterpret an ordinary request—to get supplies from the supply closet, for instance—and do it incorrectly, incompletely, or not at all.

Poor stress tolerance. Despite her passivity and her apparent lack of interest in her performance or in how others saw her, Kelly experienced her job as extremely stressful. Her inability to cope with stress increased her problems on the job; she became more withdrawn and suspicious and less reliable. She lost concentration, she worked more slowly, she made more mistakes, she gave up easily. By the time her supervisor sent her back to the vocational training program, she was having hallucinations again, sometimes at work, and sometimes beyond her ability to cope with them as she had been taught. She was beginning to feel that she needed to go back to the hospital.

Working with Schizophrenia

Kelly didn't regret losing her job. She didn't mind returning to the vocational training program; she liked it better than working and found it much less stressful. She was very concerned, however, about losing her apartment. Living independently had come to mean a great deal to her. She knew that continuing to do so was tied to her ability to take care of herself and that losing her job jeopardized her chances. Returning to the hospital would almost certainly mean returning to a group home as well.

Kelly's hallucinations became more frequent as her anxiety increased. The stress of trying to hang on, trying to maintain her routine, trying to do what she needed to do, trying to stay out of the hospital, was enormous. Ordinary tasks, like going to the grocery store, became overwhelming. She found it difficult to attend her vocational training program every day as scheduled. She wanted more than anything to keep her apartment, but she truly didn't know if she could adequately take care of herself.

She felt desperate and knew she needed help. She had many resources available to her, but wasn't sure whom she could trust. She knew from experience that increasing her medication would ease some of her symptoms, but she was afraid that if she called her psychiatrist he would hospitalize her immediately. Instead, she called her outpatient psychiatric nurse, who listened to her, spoke in a soothing voice, and reviewed the coping skills Kelly had learned to deal with her symptoms and with the stress in her life. The nurse also asked the psychiatrist to authorize an increased dosage of one of Kelly's medications, which he did.

At her nurse's suggestion, Kelly called her social worker, who arranged for her independent living aide to come more often. The social worker also urged Kelly to put her vocational program on hold for the time being and return to day treatment for therapy and support. Kelly followed this advice, and within a few weeks her condition stabilized and she was no longer frightened by the imminent prospect of hospitalization.

She became obsessed, however, by her desire to keep her apartment. It was the focus of her life, and any hint from anyone that she may have to give it up caused her great distress. Despite the efforts of all those who worked with her to help her continue to live independently, she came to believe that her psychiatrist and her social worker wanted to force her back to a group home. She was suspicious of them, avoided contact with them, and was uncommunicative in their presence.

Her obsession with her apartment grew into an obsession with getting a job; she thought that was the only way she could convince her psychiatrist and her social worker to leave her alone. Her therapist at the day treatment program tried to strike a delicate balance between encouraging Kelly to prepare herself for job seeking and trying to keep her from raising her stress level to an unmanageable point by taking on too much and moving too fast. Kelly thought that her therapist, too, wanted to take her apartment away.

On her own, without discussing it with her therapist, her social worker, her psychiatric nurse, or her independent living aide, Kelly contacted Deanna, a vocational rehabilitation counselor who worked for her state Department of Rehabilitation Services. Deanna had helped Kelly get her first job at the assembly plant. She agreed to meet with Kelly, and she listened as Kelly explained her urgent need to find a job immediately.

Deanna wasn't exactly sure what was going on with Kelly at the moment; she couldn't quite follow her story, though her need and her level of agitation in expressing it were clear enough. But Deanna had a great deal of experience working with people with serious and persistent mental illnesses, and she understood the importance of being in close touch with the other helping professionals in Kelly's life. If she was to work with Kelly again, she saw establishing such contacts as her first order of business.

Deanna already knew Kelly's psychiatrist, psychiatric nurse, and social worker; they had all worked with Kelly since the time of her first hospitalization and had worked with Deanna in helping Kelly get ready for her first job. Because of Kelly's suspicions about the motives of her psychiatrist, her social worker, and her day treatment therapist, she refused to sign releases of information allowing Deanna to talk with them and coordinate services. She was willing to sign a release only to her nurse.

Deanna didn't argue. She didn't know Kelly's reason for refusing to sign the releases, but she didn't think that pushing the point would help their relationship. She hoped that Kelly would eventually reconsider, allowing her to provide more comprehensive services, but in the meantime at least she could discuss Kelly's needs and options with one other professional who knew her well.

Deanna wanted to understand exactly what had gone wrong for Kelly in her job at the assembly plant. Kelly was too anxious to move on to a new job to have much patience for talking about her old one, and she refused to discuss it. Deanna knew she should talk to everyone involved with Kelly to get the complete picture, which she was prevented from doing. She did gain valuable insight from Kelly's psychiatric nurse. Kelly also gave Deanna permission to talk to her former supervisor and to look at her performance reviews.

Piecing together the information that she had, Deanna concluded that much of Kelly's difficulty had to do with being part of a work group and being expected to work in cooperation with others. The requirement that she function as part of a team had apparently contributed to her increased stress level. On the other hand, Deanna also knew that being alone or isolated for extended periods would seriously jeopardize Kelly's already shaky grasp of reality. She thought that Kelly's best chance for success would be in a setting where she could work by herself at her own pace, with coworkers or supervisors in the same room or nearby, doing their own work.

Deanna thought that flexible scheduling might help Kelly cope with fluctuations in the intensity of her symptoms and the effects of her medication. But, if her schedule was too flexible, she would be unable to establish the routine and predictability that she needed in order to remain stable. She needs her time structured, and her duties and expectations spelled out clearly and often, with little variation.

Kelly adapts poorly to change; a difference in her daily schedule, a new responsibility, or a new plant on her supervisor's desk would all affect her and require unusual coping skills on her part. She needs to be informed in advance of upcoming changes. Telling her, for instance, that one coworker has quit and another will be starting tomorrow, or that everyone will have Friday afternoon off next week, will help her adjust to the change.

Deanna was clear about the ideal job situation for Kelly; she would work best in a fairly structured setting doing routine and predictable work, a setting that also allowed for some flexibility and some variation of the pace. She would work best on her own, but not in isolation. The setting should be low-key, with no requirement for an unusually fast pace or for much contact with coworkers or with the public. It should not be a setting in which misinterpretation of reality could cause problems, or where Kelly's tendency to look and act a little odd would matter.

Having summed up Kelly's vocational needs to her satisfaction, Deanna's next task was to locate such a setting. She very much wanted to take advantage of Kelly's current high level of motivation; she knew that was likely to change, and she hoped to place Kelly in a suitable job before it did. She was also concerned, however, about Kelly's mental stability. Her high level of motivation also represented a high level of stress and anxiety, which could backfire at any time.

Placing her in a job too soon could cause her to overreact to too much stress and change, and waiting too long could cause her to stagnate and lose motivation.

Deanna's solution was to spend several weeks working on basic interviewing skills and workplace social skills with Kelly. She assured Kelly that no one could take her apartment away as long as her mental health was stable and she was looking for work. She convinced Kelly to take the time to find the right job, so she would be more likely to succeed at it. Kelly seemed to relax somewhat. She seemed less nervous about her situation and more able to relate to Deanna. She took a more active part in job-readiness groups in her day treatment program and worked diligently on interviewing skills with Deanna.

Meanwhile, Deanna was checking all of her resources, trying to find a suitable setting for Kelly. Finally, through a human resources counselor with whom she frequently worked, she heard of a job in a warehouse that served several grocery store chains in the area. The warehouse was large and employed several hundred people, but they were divided into fairly small departments to handle produce, meat, frozen foods, bakery goods, and all of the other products the stores sold.

The job opening involved filling trays with packaged bakery goods, loading the trays on carts, and wheeling the carts to loading docks where trucks would pick up the trays for delivery to local grocery stores. The work was predictable; semi trucks from the manufacturing plants arrived at specified times throughout the day, carrying for the most part the same amount of goods each time. The expected pace was steady, but not necessarily fast. Other workers did the same job, but each worked independently, with no expectation of teamwork among them.

Kelly became very excited about the job opportunity when Deanna explained it to her. Her characteristically flat affect and monotone voice were momentarily transformed. She loved bakery goods, she said, she would love this job, she would excel at it, it would be wonderful. Deanna didn't want to dampen her enthusiasm, but she did want Kelly to stay grounded in reality. She talked about the process of applying for the job, the possibility that she might not get hired, and the daily expectations if she did get hired.

Kelly still wanted to pursue the opportunity. Deanna helped her fill out the application, and she arranged an interview. She met with Kelly immediately prior to it to review interviewing skills. With some intervention on her behalf from Deanna, Kelly was hired for the job.

Almost immediately after being hired, Kelly experienced problems. Her excitement gave way to agitation, which required an increase in her medication. She had difficulty getting to work on time every day and had difficulty staying focused while there. The work itself was not hard for her, but she couldn't seem to learn the correct route to take with her filled carts, and several times got lost in the warehouse. Her coworkers identified her as odd, and the familiar pattern of ridicule and isolation seemed about to begin. Her motivation to do a good job suffered as she began to see herself as unable to do so.

Deanna learned of these problems by making a routine follow-up call to Kelly's supervisor. She suggested several accommodations that would help Kelly succeed. Flexible scheduling would ease her stress level. A piecework schedule, either paying her per loaded tray, or making breaks and quitting time contingent on completing a certain number of loaded trays, could help her motivation, because she would see immediate results. Informing coworkers about her tendency to be oversensitive and her need to work on her own might help them accept her and leave her alone. Conversely, assigning one coworker to be her workplace "buddy," to whom she could turn as needed for advice or support, would reduce her sense of isolation. Informing her to the extent possible of upcoming changes, even very minor ones, and especially of all decisions involving her, would help her adjust as needed. Open and direct communication would give her less reason to believe people were talking behind her back or singling her out.

Deanna also offered to be available as a resource for both Kelly and her supervisor, to help ease the transition. In time, as her supervisor and coworkers came to understand her needs, Kelly became a steady and reliable employee. She rarely took part in any social functions, and she occasionally needed time off to deal with life experiences she found stressful. Schizophrenia tends to ebb and flow, with acute periods and periods of remission. Kelly's performance at work is likely to fluctuate accordingly. But she can perform her job consistently, with some understanding on the part of those who work with her.

Some people with schizophrenia are so impaired as to be unemployable in a competitive setting. They need a sheltered workshop or a great deal of on-the-job support from someone trained to provide it. But many people with schizophrenia, like Kelly, can hold competitive jobs, in the right situation, with some understanding of their needs, and with some appropriate accommodations. The structure and routine provided by going to work every day can be a stabilizing factor in an otherwise chaotic life.

Summary: Schizophrenia's Effect on Vocational Abilities

Level of Impairment

1. no impairment
2. mild—minimal impairment with little or no effect on ability to function
3. moderate—some impairment, which limits ability to function fully
4. serious—major impairment, which may at times preclude ability to function
5. severe—extreme impairment

Understanding and Memory

Remembers locations and basic work procedures

1_____ 2____X____ 3_____ 4_____ 5_____

Understands and remembers short, simple instructions

1_____ 2____X____ 3_____ 4_____ 5_____

Understands and remembers detailed instructions

1_____ 2_____ 3____X____ 4_____ 5_____

Concentration and Persistence

Carries out short, simple instructions

1_____ 2____X____ 3_____ 4_____ 5_____

Carries out detailed instructions

1_____ 2_____ 3_____ 4____X____ 5_____

Maintains attention and concentration for extended periods of time

1_____ 2_____ 3_____ 4_____ 5____X____

Can work within a schedule, maintain attendance, be punctual

1_____ 2_____ 3____X____ 4_____ 5_____

Sustains ordinary routine without special supervision

1_____ 2____X____ 3_____ 4_____ 5_____

Can work with or close to others without being distracted by them

1_____ 2_____ 3_____ 4_____ 5____X____

Makes simple work-related decisions

1_____ 2_____ 3____X____ 4_____ 5_____

Works quickly and efficiently, meets deadlines, even under stressful conditions

1_____ 2_____ 3_____ 4_____ 5___X_____

Completes normal workday and workweek without interruptions due to symptoms

1_____ 2_____ 3_____ 4_____ 5___X_____

Works at consistent pace without an unreasonable number or length of breaks

1_____ 2_____ 3___X_____ 4_____ 5_____

Social Interaction

Interacts appropriately with general public

1_____ 2_____ 3_____ 4___X_____ 5_____

Asks simple questions or requests assistance when necessary

1_____ 2_____ 3___X_____ 4_____ 5_____

Accepts instruction and responds appropriately to criticism from supervisors

1_____ 2_____ 3_____ 4_____ 5___X_____

Gets along with coworkers without distracting them

1_____ 2_____ 3_____ 4_____ 5___X_____

Maintains socially appropriate behavior

1_____ 2_____ 3___X_____ 4_____ 5_____

Maintains basic standards of cleanliness and grooming

1_____ 2_____ 3___X_____ 4_____ 5_____

Adaptation

Responds appropriately to changes at work

1_____ 2_____ 3_____ 4___X_____ 5_____

Is aware of normal work hazards and takes necessary precautions

1_____ 2_____ 3___X_____ 4_____ 5_____

Can get around in unfamiliar places, can use public transportation

1_____ 2_____ 3___X___ 4_____ 5_____

Sets realistic goals, makes plans independently of others

1_____ 2_____ 3___X___ 4_____ 5_____

Summary: Vocational Strategies and Accommodations

To optimize the chances for vocational success, a person with schizophrenia needs:

- Flexible scheduling, to accommodate fluctuations in symptoms and effects of medication, along with structure, routine, and predictability, to help reduce stress and maintain mental health stability.
- Little expectation to work at a fast or variable pace, to help maintain stability and concentration.
- Little expectation to work as part of a team or to interact with coworkers or the general public, because of interpersonal difficulties and unusual interpretation of ordinary conversation and events.
- Social support both outside of work and on the job, possibly being assigned a workplace "buddy," to help ease isolation and maintain stability.
- Incentives, such as breaks or payment, based on piecework, to help improve motivation.
- Open and direct communication, especially with regard to any upcoming changes, to allow adjustment to the change and to avoid the impression of being singled out or talked about.
- Help from a vocational rehabilitation or mental health professional in informing supervisors and coworkers of workplace needs, in order to avoid misunderstandings and receive necessary accommodations.

Conclusions and Implications: The Role of Psychological Assessment

Helping vocational rehabilitation (VR) clients live happier, fuller, and more productive lives by optimizing their rehabilitation outcomes is the most important application of the material presented here. VR professionals understand that to achieve this end, three things are necessary: to relate to each client as a unique individual; to avoid stereotyping any individual based on gender, ethnicity, physical or mental ability, nature or extent of a disorder, or any other factor; and to work within the framework created by the client's strengths, weaknesses, and motivations.

For those clients with mental illnesses, a psychiatric diagnosis is part of the picture. Our hope for this book is that it helps VR professionals make a paradigm shift away from the limitations of traditional mental health diagnosis and toward its practical applications in vocational rehabilitation. A psychiatric diagnosis alone tells us little, and not even the most important things, about a person. However, by understanding the vocational consequences of a diagnosis and the direct, concrete effect it has on a person's life and ability to work, the VR professional can be well prepared to meet the challenges of working in the interface of mental health and vocational problems.

Mental health problems affect different people differently, so much so that some researchers (e.g., Anthony & Jansen, 1984; Drake, 1998) have argued that severity of psychiatric symptoms, per se, is a poor predictor of vocational functioning. For example, one person with bipolar disorder may return to work with little difficulty shortly after a hospitalization, another may return only after an extended absence to a job with significantly fewer responsibilities, while a third may never be able to return to a competitive job.

Still, for most people who have them, the effect of psychiatric symptoms on their lives is profound and far-reaching. Only 20%–30% of recently hospitalized psychiatric clients are employed after 18 months of VR services (Anthony, 1994), a figure that compares unfavorably to 50% for physically disabled clients. Why should this effect be so robust? One explanation is offered by Crewe and Athelstan (1984), who suggest that the effects of psychiatric diagnoses are mediated through work-related functional impairments. Based on their work as rehabilitation psychologists in a counseling center serving people with severe psychiatric and physical disabilities, they developed the Functional Assessment Inventory (FAI). The FAI measures such abilities as memory, motor speed, motor skills, physical attractiveness, judgment, problem solving, and effective interactions with coworkers and supervisors. Crewe and Athelstan (1984) concluded that psychiatric symptoms that adversely affect these work-related abilities are likely to cause vocational difficulties.

BEYOND DIAGNOSIS

Psychiatric diagnoses, like physical diagnoses, are by their nature generalized categories that include common symptoms and signs, but do not, cannot, and are not meant to communicate the individual characteristics that make people unique. We have tried to present the salient vocational considerations that individuals in diagnostic groups are likely to have in common. However, the importance of comprehensive individual assessment to the full understanding of a person's needs and abilities, and therefore to the best possible delivery of VR services, cannot be overstated.

Recent research suggests that domains such as interpersonal functioning, severity and type of psychiatric problem, job satisfaction, substance use and abuse, level of motivation, and dependability are all strongly linked to satisfactory employment outcomes for people with mental illness (Becker, Drake, Bond, Xie, Dain, & Harrison, 1998). These domains, in turn, are affected in various ways by an individual's personality, values, experiences, and symptoms. Therefore, individual assessment, provided by rehabilitation psychologists who understand how psychiatric and VR paradigms work together to produce vocational problems and solutions, is critical for effective vocational intervention.

Employers in both the public and private sectors frequently make use of psychological testing to improve job "fit," satisfaction, and success, and as an important tool in preemployment selection. A comprehensive psychological evaluation includes an in-depth personal interview, as well as personality, cognitive, and interest testing. The vast majority of psychologists who perform individual assessments for industry make use of personal interviews (95%), personality inventories (78.9%), and ability tests (74.3%) (Ryan & Sackett, 1998).

As Lowman (1991) states, "The most appropriate career path for bringing lasting growth and satisfaction to an individual is the one most congruent with individual abilities, interests, and personality" (p. 193). Furthermore, "The choice of general career path and fine tuning it to individual abilities and personality often may require considerable individualized work with a professionally trained vocational counselor or psychologist" (p. 193).

Lowman (1991) goes on to describe methods for integrating interests, abilities, and personality characteristics for this purpose. Finally, Lowman (1993) has described a "Clinically Useful Taxonomy of Psychological Work-Related Dysfunctions"(p. 43). In it, he attempts to integrate and categorize the kinds of work problems that cause or may be caused by either worker psychopathology or dysfunctional work environments.

PERSONALITY FACTORS

A thorough psychological assessment recognizes that personality traits or, in their extreme, personality disorders often constitute a significant part of the diagnostic picture and may in themselves account for the differences in vocational outcomes in different individuals with similar clinical (i.e., DSM-IV, Axis I) psychopathology. The prevalence of personality disorders in nonselected "normal" community samples tends to be higher than most people believe it is, about 10% (Maier, Lichtermann, Klingler, Heun, & Hallmayer, 1992). In samples that already have been diagnosed with Axis I disorders, the estimates are considerably higher, from 23%–90% (Zimmerman & Coryell, 1989). Moreover, the presence of a personality disorder tends to bring with it substantial functional impairments, including those in the vocational domain (Nakao, Gunderson, Phillips, Tanaka, Yorifuji, Takaishi, & Nishimura, 1992).

In the introduction to Part II, we discussed the five-factor model of personality (Costa & Widiger, 1994). Applying this model to personality disorders in the workplace, the traits of agreeableness and conscientiousness seem to be the best predictors of occupational success. Further support for this position was found in research performed with data from our own practice. Edelson (1993) followed 88 urban

VR clients over a period of two and a half years. Although the overall rehabilitation rate for competitive employment was rather low (5.7%), the Psychopathic Deviance (Pd) scale of the Minnesota Multiphasic Personality Inventory - 2 was consistently and significantly related to VR success. Specifically, VR clients who were more impulsive, rebellious, and argumentative, as measured by the Pd scale, had a significantly poorer VR outcome than those who were more conventional, agreeable, and thoughtful in their actions.

THE CASE FOR SUPPORTED EMPLOYMENT

While volunteer and "sheltered" worksites may certainly be helpful to some clients (cf., Bond & Boyer, 1988), research generally suggests that competitive (paid) work leads to the most desirable and efficacious vocational outcomes. In his summary of the literature on supported competitive employment (SE), Bond (1998) identified six principles inherent in the concept: (1) The goal of SE is competitive employment. (2) It allows for rapid job search and placement. (3) Rehabilitation and mental health services should be integrated as much as possible. (4) Services should be based largely on client preferences. (5) Assessment should be continuous and comprehensive, and (6) Job support services should continue indefinitely. Ford (1995) also argues persuasively for the desirability of supported competitive work. We therefore presented this model in making suggestions for working in VR with people with mental health problems, choosing as case illustrations people appropriate for supported competitive job placements.

A number of practical issues arise in providing this type of support, however. Perhaps the most controversial of these have to do with how to provide the best possible support through reasonable accommodations and how to handle disclosure issues in the process. Mancuso (1993) presented 10 case studies of competitively employed workers with psychiatric disabilities. She found that workers rarely discussed their disabilities directly with their supervisors, making appropriate accommodations difficult to provide.

"Explicit accommodations" include such things as flexible scheduling, extended periods of absence to accommodate periods of symptom increases, and short-term rather than long-term projects, thus allowing less regular attendance. In only two of Mancuso's cases was the worker directly involved in planning these kinds of accommodations. By assessing and responding to their employees' needs on their own, employers may make "unilateral accommodations." These could include modulating workflow in accordance with observed symptoms or allowing extra time to complete projects. Such accommodations occurred in four cases. In addition, four workers described "self-accommodations," such as learning to take brief time-outs in periods of high stress or asking for a partition to reduce distractions.

Importantly, the most common accommodation cited by both supervisors and employees in Mancuso's study was flexible or part-time scheduling. Supervisors also described a willingness to modify work assignments according to the employee's fluctuation of symptom severity.

DISCLOSURE OF DISABILITY

Many workers with psychiatric disabilities see disclosure of it to their employers or coworkers as undesirable, embarrassing, or inevitably leading to stigmatization on the job. Others, however, see it as a useful strategy to promote long-term positive adjustment at the worksite. While every situation is different, and the merits of disclosure must be assessed in each, we see disclosure as desirable in many cases, especially for workers who have had a series of unsuccessful job placements. These individuals may have sufficient general intelligence and job skills to be hired, but they have trouble retaining their jobs because of symptom exacerbations or job-related problems caused at least in part by personality or psychiatric issues. Mancuso (1993) described several potential benefits of disclosure, including enabling a worker to involve a third party, such as a VR professional, in the development of accommodations, making it easier to come to work during periods of heightened symptoms, and allowing coworkers and supervisors opportunities to provide support.

Another potential benefit could have far-reaching advantages. If the disclosure of a psychiatric disability is accompanied by appropriate education about it, supervisors are better able to attribute unusual or ineffective work behavior to forces outside the conscious control of the worker, rather than attributing to them negative personal qualities such as laziness, hostility, or noncooperation. Our observation has been that the most effective way to improve long-term job retention for many individuals is by creating a partnership with an employer who values diversity in the workplace and who is willing to take a little extra time to understand the unique needs of a potentially effective and productive employee. Such an approach appears to be timely and fully in the spirit of the Americans with Disabilities Act (Bruyère & O'Keeffe, 1994).

We began this book by describing the difficulties that VR professionals often face when working with individuals with psychiatric disabilities. We end on a note of cautious optimism. VR professionals truly must care about their clients, pay attention to their individual differences, and make their intervention decisions based upon a combination of client preferences, objective psychological data, and an understanding of how these data affect their client's functional work behavior. Then the VR process will be a mutually satisfying one for both the client and the VR professional.

Summary of DSM-IV

The following is a summary of relevant portions of DSM-IV's classification system. (American Psychiatric Association, 1994). It includes category headings for Axis I and Axis II disorders, as well as complete listings of disorders under those categories discussed in this book. In the multiaxial system, Axis III refers to general medical conditions, Axis IV to psychosocial and environmental problems, and Axis V to a global assessment of functioning.

Axis I: Clinical disorders, other disorders that may be the focus of clinical attention.

Disorders usually first diagnosed in infancy, childhood, or adolescence

Delerium, Dementia, Amnesic and other cognitive disorders

Mental Disorders due to a general medical condition not elsewhere classified

Substance-Related Disorders

Schizophrenia and other psychotic disorders:
Schizophrenia; episodic or single episode; paranoid, disorganized, catatonic, undifferentiated, or residual type
Schizophreniform disorder
Schizoaffective disorder
Delusional disorder
Brief psychotic disorder
Shared psychotic disorder
Psychotic disorder due to . . . [a general medical condition]
Substance-induced psychotic disorder

Mood Disorders:
Depressive disorders:
Major depression, single episode or recurrent
Dysthymic disorder
Bipolar disorders:
Bipolar I disorder—history of at least one previous manic or mixed episode
Bipolar II disorder—history of only depressive episodes previously
Cyclothymic disorder
Mood disorder due to . . . [a general medical condition]
Substance-induced mood disorder

Anxiety Disorders:
Panic disorder without agoraphobia
Panic disorder with agoraphobia
Agoraphobia without history of panic disorder
Specific phobia
Social phobia
Obsessive-compulsive disorder
Post-traumatic stress syndrome
Acute stress disorder
Generalized anxiety disorder
Anxiety disorder due to . . . [a general medical condition]
Substance-induced anxiety disorder

Somatoform Disorders:
Somatization disorder
Undifferentiated somatoform disorder
Conversion disorder
Pain disorder: Associated with psychological factors; associated with both psychological factors and a general medical condition
Hypochondriasis
Body dysmorphic disorder

Factitious Disorders

Dissociative Disorders

Sexual and Gender Identity Disorders

Eating Disorders

Sleep Disorders

Impulse-Control Disorders not elsewhere classified

Adjustment Disorders

Axis II: Personality disorders, mental retardation

Personality Disorders:
Paranoid personality disorder
Schizoid personality disorder
Schizotypal personality disorder
Antisocial personality disorder
Borderline personality disorder
Histrionic personality disorder
Narcissistic personality disorder
Avoidant personality disorder
Dependent personality disorder
Obsessive-compulsive personality disorder
Personality disorder not otherwise specified

References

American Psychiatric Association. (1994). *Diagnostic and Statistical Manual of Mental Disorders* (4th ed.). Washington, DC: American Psychiatric Association.

Anthony, W.A. (1994). The vocational rehabilitation of people with severe mental illness: Issues and myths. *Innovations and Research, 3,* 17–24.

Anthony, W.A., & Jansen, M.A. (1984). Predicting the vocational capacity of the chronically mentally ill. *American Psychologist, 39,* 537–544.

Becker, D.R., Drake, R.E., Bond, G.R., Xie, H., Dain, B.J., & Harrison, K. (1998). Job terminations among persons with severe mental illness participating in supported employment. *Community Mental Health Journal, 34,* 71–82.

Bond, G.R. (1998). Principles of the individual placement and support model: Empirical support. *Psychiatric Rehabilitation Journal, 22,* 11–23.

Bond, G.R., & Boyer, S.L. (1988). Rehabilitation programs and outcomes. In J.A. Ciardiello & M.D. Bell (Eds.), *Vocational Rehabilitation of Persons with Prolonged Psychiatric Disorders* (pp. 231–263). Baltimore: The Johns Hopkins University Press.

Bruyère, S.M., & O'Keeffe, J. (Eds.). (1994). *Implications of the Americans with Disabilities Act for Psychology.* Washington, DC: American Psychological Association.

Costa, P.T., & Widiger, T.A. (1994). *Personality Disorders and the Five-Factor Model of Personality.* Washington, DC: American Psychological Association.

Crewe, N.M., & Athelstan, G.T. (1984). *Functional Assessment Inventory Manual.* Menomonie, WI: University of Wisconsin—Stout.

Drake, R.E. (1998). A brief history of the individual placement and support model. *Psychiatric Rehabilitation Journal, 22,* 3–7.

Edelson, D.S. (1993). *Prediction of Vocational Rehabilitation Outcome: A Comparison of the Predictive Validity of Demographic Variables, MMPI-2, WRK, and TRT.* Doctoral dissertation. Minnesota School of Professional Psychology, Minneapolis.

Falvo, D.R. (1991). *Medical and Psychosocial Aspects of Chronic Illness and Disability.* Gaithersburg, MD: Aspen Publishers.

Ford, H.F. (1995). *Providing Employment Support for People with Long-Term Mental Illness: Choices, Resources, and Practical Strategies.* Baltimore: Paul Brookes Publishing Co.

Lowman, R.L. (1991). *The Clinical Practice of Career Assessment: Interests, Abilities, and Personality.* Washington, DC: American Psychological Association.

Lowman, R.L. (1993). *Counseling and Psychotherapy of Work Dysfunctions.* Washington, DC: American Psychological Association.

Maier, W., Lichtermann, D., Klingler, T., Heun, R., & Hallmayer, J. (1992). Prevalences of personality disorders (DSM-III-R) in the community. *Journal of Personality Disorders, 6,* 187–196.

Mancuso, L.L. (1993). *Case Studies on Reasonable Accommodations for Workers with Psychiatric Disabilities.* Washington, DC: Washington Business Group on Health.

Nakao, K., Gunderson, J. G., Phillips, K. A., Tanaka, N., Yorifuji, K., Takaishi, J., & Nishimura, T. (1992). Functional impairment in personality disorders. *Journal of Personality Disorders, 6,* 24–33.

Ryan, A.M., & Sackett, P.R. (1998). Individual assessment: The research base. In R. Jeanneret & R. Silzer (Eds.), *Individual Psychological Assessment: Predicting Behavior in Organizational Settings.* Washington, DC: American Psychological Association.

World Health Organization. (1997). *International Classification of Impairments, Activities and Participation.* Geneva, Switzerland: World Health Organization.

Zimmerman, M., & Coryell, W.H. (1989). DSM-III personality disorder diagnoses in a nonpatient sample: Demographic correlates and comorbidity. *Archives of General Psychiatry, 46,* 682–689.

Index

A

Adaptation
agoraphobia, 43–44
antisocial personality disorder, 143
avoidant personality disorder, 183
bipolar disorder, 30
manic phase, 30
borderline personality disorder,
132
dependent personality disorder,
195
depression, 19
histrionic personality disorder, 155
narcissistic personality disorder,
168
obsessive-compulsive disorder, 65,
207
paranoid personality disorder, 93
passive-aggressive personality
disorder, 218
posttraumatic stress disorder, 54
schizoid personality disorder, 117
schizophrenia, 235–236
schizotypal personality disorder,
107
social phobia, 43–44
somatization disorder, 77
Agoraphobia, 33, 34–44
adaptation, 43–44
case study, 34–42
characterized, 34–36
concentration, 42–43
effect at work, 36–38
effect on vocational abilities,
summary, 42–44
epidemiology, 34
memory, 42
persistence, 42–43
social interaction, 43
understanding, 42
vocational accommodations,
summary, 43–44
vocational strategies, summary,
43–44
working with, 38–42
Agreeableness, 239–240
Aloofness, 83–84, 96, 109
Amnesiac disorder, xv
Amotivational, 226
Anger, inappropriate expression,
122, 146–147
Antisocial personality disorder, 119,
133–144
adaptation, 143
case study, 133–141
characterized, 133–138
concentration, 142
effect at work, 133–138
effect on vocational abilities,
summary, 141–143
epidemiology, 133
memory, 142
persistence, 142

Antisocial personality disorder—
continued
social interaction, 143
understanding, 142
vocational accommodations,
summary, 143–144
vocational strategies, summary,
143–144
working with, 138–141
Anxiety, 35
avoidance of anxiety-provoking
situations, 35
physical symptoms, 36
Anxiety disorder, 33–66
Appearance, 146, 226
Appetite, 11
Argumentativeness, 211–212,
226–227
Attention seeking, 145–146,
157–158
Attitude, 73, 74
Avoidance, 46–47
Avoidant personality disorder, 169,
170–183
adaptation, 183
case study, 171–181
characterized, 172–174
concentration, 181–182
effect at work, 174–176
effect on vocational abilities,
summary, 181–183
epidemiology, 170–171
memory, 181
persistence, 181–182
social interaction, 182
understanding, 181
vocational accommodations,
summary, 183
vocational strategies, summary,
183
working with, 176–181

B

Behavior, 226

Biopsychosocial perspective, xvii
Bipolar disorder
adaptation, 30
concentration, 29
manic phase, 20–31
case study, 20–28
characterized, 9, 20–23
concentration, 29
effect at work, 23–24
epidemiology, 20
memory, 28
persistence, 29
social interaction, 29–30
understanding, 28
vocational accommodations,
summary, 30–31
vocational strategies, summary,
30–31
working with, 24–28
memory, 29
persistence, 29
social interaction, 29–30
understanding, 28
Blaming, 84–85
Bland expression, 109
Borderline personality disorder, 119,
120–133
adaptation, 132
case study, 120–130
characterized, 121–123
concentration, 131
effect on vocational abilities,
summary, 130–132
epidemiology, 120
memory, 130–131
persistence, 131
social interaction, 132
understanding, 130–131
vocational accommodations,
summary, 132–133
vocational strategies, summary,
132–133
working with, 125–130
Boredom, 137
Brief psychotic disorder, 221

C

Charm, 137–138
Cognition, 2, 3
    defined, 2, 3
Cognitive disorder, xv
Communication skills, 226
Complaining, 210–211, 212
Comprehensive psychological
    evaluation, 238–239
Compulsion, 56–57
Concentration, 12, 226
    agoraphobia, 42–43
    antisocial personality disorder, 142
    avoidant personality disorder,
        181–182
    bipolar disorder, 29
        manic phase, 29
    borderline personality disorder,
        131
    dependent personality disorder,
        194
    depression, 17–18
    histrionic personality disorder, 154
    narcissistic personality disorder,
        166–167
    obsessive-compulsive disorder, 64,
        206
    paranoid personality disorder,
        92–93
    passive-aggressive personality
        disorder, 217
    posttraumatic stress disorder,
        52–53
    schizoid personality disorder,
        115–116
    schizophrenia, 234–235
    schizotypal personality disorder,
        105–106
    social phobia, 42–43
    somatization disorder, 76
Conscientiousness, 3, 4–5, 239–240
    defined, 3, 4
Control, 198–199
Conversion disorder, 67

Criticism of authority figures,
    210–211

D

Decision making, 12, 226
Defeatist attitude, 11–12
Deference, 185–186
Delusional disorder, 221
Delusions, 22, 221, 224–226
Dependent personality disorder,
    169, 183–196
    adaptation, 195
    case study, 184–193
    characterized, 184–187
    concentration, 194
    effect at work, 187–189
    effect on vocational abilities,
        summary, 193–195
    epidemiology, 183–184
    memory, 194
    persistence, 194
    social interaction, 195
    understanding, 194
    vocational accommodations,
        summary, 196
    vocational strategies, summary,
        196
    working with, 189–193
Depression
    adaptation, 19
    case study, 10–19
    characterized, 9, 10–12
    concentration, 17–18
    effect at work, 13–14
    effect on vocational abilities,
        summary, 17–19
    epidemiology, 9–10
    memory, 17
    persistence, 17–18
    social interaction, 18–19
    understanding, 17
    vocational accommodations,
        summary, 19
    vocational strategies, summary, 19

Depression—*continued*
    working with, 13–19
Detail oriented, 199
Diagnosis, 238–239
    framework, xiv
*Diagnostic and Statistical Manual
    of the American Psychiatric Asso-
    ciation, Fourth Edition,* 1
    Axis I, xiii, xiv, 1
    Axis II, xiii, 1
    Axis III, 2
    Axis IV, 2
    Axis V, 2
    role, 1–6
    summary, 243–245
Difficult to work with, 86
Disablement, xvi
    defined, xvii
Disclosure issues, 240, 241–242
Disinterest, 96, 109, 111, 226
Distractibility, 22, 23, 59–60
Distracting to others, 24
Dramatic presentation, 70,
    119–168
Dress, 97
Dyslexia, xiv
Dysthymia
    characterized, 9
    epidemiology, 9–10

E

Eccentric thoughts, 97
Elevated mood, 21
Empathy, 122, 158
Employment
    employment history, 49
    frequent changes, 124
    inconsistent pattern, 47
Endurance, 48
Energy, 11, 12–13, 37, 48
Error rate, 48, 228
Excitement, 96–97
Exhaustion, 11
Expansive mood, 21
Explicit accommodation, 240–241

Exploitation, 158, 187
Extroversion, 80, 146

F

Fatigue, 226
Fear of abandonment, 123
Fear of losing support, 186–187
Feelings of inadequacy, 173
Feelings of worthlessness, 11–12
Flamboyance, 22
Flat affect, 109, 226
Flight of ideas, 22
Followthrough, 149
Functional Assessment Inventory,
    238

G

Goal, 98, 109–110
Grandiosity, 21, 157–158
Grooming, 97
Guilt, 11–12

H

Hallucinations, 22, 224–226
Histrionic personality disorder, 119,
    144–156
    adaptation, 155
    case study, 144–153
    characterized, 145–147
    concentration, 154
    effect at work, 147–149
    effect on vocational abilities,
        summary, 153–155
    epidemiology, 144
    memory, 153
    persistence, 154
    social interaction, 154–155
    understanding, 153
    vocational accommodations,
        summary, 155–156
    vocational strategies, summary,
        155–156
    working with, 149–153

Honesty, 3, 5
  defined, 3
Hostility, 83–84, 141
Hyperactivity, 21
Hypersensitivity, 13, 37, 123,
  146–147, 158–159, 173–174, 175
Hypochondriasis, 67

I

Illogical thinking, 224–226
Impulsivity, 122, 137
Indecisiveness, 199–200
Individual assessment, 238
Inefficiency, 37
Inflexibility, 198, 201
Information processing, 99
Initiative, 12–13
Insight, 57–58, 69–70, 226–227
Instability, 119, 121–122, 123–124
Intensity, 96–97
Interpersonal functioning, 3, 5, 37,
  71
  defined, 3
  reduced, 23
Interpersonal relationships, 98, 110,
  159–160, 201, 227
Interpersonal tension, 86
Irresponsibility, 122
Irritability, 11, 13, 21, 71

J

Job fit, 62
Job performance, psychological
  factors, 2–6
Job-specific requirements, 3, 6
Judgment, 22–23, 24, 137

L

Lack of future orientation, 49–50, 51
Lack of interest in life, 11
Language, 226
Learning disorder, xiv
Litigiousness, 85

Low self-confidence, 11–12

M

Manipulation, 160
Memory, 12, 226
  agoraphobia, 42
  antisocial personality disorder, 142
  avoidant personality disorder, 181
  bipolar disorder, 28
    manic phase, 28
  borderline personality disorder,
    130–131
  dependent personality disorder,
    194
  depression, 17
  histrionic personality disorder, 153
  narcissistic personality disorder,
    166
  obsessive-compulsive disorder,
    63–64, 205–206
  paranoid personality disorder, 92
  passive-aggressive personality
    disorder, 216–217
  posttraumatic stress disorder, 52
  schizoid personality disorder, 115
  schizophrenia, 234
  schizotypal personality disorder,
    105
  social phobia, 42
  somatization disorder, 76
Miscommunication, 228
Misinterpretation of interpersonal
  situations, 83
Mood, defined, 9
Mood disorder, 9–31
Motivation, 3, 4–5, 11, 12–13, 71,
  109–110
  defined, 3, 4
  excessive, inappropriate, 23

N

Narcissistic personality disorder,
  119–120, 156–168
  adaptation, 168

Narcissistic personality disorder—
  continued
  case study, 156–166
  characterized, 156–159
  concentration, 166–167
  effect at work, 159–161
  effect on vocational abilities,
    summary, 166–168
  epidemiology, 156
  memory, 166
  persistence, 166–167
  social interaction, 167–168
  understanding, 166
  vocational accommodations,
    summary, 168
  vocational strategies, summary,
    168
  working with, 161–166
Need to be taken care of, 184–185
Negativistic attitude, 209–210
Negativistic personality disorder.
  See Passive-aggressive personality
  disorder
Neuroticism, 80

O

Obsession, 56
Obsessive-compulsive personality
  disorder, 33, 55–66, 169–170,
  196–208
  adaptation, 65, 207
  case study, 55–63, 196–205
  characterized, 56–59, 197–200
  concentration, 64, 206
  effect at work, 59–60, 200–201
  effect on vocational abilities,
    summary, 63–65, 205–207
  epidemiology, 55, 196
  memory, 63–64, 205–206
  persistence, 64, 206
  social interaction, 64–65,
    206–207
  understanding, 63–64, 205–206
  vocational accommodations,
    summary, 65–66, 207–208

  vocational strategies, summary,
    65–66, 207–208
  working with, 60–63, 201–205
Obstructiveness, 211
Openness to experience, 80
Order, 198–199
Organic disorder, xv
Ostracism, 98
Outgoing, 146

P

Pace, 2–4, 37, 59, 200
  defined, 2, 3
Pain disorder, 67
Panic, 35
Panic attack, 35, 36
  stress, 40
Paranoid personality disorder, 81,
  82–94
  adaptation, 93
  case study, 82–92
  characterized, 83–85
  concentration, 92–93
  effect at work, 85–86
  effect on vocational abilities,
    summary, 92–94
  epidemiology, 82
  memory, 92
  persistence, 92–93
  social interaction, 93
  understanding, 92
  vocational accommodations,
    summary, 94
  vocational strategies, summary, 94
  working with, 86–92
Passive resistance, 210
Passive-aggressive personality
  disorder, 170, 208–218
  adaptation, 218
  case study, 208–216
  characterized, 209–211
  concentration, 217
  effect at work, 211–212
  effect on vocational abilities,
    summary, 216–218

memory, 216–217
persistence, 217
social interaction, 218
understanding, 216–217
vocational accommodations,
    summary, 218–219
vocational strategies, summary,
    218–219
working with, 212–216
Passivity, 185–186, 227–228
Perfectionism, 198
Persistence, 3, 4, 71
agoraphobia, 42–43
antisocial personality disorder, 142
avoidant personality disorder,
    181–182
bipolar disorder, 29
    manic phase, 29
borderline personality disorder,
    131
defined, 3, 4
dependent personality disorder,
    194
depression, 17–18
histrionic personality disorder, 154
narcissistic personality disorder,
    166–167
obsessive-compulsive disorder, 64
obsessive-compulsive personality
    disorder, 206
paranoid personality disorder,
    92–93
passive-aggressive personality
    disorder, 217
posttraumatic stress disorder,
    52–53
schizoid personality disorder,
    115–116
schizophrenia, 234–235
schizotypal personality disorder,
    105–106
social phobia, 42–43
somatization disorder, 76
Personality disorder, *see also* Specific
    type, 79
anxious cluster, 169–219

dramatic cluster, 119–168
five-factor model of personality,
    79–80
odd cluster, 81–117
Personality factors, 239–240
Persuasiveness, 137–138
Pessimism, 11–12
Pet therapy, 51
Physical symptoms
increase in times of stress, 69
not explained by medical find-
    ings, 69
Physical violence, 86
Posttraumatic stress disorder, 33,
    44–54
case study, 45–52
characterized, 45–47
concentration, 52–53
effect at work, 47–48
effect on vocational abilities,
    summary, 52–54
epidemiology, 44–45
memory, 52
persistence, 52–53
social interaction, 53–54
understanding, 52
vocational accommodations,
    summary, 54
vocational strategies, summary,
    54
working with, 48–52
Preoccupation with death, 12
Pressured speech, 22
Psychiatric disorder
number codes, 2
problems with reality, 221–236
treatment, xvi
Psychological evaluation, 72
Psychological factors, job perfor-
    mance, 2–6
Psychological testing, 238–239

R

Racing thoughts, 22
Rationality, 85

Reality operations, 224–226
Reality testing, 22
Reasonable accommodation, 240–241
Reliability, 3, 4, 71
   defined, 3, 4
Remorse, 122
Rigidity, 201
Risk taking, 160–161, 175–176
Rule-bound, 201

S

Schizoaffective disorder, 221
Schizoid personality disorder, 81–82, 107–117
   adaptation, 117
   case study, 108–115
   characterized, 108–110
   concentration, 115–116
   effect at work, 110–111
   effect on vocational abilities, summary, 115–117
   memory, 115
   persistence, 115–116
   social interaction, 116–117
   understanding, 115
   vocational accommodations, summary, 117
   vocational strategies, summary, 117
   working with, 111–115
Schizophrenia, 221, 223–236
   adaptation, 235–236
   case study, 223–233
   characterized, 224–227
   concentration, 234–235
   effect at work, 227–228
   effect on vocational abilities, summary, 234–236
   epidemiology, 223
   memory, 234
   persistence, 234–235
   social interaction, 235
   understanding, 234
   vocational accommodations, summary, 236

   vocational strategies, summary, 236
   working with, 228–233
Schizophreniform disorder, 221
Schizotypal personality disorder, 81–82, 94–107
   adaptation, 107
   case study, 95–105
   characterized, 95–97
   concentration, 105–106
   effect at work, 97–99
   epidemiology, 95
   memory, 105
   persistence, 105–106
   social interaction, 106
   understanding, 105
   vocational accommodations, summary, 107
   vocational strategies, summary, 107
   working with, 99–105
Self-accommodation, 241
Self-centeredness, 145–146, 148–149, 157–158, 160
Self-concept, inflated, 23
Self-destructiveness, 122–123
Self-employment, 25–26
Self-esteem, 21, 111–112, 186–187
Self-presentation as incompetent, 188–189
Sense of entitlement, 159
Sleep, 11, 20, 25, 27, 226
   reduced need, 21
Sociability, 21
Social inhibition, 172–173
Social interaction
   agoraphobia, 43
   antisocial personality disorder, 143
   avoidant personality disorder, 182
   bipolar disorder, 29–30
      manic phase, 29–30
   borderline personality disorder, 132
   dependent personality disorder, 195
   depression, 18–19

histrionic personality disorder,
154–155
narcissistic personality disorder,
167–168
obsessive-compulsive disorder,
64–65
obsessive-compulsive personality
disorder, 206–207
paranoid personality disorder, 93
passive-aggressive personality
disorder, 218
posttraumatic stress disorder,
53–54
schizoid personality disorder,
116–117
schizophrenia, 235
schizotypal personality disorder,
106
social phobia, 43
somatization disorder, 77
Social isolation, 51
Social phobia, 33
adaptation, 43–44
case study, 34–42
characterized, 34–36
concentration, 42–43
effect at work, 36–38
effect on vocational abilities,
summary, 42–44
epidemiology, 34
memory, 42
persistence, 42–43
social interaction, 43
understanding, 42
vocational accommodations,
summary, 43–44
vocational strategies, summary,
43–44
working with, 38–42
Social support, 27–28, 31, 40, 52,
62, 152, 153, 187–189
Socially withdrawn, 226
Somatization disorder, 67, 68–78
adaptation, 77
case study, 68–75
characterized, 68–70
concentration, 76

effect at work, 70–71
effect on vocational abilities,
summary, 75–77
epidemiology, 68–78
memory, 76
persistence, 76
social interaction, 77
understanding, 76
vocational accommodations,
summary, 77–78
vocational strategies, summary,
77–78
working with, 71–75
Somatoform disorder, 67–78
characterized, 67
Speech, 226
Standards of workplace behavior, 74
Staying on task, 13
Stress tolerance, 3, 5–6, 13, 24, 37,
47–48, 59, 71, 73, 124, 228
defined, 3
panic attack, 40
Submissiveness, 185–186
Substance abuse, xv
Supervision, 86, 110, 129, 141,
152–153, 216
Supported employment, 240–241
Suspiciousness, 226–227

T

Team member, 110
Tearfulness, 10
Training, 50–51
Trauma
exposure, 45–46
reexperiencing, 46
Trustworthiness, 3, 5
defined, 3

U

Unassertiveness, 189
Understanding
agoraphobia, 42
antisocial personality disorder,
142

avoidant personality disorder, 181
bipolar disorder, 28
    manic phase, 28
borderline personality disorder,
    130–131
dependent personality disorder,
    194
depression, 17
histrionic personality disorder,
    153
narcissistic personality disorder,
    166
obsessive-compulsive disorder,
    63–64
obsessive-compulsive personality
    disorder, 205–206
paranoid personality disorder, 92
passive-aggressive personality
    disorder, 216–217
posttraumatic stress disorder, 52
schizoid personality disorder, 115
schizophrenia, 234

schizotypal personality disorder,
    105
social phobia, 42
somatization disorder, 76
Unilateral accommodation,
    240–241
Unreliability, 122
Unusual behavior, 97
Unusual interpretation of ordinary
    events, 96

V

Vindictiveness, 84–85
Vocational history, 49
Vocational preference, 49–50

W

Work environment, 50, 62
Workplace danger, 24, 86, 124–125,
    130, 137